Joydip Kanjilal and
Sriram Putrevu

WITHDRAWN

Sams **Teach Yourself**

ASP.NET
Ajax

in **24**
Hours

SAMS   800 East 96th Street, Indianapolis, Indiana, 46240 USA

Sams Teach Yourself ASP.NET Ajax in 24 Hours

ISBN-13: 978-0-672-32967-8
ISBN-10: 0-672-32967-0

The Library of Congress Cataloging-in-Publication Data is on file.

Printed in the United States of America

First Printing July 2008

Trademarks

All terms mentioned in this book that are known to be trademarks or service marks have been appropriately capitalized. Sams Publishing cannot attest to the accuracy of this information. Use of a term in this book should not be regarded as affecting the validity of any trademark or service mark.

Warning and Disclaimer

Every effort has been made to make this book as complete and accurate as possible, but no warranty or fitness is implied. The information provided is on an "as is" basis. The authors and the publisher shall have neither liability nor responsibility to any person or entity with respect to any loss or damages arising from the information contained in this book.

Bulk Sales

Sams Publishing offers excellent discounts on this book when ordered in quantity for bulk purchases or special sales. For more information, please contact

    U.S. Corporate and Government Sales
    1-800-382-3419
    corpsales@pearsontechgroup.com

For sales outside the U.S., please contact

    International Sales
    international@pearson.com

Editor-in-Chief
Karen Gettman

Executive Editor
Neil Rowe

Development Editor
Mark Renfrow

Managing Editor
Kristy Hart

Project Editor
Betsy Harris

Copy Editor
Water Crest Publishing, Inc.

Indexer
Lisa Stumpf

Proofreaders
San Dee Phillips
Language Logistics

Technical Editor
J. Boyd Nolan

Publishing Coordinator
Cindy Teeters

Book Designer
Gary Adair

Compositor
Bronkella Publishing

This Book Is Safari Enabled

The Safari® Enabled icon on the cover of your favorite technology book means the book is available through Safari Bookshelf. When you buy this book, you get free access to the online edition for 45 days.

Safari Bookshelf is an electronic reference library that lets you easily search thousands of technical books, find code samples, download chapters, and access technical information whenever and wherever you need it.

To gain 45-day Safari Enabled access to this book:

▶ Go to http://www.informit.com/onlineedition.

▶ Complete the brief registration form.

▶ Enter the coupon code RDMF-KFKM-MCJK-C9LD-99E1.

If you have difficulty registering on Safari Bookshelf or accessing the online edition, please email customer-service@safaribooksonline.com.

Contents at a Glance

Part IV: Using ASP.NET Ajax to Build a Sample E-Commerce Application

Table of Contents

About the Authors

Joydip Kanjilal is a Microsoft Most Valuable Professional in ASP.NET since 2007. He has more than 12 years of industry experience in IT, with more than 6 years in Microsoft .NET and its related technologies. He has authored many articles for some of the most reputable sites, such as www.asptoday.com, www.devx.com, www.aspalliance.com, www.aspnetpro.com, www.sql-server-performance.com, www.sswug.com, and so on. A lot of these articles have been selected at www.asp.net—Microsoft's official site on ASP.NET. Joydip was also a community credit winner at www.community-credit.com a number of times.

He is currently working as a Lead Architect at a reputable company in Hyderabad, India. He has years of experience in designing and architecting solutions for various domains. His technical strengths include C, C++, VC++, Java, C#, Microsoft .NET, Ajax, Design Patterns, SQL Server, Operating Systems, and Computer Architecture. Joydip blogs at http://aspadvice.com/blogs/joydip and spends most of his time reading books, blogging, and writing books and articles. His hobbies include watching cricket and soccer and playing chess. Joydip can be reached at joydipkanjilal@yahoo.com.

Sriram Putrevu has an MCA (Master of Computer Applications) from Osmania University, India. He is currently working as a Lead Developer at a multinational company (MNC) in Hyderabad, India. Sriram specializes in the Microsoft .NET technologies and has been working with this technology for the last 5 and 1/2 years. He is also a Microsoft Certified Technology Specialist in .NET Framework 2.0 and Web Applications.

Over the years, Sriram has gained vast experience in developing several high-scale applications across various domains in healthcare, supply chain/logistics, EAI, and e-commerce. His current ambitions involve architecting and implementing next-generation .NET-based applications.

When not at work, Sriram likes to spend time with family and friends. He is also very passionate about the sport cricket and keenly follows this game. Sriram blogs at http://sriramputrevu.blogspot.com/ and can be reached at sriramputrevu@yahoo.com.

Dedication

This book is dedicated to our parents for their love, inspiration, and support.

Acknowledgments

Writing a book is always a rewarding experience. It is a great feeling when ideas eventually turn into books. My special thanks to Neil Rowe for providing me with the opportunity to author this book—turning this idea into a reality. I am thankful to the entire Sams team for their support.

My thanks to Sriram Putrevu for his hard work, dedication, and keeping me focused with the latest trends and happenings in and around Ajax. I am also thankful to Abhishek Kant (Microsoft), Steve Smith (AspAlliance), Russell Jones (DevX), Steve Jones (SSWUG), Jude Kelly (SQL Server Performance), Douglas Paterson (Packt Publishing), and Anand Narayaswamy (AspAlliance) for their inspiration and support. My heartiest thanks to my friends Tilak Tarafder and Rituraj Singh for their continued encouragement.

My deepest respect and gratitude to my parents for their love, blessings, and encouragement throughout my life. My thanks to my other family members too, for their support, and to little Jini in particular, for her continued inspiration and love.

Thank you all so much!

—Joydip Kanjilal

First and foremost, I would like to thank my coauthor Joydip Kanjilal for having faith and confidence in me to deliver this book. Without his encouragement, I couldn't have made this huge step forward in writing this book.

My special thanks to the entire Sams team, for their continuous support during several phases of this project. Their input and suggestions helped me to do a better job.

I would also like to express my gratitude to all my employers, who have given me an opportunity to work with them and experience different facets of professional life.

And finally, my heartfelt thanks to my entire family—especially my dad (P.V.D. Nageswara Rao), my mom (P. Rajeswari), my brother (P. Loknath), and to the little Poorvika and Rushil, and my inspirational grandfather (P.V.K. Punneswara Rao), and to every other member in the family for all their love and endless support, not only during this phase of the project, but also throughout my life. Thank you all very much!

—Sriram Putrevu

We Want to Hear from You

As the reader of this book, *you* are our most important critic and commentator. We value your opinion, and we want to know what we're doing right, what we could do better, what areas you'd like to see us publish in, and any other words of wisdom you're willing to pass our way.

You can email or write me directly to let me know what you did or didn't like about this book—as well as what we can do to make our books stronger.

Please note that I cannot help you with technical problems related to the topic of this book, and that because of the high volume of mail I receive, I might not be able to reply to every message.

When you write, please be sure to include this book's title and authors, as well as your name and phone number or email address. I will carefully review your comments and share them with the authors and editors who worked on the book.

Email: feedback@samspublishing.com

Mail: Neil Rowe
         Executive Editor
         Sams Publishing
         800 East 96th Street
         Indianapolis, IN 46240 USA

Reader Services

Visit our website and register this book at informit.com/register for convenient access to any updates, downloads, or errata that might be available for this book.

There is a ReadMe.doc file on the website along with the sample application. This file contains instructions on how to use the application (developed in Part IV) on your system.

PART I

Getting Started with Ajax

HOUR 1

Getting Started with ASP.NET Ajax

What You'll Learn in This Hour:

▶ Introducing Ajax
▶ Technologies that make up Ajax
▶ The pros and cons of using Ajax
▶ ASP.NET Ajax
▶ Goals of ASP.NET Ajax
▶ Installing Ajax
▶ Creating your first Ajax application

The solution to building applications with fast, user-friendly, and responsive user interfaces is here. Yes! Ajax is in. Ajax is an acronym for Asynchronous JavaScript and XML—a technology that can reduce web page postbacks significantly and yield better response times for your web applications. Using Ajax, the hits to the web server are reduced—thus, you have fewer page refreshes. Moreover, you can use Ajax to ensure that a specific portion of the page is refreshed and not the entire page content.

Usage of Ajax provides rich user experience with a responsive user interface, which eventually results in an awesome user experience. The ASP.NET 2.0 Server development platform is now integrated with the client-side libraries that incorporate cross-browser JavaScript and DHTML technologies. ASP.NET Ajax was available as a separate package in ASP.NET 2.0. With ASP.NET 3.5, you have the Ajax framework built in. In other words, you need not download and install the Ajax package separately in your system; you have built-in support for all Ajax features. There have been a lot of improvements to Ajax in ASP.NET 3.5. We discuss these improvements later in this book. In this hour, we take a look at ASP.NET Ajax, its ingredients, and how we can get started with it.

Things You Should Know

To understand the concepts covered in this book, you need a basic understanding of the following:

- ▶ JavaScript

- ▶ ASP.NET 2.0

- ▶ C#

Ajax—A Paradigm Shift

The advent of Ajax has put an end to the arduous struggle of web application development communities worldwide to find a technology that can not only improve response times, but also allow for asynchronous processing. Ajax is a technology with cross-platform, cross-architecture, and even cross-browser support. In fact, Ajax has already become recognized in Microsoft and Sun development communities for building lightning-fast web applications with improved response times, which results in awesome user experiences. Note that Ajax is a technology; it is not specific to ASP.NET or Java. You can use Ajax in both of the preceding technologies. Moreover, you can use Ajax in any web browser, such as IE, Mozilla, Firefox, and so on.

By the Way

> Prior to Ajax, we could register client-side scripts ASP.NET 2.0 Ajax Page level methods. Here is an example:
>
> ```
> Page.ClientScript.GetPostBackEventReference(this, String.Empty);
> ```

There's an old proverb that says, "The old order changeth yielding place to new." With the introduction of Ajax, there has been a paradigm shift—we have moved away from the earlier trend in which we had to force a postback to retrieve data from the server. With Ajax, we can do the same even without a postback to the web server. The result is improved response times and better performance of the application as a whole.

Ajax uses the `XMLHttpRequest` object, a JavaScript object that can communicate directly with the web server to retrieve data, without the need to reload web pages each time data is requested. We discuss more on `XMLHttpRequest` object in Hour 3, "Working with the `XMLHttpRequest` Object."

Technologies That Make Up Ajax

Ajax is, in itself, a combination of existing technologies. These include the following:

- ▶ `XMLHttpRequest` object
- ▶ JavaScript
- ▶ DHTML
- ▶ DOM
- ▶ XML

Let's briefly discuss each of them.

JavaScript is a scripting language developed initially by Netscape, but having the capability to be used on all known browsers. It is an interpreted language that can be used both on the client and server side as a scripting language. JavaScript can be easily used to interact with the HTML elements, validate user input, and manage your settings, such as the color and background color of different controls on a form. Like any other programming language, JavaScript contains variables, arrays, loops, functions, operators, exception handling in the form of "try" and "catch" statements, and so on. You can place your JavaScript code directly on the same HTML page or even in a separate .js file and link your web page with it.

All the HTML elements in your web page are organized in a Document Object Model, a W3C recommendation that every browser follows. This model describes how all the elements in an HTML page, such as input fields, paragraphs, images, anchors, and so on, are related to the topmost structure: the "document." This model defines the structure in a tree consisting of all the attributes and methods defined for an object in the document.

Fine, but what is DHTML? DHTML is the acronym for Dynamic Hypertext Markup Language, a technology that you can use to make your web page dynamic with the use of JavaScript. The word "dynamic" implies the capability of the browser to alter the look and style of HTML elements after the document has been loaded onto the browser. This dynamic content can be realized in several ways, either by applying properties to elements or by applying layers to a document.

CSS, or Cascading Style Sheets, are files that store the styles of your web page HTML elements. These files typically have the .css extension. Note that CSS is basically used to provide a customized look and feel to your HTML elements. You can use CSS files to store the formatting and style information of elements at a common place and then reuse it in your web forms to facilitate easy maintenance and enforce the consistency of the look and feel of the user interface elements.

As an example, you can store all the headings in all the web pages of an application by defining them as a class in the `.css` file. Later, if the heading style needs to be changed, you can do this just in one place—the `.css` file. The changes would be reflected across all web pages of your application wherever this class has been used.

The Pros and Cons of Using Ajax

Some of the many benefits of using Ajax in web-based applications include the following:

▶ Improved user experience

▶ Asynchronous processing

▶ Reduced server hits and network load

▶ Platform and architecture neutrality

▶ Multibrowser support

▶ Faster page renders and improved response times

We discuss each of these as we progress through the hours of this book.

The Downsides of Using Ajax

Now let's discuss the drawbacks of using Ajax or, more precisely, areas where Ajax can fit and those where it can't. Although Ajax comes with a lot of advantages, there are quite a few downsides to using Ajax in your web applications. The major drawback is its massive usage and dependency on JavaScript. It should be noted that JavaScript is implemented differently for various browsers, such as Internet Explorer, Netscape, Mozilla, and so on. This becomes a constraint especially when you need to make Ajax work across browsers.

Added to this, you do not have support for JavaScript in mobile browsers. So, taking Ajax's dependency on JavaScript into consideration, Ajax might not be well suited for designing mobile applications.

Usage of Ajax makes your web page difficult to debug, increases the code size of your web page, and makes your web page prone to potential security threats. Moreover, its usage—and the asynchronous operations thereafter—tend to increase the load on the web server. When using Ajax, making your application cross-browser compliant is rather difficult (although not impossible, of course), and the Back button of your web browser does not work.

Looking Back in Time

The technologies that make up Ajax are not new; they've been around for years. Netscape's LiveScript (eventually called JavaScript) allowed for asynchronous processing some time ago.

Netscape came up with support for Dynamic XML and Microsoft with the XMLHttpRequest object within the browser that can be used to retrieve data from the server asynchronously. This phenomenon was later called Ajax by Jesse James Garrett of Adaptive Path in early 2005. Ajax was born. However, it was only in the fall of the same year that Ajax made its presence felt within development communities worldwide.

Google led the drive to make Ajax known to these communities by announcing the first public implementation of Ajax in Google Suggest. Because of these efforts, examples of the public use of Ajax can be found worldwide; a few of these examples are as follows:

- ▶ Google Maps
- ▶ Google Suggest
- ▶ GMail
- ▶ Live.com

And, the list goes on!

What Is ASP.NET Ajax?

ASP.NET Ajax, formerly known as Atlas, is an extension of ASP.NET 2.0. It allows you to leverage the power of Ajax while developing ASP.NET Ajax web applications. The MSDN states, "ASP.NET Ajax is a set of technologies to add Ajax (Asynchronous JavaScript and XML) support to ASP.NET. It consists of a client-side script framework, server controls, and more. Although Ajax is essentially a client-side technique, most of its real-world deployments call for server-side processing."

The ASP.NET Ajax architecture has a framework developed for both client side and server side. The client-side framework comes in the form of the Microsoft Ajax Library. This Library includes a collection of client-side libraries that include support for creating client-side components, browser compatibility, managing asynchronous requests, web and application services, different core services in serialization, JavaScript base class extensions, and so on.

The ASP.NET Ajax server components consist of several web server controls and components to handle the flow and the user interface. It also shows the functionality of ASP.NET 2.0 Ajax server extensions, which include support for localization, globalization, debugging, tracing, web services, and application services.

Moreover, ASP.NET Ajax has come up with several server controls—namely, ScriptManager, UpdatePanel, UpdateProgress, and Timer—that enable a faster response. These controls are responsible for faster updates, better response times, and improved performance and efficiency. We'll look at each of these controls in detail in the hours that follow.

ASP.NET Ajax also provides web services that can be used from the client script to work with different application services for forms authentication and user profiles. There are several ASP.NET application services provided with the Ajax server extensions, which can be accessed by web service calls from the client script. This data transfer can be handled by different network components that make it easy to return results of a web service call.

Other Ajax Frameworks

Apart from Microsoft's ASP.NET Ajax, there are plenty of other Ajax frameworks. We discuss only the major ones—that is, those frameworks that are widely in use. Our list includes the following:

- ▶ Atlas
- ▶ AJAXPro.NET
- ▶ MagicAJAX.NET
- ▶ Anthem.NET

Atlas, as mentioned previously, is the older form of Microsoft Ajax Library. It is a framework that integrates the Client-Side JavaScript Library and is freely available and can be used with ASP.NET 2.0 to develop Ajax applications. It has cross-browser support and exposes a number of object-oriented APIs, which can be used to develop web applications that minimize server hits or postbacks and perform asynchronous calls.

AJAXPro.NET is an Ajax library for use with the ASP.NET engine. The best part of AJAXPro.NET is that you can use it in the Internet Explorer event if the `ActiveX` object is disabled in your browser. Furthermore, it has certain distinct advantages over Atlas. It does not have any web service layer and is compliant with both versions of .NET—.NET 1.x and .NET 2.0—and is simple to understand and implement in your web applications.

MagicAJAX.NET, or the Magic Ajax engine for use with the ASP.NET engine, is also a freely available Ajax framework. It is a flexible Ajax framework for use in the ASP.NET platform. It was published in an article at www.codeproject.com. Since then, it was improved a lot and was later provided free at www.sourceforge.net.

Anthem.NET is an open source Ajax framework that is compliant with ASP.NET 1.x and 2.0 versions. This framework was developed by Jason Diamond and contains a rich set of Ajax-enabled controls that can be used to Ajax-enable your web applications. You have support for View State in Anthem.NET with a rich set of controls and server-side events.

Goals of ASP.NET Ajax

There are many goals for Ajax. The following are some of the most important:

- ▶ Improving performance and efficiency by negating page postbacks
- ▶ Introducing partial page updates to refresh only parts of a web page
- ▶ Reducing the network load
- ▶ Providing a framework with a collection of integrated server- and client-side components to ease development of web applications that can leverage the power of Ajax

The section that follows discusses the steps for installing Ajax.

Installing Ajax

To start developing ASP.NET Ajax applications using Visual Studio 2005, you first need to install and configure ASP.NET Ajax.

By the Way

> In discussing how to install Microsoft ASP.NET Ajax in your system, this section assumes that you have already downloaded the ASP.NET Ajax installer package from the download link provided later in this hour.

Setting Up Your Environment

Before you install ASP.NET Ajax in your system, make sure your system meets the minimum installation requirements as outlined in this section. The installation prerequisites are as follows:

- A Windows OS that can host the Microsoft .NET framework (Windows 2000, 2003, XP, Vista, and so on)

- Microsoft .NET framework 2.0 or Version 3.0

- Internet Explorer 5.01 or higher

- Microsoft Visual Studio 2005 or Visual Web Developer Express Edition (optional)

By the Way

> Before you proceed through the installation steps discussed here, make sure that you uninstall any previous versions of ASP.NET Ajax in your system.

Installing ASP.NET Ajax

The following are the steps for installing ASP.NET Ajax in your system:

1. Log in with the administrator's privileges and initiate the installation procedure.

2. Download the ASP.NET AJAX 1.0 from the ASP.NET Ajax downloads website:

   http://www.microsoft.com/downloads/details.aspx?FamilyID=ca9d90fa-e8c9-42e3-aa19-08e2c027f5d6&displaylang=en

3. Execute the ASPAJAXExtSetup.msi installation package to install ASP.NET Ajax in your system by double-clicking the .msi file and following the steps shown in Figures 1.1 through 1.5.

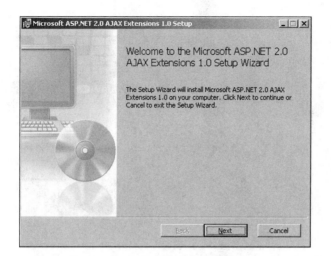

FIGURE 1.1
Installation
Wizard—Step 1

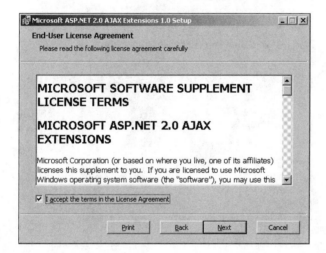

FIGURE 1.2
Installation
Wizard—Step 2

FIGURE 1.3
Installation
Wizard—Step 3

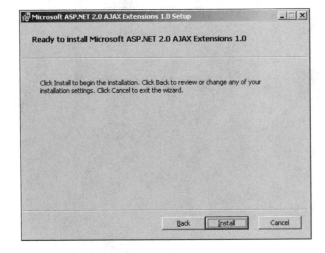

FIGURE 1.4
Installation
Wizard—Step 4

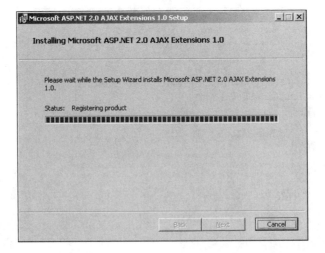

Alternatively, you can execute the ASPAJAXExtSetup.msi package from the command line:

```
msiexec /i ASPAJAXExtSetup.msi [/q] [/log <log file name>]
  [INSTALLDIR =<installation path>]
```

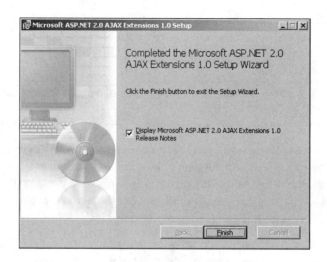

FIGURE 1.5
Installation
Wizard—Step 5

You are done! By default, the ASP.NET Ajax assembly (`System.Web.Extensions.dll`) is installed in the following path:

```
drive:\..\Program Files\Microsoft ASP.NET\ASP.NET 2.0 AJAX
Extensions\v1.0.nnnn.
```

> **By the Way**
>
> You can suppress the user prompt by using the /q option when specifying the preceding command. Remember not to include the assembly in the bin folder of your Ajax-enabled website.
>
> You can install and use ASP.NET Ajax with Microsoft Visual Studio 2005 or the Microsoft Visual Web Developer Express Edition. However, you do not need Visual Studio 2005 to use ASP.NET Ajax to create ASP.NET web applications.
>
> You can also install and use the Microsoft Ajax Library without the .NET framework, and even on a non-Windows environment, to create client-based web applications for any browser that supports ECMAScript (JavaScript).

The Microsoft ASP.NET Ajax is now installed in your system and ready to use.

Creating Your First Ajax Application

The heart of any Ajax-enabled web page is the `XMLHttpRequest` object, an object that facilitates communication with the server without posting the web page back to the web server. This communication can be done synchronously or asynchronously without postbacks. In this section, we examine how we can implement a simple application using this object. The `XMLHttpRequest` object is discussed at length later in this book.

You have to instantiate the `XMLHttpRequest` object differently for different browsers, such as Mozilla and IE.

Let's now take a look at how you can use this object using JavaScript with different browsers. After we get an understanding of how the `XMLHttpRequest` object works, we can get into the details of the Microsoft Ajax Library and its usage. This Library encapsulates all the JavaScript code in the form of an API and presents us with a set of method calls that facilitate easier development in Ajax.

You need to follow specific steps to create your first sample application using the `XMLHttpRequest` object. These steps are discussed in this section and the next section.

1. Create an instance of the `XMLHttpRequest` object, as shown in the following code snippet:

```
var xmlHttp = new ActiveXObject("Microsoft.XMLHTTP")
```

In the next section we discuss how we can implement a generic function that we can use across all common browsers. Moving ahead, we will make use of this function to create an instance of XMLHttpRequest

In Mozilla and Safari browsers, the `XMLHttpRequest` is a built-in native object. Creation of this object in these browsers is as follows:

```
var xmlHttp = new XmlHttpRequest();
```

Creating a Generic Function for Instantiating the `XMLHttpRequest` Object

In this section we implement a generic function that can be used to create an instance of the `XMLHttpRequest` object based on the type of the browser on which it is intended to be used. This function is as follows:

```
<script language="javascript" type="text/javascript">
    var xmlHttp = false;
    function getXmlHttpRequestObject()
    {
        try
        {
            //IE implementation
            xmlHttp = new ActiveXObject("Microsoft.XMLHTTP");
        }
        catch(e)
```

```
{
    try
    {
     //Legacy implementation
     xmlHttp = new ActiveXObject("MsXml2.XMLHTTP");
    }
    catch(exp)
    {
        xmlHttp = false;
    }
}
if (!xmlHttp && typeof XmlHttpRequest != 'undefined')
{
    //Mozilla based browsers
    //creating a native request object
    xmlHttp = new XmlHttpRequest();
}
}
</script>
```

How Does It Work?

What does the previous code do? It illustrates the creation of the XMLHttpRequest object appropriate for the browser type making the request. It is done with the help of a simple exception-handling mechanism using the "try" and "catch" exception blocks. Note that this method can be called from any page in the application by simply placing this in a .js file and calling the getXmlHttpRequestObject method wherever it is required. If we place this in a .js file, we need not write the same code repeatedly in every web page.

2. Open Visual Studio 2005, and click File, New, Web Site to create a new web site. Name this web site and save it (see Figure 1.6).

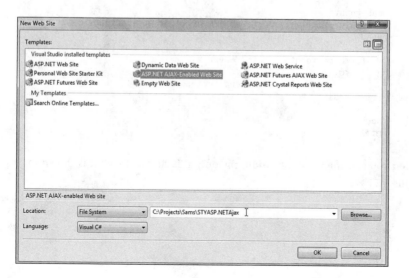

FIGURE 1.6
Creating the web site

3. Now place the following code in the `Default.aspx` HTML source:

```
<%@ Page Language="C#" AutoEventWireup="true"
CodeFile="Default.aspx.cs" Inherits="_Default" %>
<!DOCTYPE html PUBLIC "-//W3C//DTD XHTML
Transitional//EN"
"http://www.w3.org/TR/xhtml1/DTD/xhtml1-transitional.dtd">
<html xmlns="http://www.w3.org/1999/xhtml">
<script language="javascript" type="text/javascript">
    var xmlHttp = false;
    function getXmlHttpRequestObject()
    {
        try
        {
            //IE implementation
            xmlHttp = new ActiveXObject("Microsoft.XMLHTTP");
        }
        catch(e)
        {
            try
            {
             //Legacy implementation
             xmlHttp = new ActiveXObject("MsXml2.XMLHTTP");
            }
            catch(exp)
            {
                xmlHttp = false;
            }
        }
        if (!xmlHttp && typeof XmlHttpRequest != 'undefined')
        {
            //Mozilla based browsers
            //creating a native request object
            xmlHttp = new XmlHttpRequest();
        }
    }
    </script>

<head runat="server">
    <title>Creating your first ASP.NET Ajax Application</title>
</head>
<body>
    <form id="form1" runat="server">
        <div>
            Your First AJAX application at work !
        </div>
    </form>
</body>
</html>
```

When you execute the application, the output is similar to what is shown in
Figure 1.7.

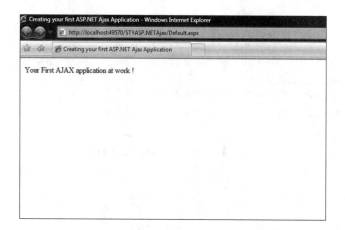

FIGURE 1.7
The first Ajax
program

We now discuss how we can use Ajax to fetch data from the server asynchronously and display it in the client browser.

4. We have the JavaScript function in place. Now let's call and instantiate it, as shown in the following code snippet:

```
getXmlHttpRequestObject();
```

Now, the instance is ready for use:

```
xmlHttp.open("GET", "TestFile.txt", true);
xmlHttp.onreadystatechange = function()
{
    if (xmlHttp.readyState == 4)
    {
        alert(xmlHttp.responseText);
    }
}
xmlHttp.send(null);
```

What Does the Previous Code Do?

What does the previous code do? It uses the XMLHttpRequest object's GET/Open method to read a text file on the server and display its content at the client side in a message box using JavaScript.

Here is how the complete code inside the <Script> tag now looks like:

```
<script language="javascript" type="text/javascript">
    var xmlHttp = false;
    getXmlHttpRequestObject();
    xmlHttp.open("GET", "TestFile.txt", true);
    xmlHttp.onreadystatechange = function()
    {
```

```
        if (xmlHttp.readyState == 4)
        {
            alert(xmlHttp.responseText);
        }
    }
    xmlHttp.send(null);
    function getXmlHttpRequestObject()
    {
        try
        {
           //IE implementation
           xmlHttp = new ActiveXObject("Microsoft.XMLHTTP");
        }
        catch(e)
        {
            try
            {
              //Legacy object implementation
              xmlHttp = new ActiveXObject("MsXml2.XMLHTTP");
            }
            catch(exp)
            {
                xmlHttp = false;
            }
        }
        if (!xmlHttp && typeof XmlHttpRequest != 'undefined')
        {
            //Mozilla based browsers
            //creating a native request object
            xmlHttp = new XmlHttpRequest();
        }
    }
    </script>
```

5. Add a file called `TestFile.txt` to your project, open it, and type some content, such as "Welcome to the world of Ajax."

6. Save your work and start executing your project. You'll be prompted to add the `Web.Config` file to your application to enable debugging.

7. Accept all the defaults, and click the OK button. This executes the application and opens up a browser, showing the contents of the text file retrieved from the server on an alert in your web page. We are done!

The output is captured, as shown in Figure 1.8.

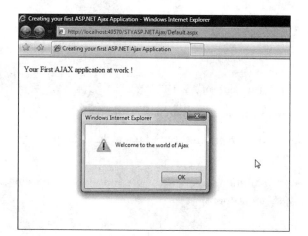

FIGURE 1.8
Welcome to the world of Ajax.

In the code snippet shown earlier, the open method was used to communicate with the server, and "readyState" returned a status code of 4, which implies that a transaction completed successfully.

So, after reading this section, you now should have a basic idea of how Ajax can be put in action.

Summary

With Microsoft taking Ajax to new heights and quickly coming up with newer releases, Ajax is all set to become the next-generation technology of choice for building fast and responsive web applications. In this hour, we discussed the various set of technologies that make up Ajax, the key ingredients of ASP.NET Ajax, the major goals of ASP.NET Ajax, and why Ajax has become indispensable in web application development communities worldwide. Apart from this, we've also learned how to install ASP.NET Ajax and what comes with it. In the next hour, we'll explore the internals of the ASP.NET Ajax architecture. So, stay tuned!

Workshop

Quiz

1. What are the basic goals of ASP.NET Ajax?

2. What are the constituent technologies in Ajax?

3. Name some of the server controls that are included as part of the ASP.NET Ajax framework.

4. What are the minimum requirements/prerequisites for installing and running ASP.NET Ajax applications?

5. Name some popular ASP.NET Ajax frameworks.

Answers

1. The basic goals of ASP.NET Ajax are as follows:

   ▶ Reduced web server hits and network load

   ▶ Rich and interactive user interface

   ▶ Platform and architecture neutrality

   ▶ Support for both synchronous and asynchronous communication

   ▶ Provide a server- and client-side framework for seamless usage of Ajax in applications

2. The constituent technologies that make up Ajax are as follows:

   ▶ XMLHttpRequest object

   ▶ JavaScript

   ▶ DHTML

   ▶ DOM

   ▶ XML

3. ASP.NET Ajax has come up with several server controls. These are the following:

- ▶ ScriptManager
- ▶ UpdatePanel
- ▶ UpdateProgress
- ▶ Timer

These controls are responsible for faster updates, better response times, and improved performance and efficiency.

4. To install and run ASP.NET Ajax applications, you should have all of the following in your system:

- ▶ A Windows OS that can host the Microsoft .NET framework (Windows 2000, 2003, XP, Vista, and so on)
- ▶ Microsoft .NET framework 2.0 or Version 3.0
- ▶ Internet Explorer 5.01 or higher
- ▶ Microsoft Visual Studio 2005 or Visual Web Developer Express Edition (optional)

5. Some of the most popular ASP.NET Ajax frameworks include the following:

- ▶ Michael Schwarz's Ajax.NET
- ▶ Jason Diamond's Anthem
- ▶ MagicAJAX.NET
- ▶ ComfortASP.NET
- ▶ Microsoft's Atlas
- ▶ ASP.NET Ajax from Microsoft

HOUR 2

Understanding the ASP.NET Ajax Architecture

What You'll Learn in This Hour:

- ▶ Introducing ASP.NET
- ▶ Understanding the ASP.NET architecture
- ▶ The ASP.NET page life cycle events
- ▶ Introducing ASP.NET Ajax
- ▶ Goals of ASP.NET Ajax
- ▶ The downsides of using ASP.NET Ajax
- ▶ The architecture of ASP.NET Ajax
- ▶ Other Ajax frameworks

Ajax is fast becoming an indispensable technology within web development communities. In this hour, we take a look at the architecture of ASP.NET Ajax and its blocks. But, before we delve deep into the architecture of Ajax, we examine the architecture of ASP.NET and learn about ASP.NET Ajax.

Introducing ASP.NET

Microsoft's ASP.NET is a platform that enables you to build web applications in a managed environment. It offers you power, flexibility, manageability, extensibility, and more! Before we delve deep into the architecture of ASP.NET Ajax, let's take a bird's-eye view of what actually happens from the time your web browser sends a request to the web server that runs the ASP.NET engine until the time the web browser receives a response back.

A Quick Look at the ASP.NET Architecture

In this section we take a look at the ASP.NET architecture. We divide our discussion in two parts: the application life cycle events and the page life cycle events.

The Application Life Cycle Events

1. Whenever you press the Submit button on the web page, the request is sent to the web browser; in our case, let the web server be IIS.

2. The IIS picks up this request and looks for the server extensions. Each server extension is actually mapped to the IIS. Now, if the server extension of this request is .aspx, it maps to aspnet_isapi.dll. After this .dll is invoked, it hosts the ASP.NET worker process that initializes the Http Pipeline.

> **By the Way**
>
> In the Http Pipeline, you have a set of objects, such as HttpRuntime, HttpWorkerRequest, HttpApplicationFactory, and so on.

3. If the HttpApplication object does not exist for the application, it creates one—or else it picks it from the pool of these HttpApplication objects and passes the incoming request to it to handle.

> **By the Way**
>
> The HttpApplicationFactory is simply a factory that creates HttpApplication objects. It is a pool that contains these HttpApplication objects so that the request can be served.

4. The worker process calls the HttpRuntime.ProcessRequest() method.

5. The HttpRuntime creates the HttpContext and calls the HttpApplicationFactory.

6. The HttpApplicationFactory creates an instance of the web page object from a dynamically created assembly and selects the appropriate HttpApplication object that can serve the incoming request.

7. The HttpApplication instance processes the request and, in turn, selects the appropriate PageHandlerFactory.

By the Way

The HttpApplication object is responsible for selecting the appropriate PageHandlerFactory for that requesting page; this creates an instance of the page class of the web page that has initiated the request. All handler factories implement the IHttphandler interface. How does the HttpApplication object know which is the handler for that page? It first determines the type of the incoming request and invokes the appropriate handler factory.

If the request is for a page, then it calls the PageHandlerFactory for that page. It finds the handler for the page by searching the <httpHandlers> section of the machine.config file. The HttpModule is one that fits into the HttpPipeLine of objects and can filter or edit the requests or the responses that come its way. On the other hand, the HttpHandler is responsible for initiating rendering and is defined in the configuration files. Your web page class actually derives from the System.Web.UI.Page class and implements the IHttpHandler interface.

8. The PageHandlerFactory now creates the page instance by making use of the page handler of the web page. It does this to return the page instance to the HttpRuntime through the HttpApplicationFactory.

9. The HttpRuntime uses this page instance and calls the ProcessRequest() method of the web page.

10. The ProcessRequest() method first calls the FrameworkInitialize() method and then calls the page life cycle methods.

By the Way

Each page handler implements the IHttpHandler interface that contains the ProcessRequest() method, which is actually responsible for processing the request. The response is complete and served to the client browser after the page is unloaded from the memory.

The next section discusses the sequence of events that are executed in the life cycle of an ASP.NET web page.

The Page Life Cycle Events

Now, let's discuss the sequence of events that are executed in the life cycle of a page. The following are these events, listed in the order in which they are executed:

1. Page_Init

2. LoadViewState

3. LoadPostData

4. Page_Load

5. RaisePostDataChangedEvent

6. RaisePostBackEvent

7. Page_PreRender

8. SaveViewState

9. Page_Render

10. Page_UnLoad

These events can be overridden—that is, you can override them to implement your custom handlers—and are associated with their respective event handlers. The ASP.NET page life cycle events are discussed in the following steps:

1. The page life cycle starts with the invocation of the Page_Init event. This event is responsible for initializing the controls that you use in your page to their default values. This event can also be used to create or even re-create the controls in your web page that need to be created dynamically.

2. The next event handler that gets executed is the LoadViewState method that restores the View State for the web page. This method is only executed if and when the web page has been posted back and restores any previously stored View State data associated with the web page.

By the Way

> But, what is View State? Well, View State is actually a hidden field stored within your web page. The name of this hidden field is __viewstate. View State contains the control state for the controls that your web page contains—in case the controls in your web page lose the data contained in them, if a postback to the web server occurs. The View State of a web page can be stored using the SaveViewState method.

3. The next method to be executed in this chain of events is the LoadPostBackData. This method is responsible for processing the data of the server controls, and these controls are populated with the previously posted data.

4. The Page_Load event is triggered. This method can be used to populate and bind data to your controls either from the database or any other sources, states, and so on.

5. The RaisePostBackData and RaisePostBack events are triggered if, and only if, there was a postback. The PreRender event is fired next, and you can use

this event to make any changes to the data contained in your controls prior to their rendering.

6. The Render event is triggered, which creates the Response object for the web page. Now the page is eventually rendered through the Render event, which uses a text writer to write the response stream to the Response.

The Response object is actually a property of the Page class. The Render event, like the other events in the page's life cycle, can be overridden. You can customize the eventual output by overriding the associated event handler for the page's Render event.

7. The page is unloaded from the memory, and the Response object is sent to the browser in the Page Unload event. You can override this method to perform your necessary cleanup activities. According to MSDN, "Unload is called after the page has been fully rendered, sent to the client, and is ready to be discarded. At this point, page properties such as Response and Request are unloaded and any cleanup is performed."

Figure 2.1 depicts the page life cycle methods and the sequence in which they are executed.

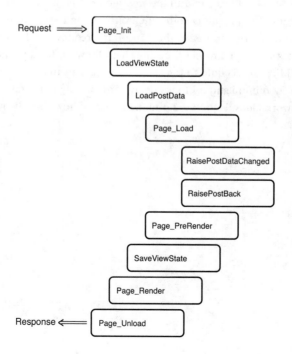

FIGURE 2.1
The ASP.NET page life cycle

You can learn more about ASP.NET architecture by reading Rick Strahl's excellent article at the following link:

www.west-wind.com/presentations/howaspnetworks/howaspnetworks.asp

Well, we have had a look at the architecture of ASP.NET—that is, the sequence of events that occur from the time a request is generated until the time the response is received by the web page initiating the request.

The next section discusses the architecture of ASP.NET Ajax.

A Bird's-Eye View of the ASP.NET Ajax Architecture

Before we delve deep into the ASP.NET Ajax architecture, let's discuss how both an Ajax and a non-Ajax web application work. In a non-Ajax web application environment, the Http request that is sent by the client browser is directly processed at the web server at the server side. The web server processes this incoming request and returns the response back to the client browser in the form of HTML and CSS. This happens synchronously—that is, the browser has to wait until the request is complete. On the contrary, in an Ajax web application environment, the Ajax engine sits in between the client browser and the web server. It is the Ajax layer that is responsible for initiating requests both synchronously and asynchronously to the web server. The web server processes these incoming requests and returns the response to the Ajax engine rather than the client browser directly. The Ajax engine returns the HTML and CSS data to the client browser. This model facilitates faster responsiveness by minimizing postback delays and also by reducing the server overheads and network loads. Figures 2.2 and 2.3 illustrate how these two models work.

NonAjax-Web Application

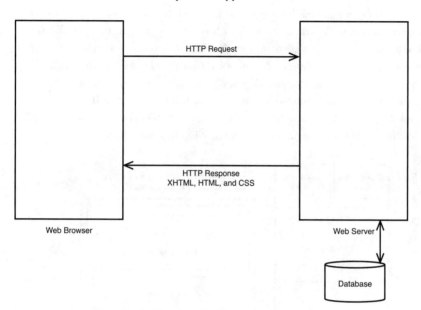

FIGURE 2.2
Non-Ajax web
application
development
model

Ajax Web Application

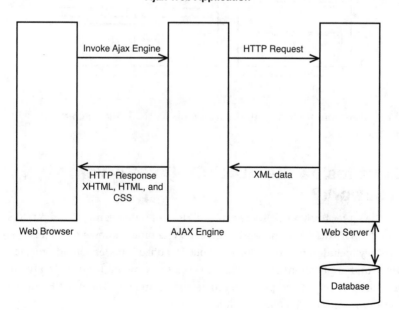

FIGURE 2.3
Ajax web appli-
cation develop-
ment model

Note that there are two perspectives to the ASP.NET Ajax architecture: the server and the client. In other words, you get two APIs with this framework: the server-side API and the client-side API. We will learn both of them as we progress through this section. Note that we refer to the client API as the client framework and the server API as the server framework. It should also be noted that the client framework is not tightly coupled to the server framework—that is, the client framework can work independent of the server framework. Thus, you can use the client framework to design and develop applications even in PHP or other web-based languages as well! Figure 2.4 illustrates the components of the ASP.NET Ajax architecture.

FIGURE 2.4
The ASP.NET
Ajax architecture

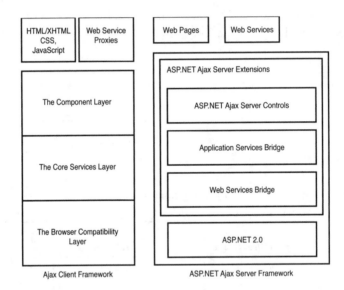

In the next section, we begin our discussion on ASP.NET Ajax architecture with the server framework.

What's Inside the ASP.NET Ajax Server Framework?

Inside the server framework, there is a collection of server controls and services that extend the ASP.NET 2.0 framework. These are commonly known as server extensions. They include support for localization, globalization, debugging, tracing, web services, and application services and are essentially meant for reducing the round-trips to the web server and providing incremental updates. The ASP.NET Ajax server extensions framework includes the following:

- ▶ ASP.NET Ajax server controls

- ▶ Application services bridge

- ▶ Web services bridge

The ASP.NET Ajax Server Controls

You can group the ASP.NET Ajax server controls into two distinct groups: Script Management and Partial Update.

The Script Management Group

You have the following controls within the Script Management group:

- ▶ ScriptManager

- ▶ ScriptManagerProxy

The ScriptManager is the most important control for an Ajax-enabled web page. It facilitates partial page rendering of a web page using the UpdatePanel, provides access to web services, and enables registering the scripts. The other control in this group—the ScriptManagerProxy—as the name suggests, acts as a "proxy" to the ScriptManager control instance.

The Partial Update Group

The Partial Update or the Partial Page Rendering group contains the following controls:

- ▶ UpdatePanel

- ▶ UpdateProgress

- ▶ Timer

The UpdatePanel acts as a container of controls that you can use for specifying the portion of your web page where you need partial page rendering. This is the control that works together with the ScriptManager control to provide you with an asynchronous callback feature—that is, an asynchronous mode of operation that requires less network and server load and provides you with an awesome user experience. The UpdateProgress controls work together with the UpdatePanel control and are displayed automatically whenever an asynchronous update operation is started.

The Application Services Bridge

The application services bridge is an API that enables the different application services like authentication and profile management to be invoked from the client-side script.

The Web Services Bridge

The web services bridge is an API that provides access to external web services from the client-side script. You have JavaScript proxies available to access these web services. Both of these bridges are responsible for asynchronous communication support.

The following section discusses the ASP.NET Ajax client framework.

What's Inside the ASP.NET Ajax Client Framework?

The ASP.NET Ajax client framework is essentially comprised of a set of JavaScript files that form part of a library commonly called the Microsoft Ajax Library. The major components that are included in this library are the following:

- ▶ The Component Layer
- ▶ The Core Services Layer
- ▶ The Browser Compatibility Layer

Let's now take a quick look at each of these components.

The Core Component Layer

The Component Layer is comprised of a set of nonvisual components that provide support for asynchronous communication, networking, localization, XML and JSON serialization, ASP.NET application services, and so on.

The Core Services Layer

The Core Services Layer contains the ASP.NET Ajax Base Class Library and its extensions, which facilitate object-oriented programming and an extension to the existing JavaScript types.

The Browser Compatibility Layer

The Browser Compatibility Layer is responsible for providing cross-browser support for Ajax-enabled web pages—that is, support for browsers such as IE, Mozilla, Firefox, and so on.

> JSON, the abbreviated form of JavaScript Object Notation, is a subset of JavaScript. It is actually a good replacement for XML as a data interchange format. Moreover, it is lightweight and much simpler to read and write compared to XML. We'll learn more about JSON later in this book.

By the Way

Summary

Those days of unavoidable page refreshes and slow response times are now history. With Ajax, you can now use client-side scripting to talk to the web server and exchange data with a massive usage of JavaScript. Using Ajax, you can cut down on the network load and the bandwidth usage and retrieve only the data that is required to give you faster interfaces, richer user interfaces, and better response times. We have had a bird's-eye view of the architecture of ASP.NET Ajax in this hour; we learn about the XMLHttpObject in the next hour.

Workshop

Quiz

1. What is the purpose of the PageHandlerFactory?

2. What are the names of the sequence of events in the page life cycle?

3. What are the components of the ASP.NET Ajax server extensions framework?

4. Name the controls that are part of the Partial Page Rendering group.

5. Name the components of the ASP.NET Ajax Client Library.

6. Name some common Ajax frameworks, apart from the ASP.NET Ajax framework.

7. Name the controls that are part of the Script Management group.

8. What is JSON?

Answers

1. The PageHandlerFactory is responsible for creating a page instance and returning it to the HttpRuntime through the HttpApplicationFactory.

2. The sequence of events that occur in the page life cycle are as follows:

    1. Page_Init

    2. LoadViewState

    3. LoadPostData

    4. Page_Load

    5. RaisePostDataChangedEvent

    6. RaisePostBackEvent

    7. Page_PreRender

    8. SaveViewState

    9. Page_Render

    10. Page_UnLoad

3. The ASP.NET Ajax server extensions framework includes the following:

    ▶ ASP.NET Ajax server controls

    ▶ Application services bridge

    ▶ Web services bridge

4. The Partial Page Rendering group contains the following controls:

    ▶ UpdatePanel

    ▶ UpdateProgress

    ▶ Timer

5. The major components that are included as part of the ASP.NET Ajax Client Library are the following:

    ▶ Component Layer

    ▶ Core Services Layer

    ▶ Browser Compatibility Layer

6. Some common Ajax frameworks are the following:

 ▶ Atlas

 ▶ AJAXPro.NET

 ▶ MagicAJAX.NET

 ▶ Anthem.NET

7. The controls that are part of the Script Management group are as follows:

 ▶ ScriptManager

 ▶ ScriptManagerProxy

8. JSON, the abbreviated form of JavaScript Object Notation, is a subset of JavaScript. It is lightweight and actually a good alternative to XML as a data interchange format.

HOUR 3

Working with the
XMLHttpRequest **Object**

What You'll Learn in This Hour:

▶ An overview of the XMLHttpRequest object
▶ Creating the XMLHttpRequest object
▶ Synchronous and asynchronous data retrieval using XMLHttpRequest
▶ Working with the XMLHttpRequest object
▶ Simulating Ajax without XMLHttpRequest

In the preceding hours, we looked at Ajax and its architecture. In this hour, we examine the XMLHttpRequest object, which forms the heart of an Ajax application—this is the foundation that acts as a communication layer between the server and the client. We take a look at how the page requests are made, both synchronously and asynchronously, using this object and also how the responses are handled.

An Overview of the XMLHttpRequest **Object**

To put it simply, the XMLHttpRequest object uses JavaScript to make requests to the server and process the response, thereby minimizing the postback delays. It can be called as an API that can be used by JavaScript to transfer XML and other formats of data between the server and client using HTTP. Microsoft invented this object; it was initially designed to load XML documents from JavaScript. The name XMLHttpRequest might be misleading because of the term XML, but, in fact, you can transfer the data in XML or other text-based formats. These formats can be plain text, HTML, or JSON. JSON is an acronym for JavaScript Object Notation. The XMLHttpRequest object plays an important role in the development of Ajax-style applications to implement responsive and dynamic web applications.

Looking Back in Time

The XMLHttpRequest object came into existence as early as 1998, when Microsoft first introduced it in its IE 4.0 web browser. However, it had limited functionality, and it came in as an ActiveXObject in IE 5.0.

The usage of this object became more popular courtesy of Google, with its implementation of Google Maps and GMail. Later, Microsoft created its own implementation of Virtual Earth. The World Wide Web Consortium (W3C) published the latest working draft and specification of the XMLHttpRequest object's API on June 18, 2007. You can view a draft of this at this link: www.w3.org/TR/XMLHttpRequest/.

There are several other browser vendors who have started implementing this object to benefit this approach. The list of browsers that support this object include IE 5.0 and above, Mozilla 1.0 and above, Firefox, Safari 1.2 and above, and Opera 8.0 and above.

Creating the XMLHttpRequest Object

You can create the object for ActiveX by passing the name of the object to its constructor:

```
var xmlHttp = new ActiveXObject("Microsoft.XMLHTTP");
```

The preceding syntax works for IE browsers; however, for Mozilla and Safari browsers, you can just make a call to the constructor of the XMLHttpRequest class without any arguments:

```
var xmlHttp = new XmlHttpRequest();
```

For Mozilla, Safari, and Opera browsers, this object is a native JavaScript object, as compared to IE 5.0 and 6.0 versions, where this comes as an ActiveXObject. Ironically, IE 7.0 has also made the XMLHttpRequest object a native JavaScript object. Because this object has different implementations for different browsers, and because this object is used in every web page for performing request and response, we can encapsulate all this into a single JavaScript file and expose a method called getXmlHttpRequestObject().

Let's put this method and the variable xmlHttp in a JavaScript file called xmlhttp.js and include this JavaScript file in every web page. The later hours that use the XMLHttpRequest object will use this JavaScript file. The variable xmlHttp now holds the instance of the XMLHttpRequest object.

The XMLHttpRequest object does not work on IE 6.0 if ActiveX is disabled.

The following is the code snippet in the `xmlhttp.js` JavaScript file:

```
var xmlHttp = false;
function getXmlHttpRequestObject() {
    // check for native XMLHttpRequest object
    if(window.XMLHttpRequest && !(window.ActiveXObject)) {
    try {
            xmlHttp = new XMLHttpRequest();
        }
    catch(e) {
            xmlHttp = false;
        }
    }
    // check for IE/Windows ActiveX version
    else if(window.ActiveXObject) {
        try {
            xmlHttp = new ActiveXObject("Msxml2.XMLHTTP");
        }
    catch(e) {
            try {
                xmlHttp = new ActiveXObject("Microsoft.XMLHTTP");
            }
            catch(e) {
                xmlHttp = false;
            }
        }
    }
}
```

The `getXmlHttpRequestObject()` method encapsulates the functionality of instan-
tiating the XMLHttpRequest object for different browsers. To perform any request
using this object, we simply check the status of the variable xmlHttp. If it validates
to false, then the object has not been instantiated—or else you get an instance of the
XMLHttpRequest in this variable for use. The function getXmlHttpRequest() first
checks for the native XMLHttpRequest object. Refer to the following code snippet:

```
if(window.XMLHttpRequest && !(window.ActiveXObject))
```

If window.XMLHttpRequest validates to true and window.ActiveXObject validates
to false, then the native object instance is created and set to the variable xmlHttp.
This is executed for the Mozilla, Safari, Opera, and IE 7.0 browsers. The "else if"
block checks for the existence of ActiveXObject. Refer to the following code snippet:

```
    try {
        xmlHttp = new ActiveXObject("Msxml2.XMLHTTP");
        }
    catch(e) {
            try {
```

```
            xmlHttp = new ActiveXObject("Microsoft.XMLHTTP");
        }
    catch(e) {
        xmlHttp = false;
    }
```

If the browser type is IE, an instance of type `ActiveXObject` is created and is set to
the variable xmlHttp.

> The XMLHttpRequest object can make requests only to the same domain as the
> currently loaded page. This security policy is also known as the "same origin"
> policy.

Synchronous and Asynchronous Data Retrieval Using the XmlHttpRequest Object

Now that we have learned how to create the XMLHttpRequest object, we examine
how the request and response is handled. Let's illustrate this by calling a resource on
the server. To make this simpler, we call an XML file from the server onto the browser. This process can be handled in two ways: synchronously and asynchronously.
First, we see how the request is handled synchronously.

Synchronous Data Retrieval

Let's use the method getXmlHttpRequestObject() to create an instance of the
XMLHttpRequest object. Now this instance is set to the xmlHttp variable, as shown
in the following code snippet:

```
<script language="javascript" type="text/javascript" src=xmlhttp.js></script>
<script language="javascript">
function getXMLDocument(url) {
        getXmlHttpRequestObject();
        if(xmlHttp) {
                xmlHttp.open("GET", url, false);
                xmlHttp.send(null);
                alert("Request / Response handled synchronously");
        }
}
//here is the method call for getXMLDocument
getXMLDocument ("http://" + location.host + "AJAX/Items.xml");
</script>
```

Note that all the processing is bundled in the method called getXMLDocument. This method expects an URL as a parameter. This is the URL of the web server to be accessed. After this method is invoked, the getXmlHttpRequestObject() method is called and an instance of XMLHttpRequest is set to the variable xmlHttp. Next, this variable is validated to check if it is null or an instance is associated with it. If this variable holds the instance, the open() method is invoked with three parameters. Although the first two parameters are mandatory, the third parameter is an optional one. The first parameter is the type of request. This can be any of the standard HTTP verbs: GET, POST, PUT, or HEAD. GET is primarily for operations on data retrieval requests. POST is used to send data to the server, especially data greater than 512 bytes in size.

In our example, we've used GET as the first parameter because we are retrieving an xml file from the server. The second parameter is the URL, and this is the address of the web server where the application resides. Refer to the following code snippet:

```
("http://" + location.host + "AJAX/Items.xml");
```

In the preceding URL, we've used location.host property. Location is the address of the web server, and host property is the port number. Suppose our URL is the following:

> http://localhost:3041/AJAX/Items.xml

The location here is "localhost," and the port number is 3041.

A port is an unsigned integer that uniquely identifies a process running over a network. On the contrary, a socket is the end point of a two-way communication between two processes running over a network.

By the Way

The third optional parameter in the Open method is a Boolean value, which is "true" for an asynchronous request and "false" for a synchronous request. (The default value is "true.") In our example, we've set it to "false," because we require a synchronous operation—that is, the script would wait for the request to be sent and for a response to be received from the server.

Next, the send method is called, which performs the actual request. Note that we've specified an alert statement to display a message box that is displayed only after the request is processed and returned from the server.

What we've seen is a synchronous operation that is similar to the normal request/ response process in any web application. But the real power of the XMLHttpRequest object is that it facilitates asynchronous operations. We discuss how you can use the XMLHttpRequest object to perform asynchronous operations in the next section.

Asynchronous Data Retrieval

Let's run through the same example we used in the preceding section in an asynchronous mode of operation for data retrieval. All we have to do here is change the third parameter of the open method to true (indicating the asynchronous mode of retrieval). Refer to the following code snippet:

```
function getXMLDocument(url) {
        getXmlHttpRequestObject();
        if(xmlHttp) {
                xmlHttp.open("GET", url, true);
                xmlHttp.onreadystatechange = processRequest
                xmlHttp.send(null);
        }
}
function processRequest(url) {
        if(xmlHttp.readyState == 4) {
            //Processing…to be done here........
            alert("Request / Response handled Asynchronously");
        }
}
```

Note that in the preceding snippet, the third parameter of the open method is set to "true," which is indicative of an asynchronous mode of data retrieval. This implies that the user need not wait until the script has completed execution on the server. After the state has been changed, it triggers the callback method associated with the onreadystatechange event. In the previous example, the request to url on the server is done asynchronously, and a callback method called processRequest is set to the onreadystatechange event. The processRequest method on the client is executed accordingly. The following code snippet illustrates the processRequest method:

```
        if(xmlHttp.readyState == 4) {
            //Processing...to be done here........
            alert("Request / Response handled Asynchronously");
        }
```

There are several values associated with the state change process. In our example, we are checking whether the value of the readyState property is 4 (meaning "complete").

Tables 3.1, 3.2, and 3.3 list the status codes, properties, and methods of the XMLHttpRequest object.

TABLE 3.1 Status Codes for the readyState Property of the XMLHttpObject

Status Code	Status Code Description	Status of the XMLHttpRequest Object
0	Uninitialized	The object has been created but not initialized. (The open method has not been called.)
1	Loading	The object has been created, but the send method has not been called.
2	Loaded	The send method has been called, but the status and headers are not yet available.
3	Interactive	Some data has been received. Calling the responseBody and responseText properties at this state to obtain partial results will return an error, because status and response headers are not fully available.
4	Completed	All the data has been received, and the complete data is available in the responseBody and responseText properties.

TABLE 3.2 The XMLHttpObject Properties

Property	Description	
onreadystatechange	An event handler for an event that fires at every state change	Read/Write
readyState	Returns the current state of the request	Read Only
responseText	Response in string format	Read Only
responseXML	Response in XML format	Read Only
Status	Status code returned by server	
	Example: 200 (OK), 404 (Not Found), and so on	Read Only
statusText	String for the corresponding status code	Read Only

TABLE 3.3   The XMLHttpObject **Methods**

Method	Description
abort()	Cancels the current request.
getAllResponseHeaders()	Returns a complete set of HTTP headers (labels and values) as string.
getResponseHeader("headername")	Returns the specified string value of the HTTP header.
open("method", "URL"[, asyncFlag[, "userName"[, "password"]]])	Specifies the method, URL, and other optional parameters of a request.
	The method parameter can have any of the values GET, POST,PUT, or HEAD.
	The URL parameter may be a relative URL or complete URL.
	The asyncFlag parameter specifies whether the request should be handled asynchronously. "True" indicates that the script processing carries on after the send() method, without waiting for a response, and "false" indicates that the script waits for a response before continuing script processing. By default, it is set to true.
Send(content)	Sends the request to the server and receives the response.
setRequestHeader(label, value)	Adds a label/value pair to the HTTP header to be sent.

Working with the XMLHttpRequest Object

So far, we've seen the creation and usage of the XMLHttpRequest object in both synchronous and asynchronous fashion. Let's now see how the XMLHttpRequest object can be used to load an XML file and display its contents in the web browser. We will also discuss the usage of the responseXML property of the XMLHttpRequest object in this section.

Let's open the same solution file (.sln file) that we created earlier and proceed with the following steps:

1. Add a new item, the Web Form, and name it FetchXml.aspx.

2. Create an XML file called Items.xml populated with the following sample data:

```xml
<?xml version="1.0" encoding="utf-8" ?>
<ItemList>
  <Item>
    <Name>HP</Name>
    <Model>5446 A</Model>
    <Make>2007</Make>
    <Price>$ 896.00</Price>
  </Item>
  <Item>
    <Name>Compaq</Name>
    <Model>654AN</Model>
    <Make>2006</Make>
    <Price>$ 655.00</Price>
  </Item>
  <Item>
    <Name>DELL</Name>
    <Model>34543656</Model>
    <Make>2007</Make>
    <Price>$ 720.00</Price>
  </Item>
</ItemList>
```

3. Add the Items.xml file to the solution.

4. Switch to the FetchXML.aspx page and paste the following code in the source view:

```
<%@ Page Language="C#" AutoEventWireup="true" CodeFile="FetchXML.aspx.cs"
Inherits="FetchXML" %>
<!DOCTYPE html PUBLIC "-//W3C//DTD XHTML 1.0 Transitional//EN"
"http://www.w3.org/TR/xhtml1/DTD/xhtml1-transitional.dtd">
<html xmlns="http://www.w3.org/1999/xhtml">
<script language="javascript" type="text/javascript"
src=xmlhttp.js></script>
<script language="javascript" type="text/javascript">
    function LoadItemNames() {
        getXmlHttpRequestObject();
        xmlHttp.open("GET", "Items.xml", true);
        xmlHttp.onreadystatechange = function()
        {
            if (xmlHttp.readyState == 4) {
                //If the Http Status code is 200, i.e., if the request
is ok.
                if (xmlHttp.status == 200) {
                    var xml = xmlHttp.responseXML.documentElement;
                    //itemList variable below contains the list of items.
                    var itemList = xml.getElementsByTagName("Name");
```

```
                            //Fetching the reference of the <select> tag -
➥ddlItems
                            var ddlItems = document.getElementById("ddlItems");
                            for(var i = 0; i < itemList.length; i++) {
                                //creating new <option> tag
                                var newOption =
document.createElement('option');
                                //assigning value and text to the new option tag.
                                newOption.value = itemList[i].firstChild.data;
                                newOption.text = itemList[i].firstChild.data;
                                //adding new item in the <select> tag ddlItems.
                                ddlItems.options.add(newOption);
                            }
                        }
                    }
                }
            xmlHttp.send(null);
        }
        function LoadItemText() {
            getXmlHttpRequestObject();
            xmlHttp.open("GET", "Items.xml", true);
            xmlHttp.onreadystatechange = function()
            {
                    if (xmlHttp.readyState == 4) {
                        //If the Http Status code is 200, i.e, if the request
➥is ok.
                        if (xmlHttp.status == 200) {
                            document.getElementById("lblText").innerText =
➥xmlHttp.responseText;
                        }
                    }
            }
            xmlHttp.send(null);
        }
        </script>
<head runat="server">
    <title>Example of XmlHttpRequest Object</title>
</head>
<body>
    <form id="form1" runat="server">
        <input type="button" id="btnLoadItemNames"
value="Load Item Names"
onclick="LoadItemNames();" /> 
<span id="spnItemNames">Items</span>
        <select id="ddlItems">
            <option value="">— — — — —-</option>
        </select><br /><br />
        <input type="button" id="btnLoadItemText"
value="Load XML as Text"
onclick="LoadItemText();" /> 
        <div id="lblText"></div>
    </form>
</body>
</html>
```

5. Now that the entire infrastructure is ready, let's execute the application to see
   the results. Right-click FetchXML.aspx and click the option Set As Start Page,
   as shown in Figure 3.1.

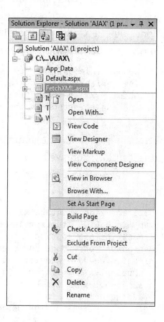

FIGURE 3.1
Setting the
start-up page
for the applica-
tion

6. Now execute the application by pressing the function key F5. If debugging is
   set to false in the web.config file, you'll be prompted to enable it to true.
   After this is done, the application opens up in a browser, as shown in
   Figure 3.2.

FIGURE 3.2
The
FetchXML.aspx
page in the
browser

Initially, the DropDownList is empty. When you click the button Load Item Names,
the items are loaded from the XML file Items.xml into the DropDownList Items.
This is done by calling the JavaScript method LoadItemNames(), as shown in the
following code snippet:

```
<input type="button" id="btnLoadItemNames"
value="Load Item Names"
onclick="LoadItemNames();" />
```

In the LoadItemNames() method, we fetch the Items.xml file from the server through the XMLHttpRequest object. After the processing is done, the callback function of the onreadystatechange event is invoked, which checks the readyState property to see if the process is complete. It then checks with the status of the HTTP request to see if the code is 200—that is, whether a successful request has been made. Next, the response is sent back in XML format and is set to the responseXML property of the xmlHttp, as shown in the following code snippet:

```
var xml = xmlHttp.responseXML.documentElement;
                        //itemList variable below contains the list of items.
                        var itemList = xml.getElementsByTagName("Name");
                        //Fetching the reference of the <select> tag - ddlItems
```

The variable xml defined previously now holds the documentElement object, which can navigate to any of the tags it holds. Here we get hold of the list of Name tags and iterate through them to dynamically populate the DropDownList Items, as shown in the following code snippet:

```
                        var ddlItems = document.getElementById("ddlItems");
                        for(var i = 0; i < itemList.length; i++) {
                            //creating new <option> tag
                            var newOption = document.createElement('option');
                            //assigning value and text to the new option tag.
                            newOption.value = itemList[i].firstChild.data;
                            newOption.text = itemList[i].firstChild.data;
                            //adding new item in the <select> tag ddlItems.
                            ddlItems.options.add(newOption);
                        }
```

Figure 3.3 looks at the web page after the data is populated.

FIGURE 3.3
The
FetchXML.aspx
page after the
data is loaded
from the XML
file

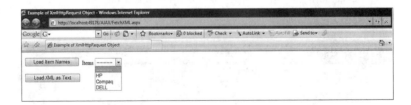

The second button in the web page, Load XML as Text, illustrates loading the same XML file Items.xml from the server as a text on the browser. This has similar functionality to the preceding except that the responseText property is used, and the output of this string is bound to the div tag called lblText on the web page. Refer to the following code snippet:

```
if (xmlHttp.status == 200) {
        document.getElementById("lblText").innerText = xmlHttp.responseText;
}
```

Figure 3.4 shows the output in the browser.

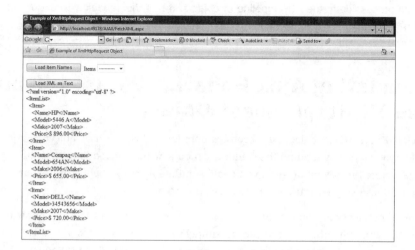

FIGURE 3.4
The
FetchXML.aspx
page displaying
the xml data as
string from the
Items.xml file

In the preceding example, we've used both the response properties. The
responseText property was used to directly fetch the xml as string and bind it to
the div tag; the responseXML was used to load the xml data into a DropDownList
control with the help of its documentElement, which holds the reference of the XML
object returned. This documentElement can be used to iterate through its nodes.
Here we've picked up its first node using the property firstChild and populated its
data into the DropDownList control.

The XMLHttpRequest object requires an URL to initiate a request to the server.
Typically, the processing on the server involves a page with its complete life cycle.
However, imagine a scenario where you only require processing a logic and returning data without the need of displaying any user interface to the user. In such situations, if you use the XMLHttpRequest object to invoke a web page that has such
logic in it, it becomes an overhead as the web page will only be rendered in your
web browser after it is done executing the entire page life cycle events. Instead,
there are other alternatives and better approaches in the form of web services, or
even HTTP handlers for that matter. We discuss these approaches later in this book.

> An Http handler is used to handle requests and hooks itself before the actual page processing in the Http Pipeline of objects. It has the capability to act on the response object after processing the request.

Simulating Ajax Behavior Without Using the XMLHttpRequest Object

The XMLHttpRequest object has become a popular and widely used object for Ajax-style applications by loading the content of a page without reloading the entire page. Before the advent of Ajax, you could simulate Ajax-like behavior in your applications using IFrames, Flash, Cookies, and so on.

IFrames make asynchronous calls to the web server and can load the content without reloading the entire page. A few advantages and disadvantages of this approach are listed next, which makes it clear as to how it compares to XMLHttpRequest.

The advantages of this approach are as follows:

▶ Ability to access web pages asynchronously

▶ Support for file uploads

However, the disadvantages of this approach are the following:

▶ Cannot perform a synchronous operation

▶ Provides less-intuitive user experience

Because IFrame supports only accessing pages through its src attribute, the entire page life cycle has to be executed to generate output.

> In the case of XMLHttpRequest, there are many other options of processing on the server, as discussed earlier.

> If your Ajax-style applications need to be supported on lower-version browsers where XMLHttpRequest is not supported, you can proceed by using IFrames.

So, we looked at the alternatives to the XMLHttpRequest object for simulating Ajax-like operations. However, modern-day web browsers have support for the XMLHttpRequest object—the core of all Ajax operations in any Ajax-enabled web application.

Summary

The XMLHttpRequest object forms the heart of Ajax applications and has a good programming model to handle requests and responses effectively. It has taken the dynamic content loading to newer heights by improving the performance considerably. The only drawback is that its implementation differs for different browsers. However, there are alternate approaches to get around this, and you can implement Ajax-like web applications using IFrames.

Workshop

Quiz

1. How do you instantiate an XMLHttpRequest object on the IE 6.0 and Mozilla browsers?

2. What are the properties used for handling responses through an XMLHttpRequest object?

3. True or False: The cancel() method is used to stop a current XMLHttpRequest.

4. True or False: url is the third parameter of the open() method of the XMLHttpRequest object.

5. What does the readyState property 4 indicate?

6. What is the purpose of the onreadystatechange event handler?

7. What are the alternate ways of achieving Ajax functionalities without using an XMLHttpRequest object?

Answers

1. XMLHttpRequest instantiation on IE 6.0 is as follows:

```
try {

        xmlHttpObj = new ActiveXObject("Msxml2.XMLHTTP"):
}
catch(e) {
        xmlHttpObj = new ActiveXObject("Microsoft.XMLHTTP");
}    //detecting the available version of MSXML parser in try...catch
```

XMLHttpRequest instantiation on Mozilla is as follows:

```
xmlHttpObj = new XMLHttpRequest();
```

2. responseText and responseXML. responseText holds the response in string format, whereas responseXML property holds the response in XML format.

3. False. Abort() is the method used to stop the current running XMLHttpRequest.

4. False. url is the second parameter of the open() method in XMLHttpRequest. This parameter is used to request the page in the url mentioned. The third parameter is a Boolean value indicating a synchronous or an asynchronous mode of retrieval of data. The default value is "true," which indicates an asynchronous mode of data retrieval.

5. The value 4 in the readyState property indicates that the request is complete.

6. The onreadystatechange event handler is used for an asynchronous mode of operation. After an asynchronous request is sent to the web server, the user can perform any other action on the page. After the processing is complete for this request, the callback method associated with the onreadystatechange event handler is triggered and processed.

7. There are several ways of achieving Ajax-style applications without using the XMLHttpRequest object, such as IFrames, Flash, Cookies, and so on.

HOUR 4

Understanding Client-Side Scripting

What You'll Learn in This Hour:

- ▶ An introduction to DHTML
- ▶ Key ingredients that impact client-side behavior and scripting
- ▶ Understanding the Document Object Model

Web development has made rapid progress over the years, from displaying static web content in HTML pages to manipulating dynamic content with the help of components on the client like CSS, as well as scripting languages like JavaScript. Ajax-style applications rely heavily on client-side scripting to achieve asynchronous communication with the web server. In this hour, we learn how client-side scripting works and how it is achieved with the help of DHTML, JavaScript, and DOM. This hour is only a refresher of DHTML, core JavaScript, and DOM, and reviews the key concepts of each. If you are completely new to JavaScript, you can refer to books such as *JavaScript: A Beginner's Guide* by John Pollock or *Learning JavaScript* by Shelley Powers.

Introducing DHTML

Dynamic HTML paved the way for developing interactive web applications by manipulating web content on a page dynamically. When we say "dynamic," we are referring to the manipulation of content and style of HTML elements in a web page, which can occur after or during the page rendering on the client browser. Therefore, this dynamic processing is done on the client side without any page refreshes.

Dynamic HTML basically constitutes the technologies Hypertext Markup Language (HTML), Cascading Style Sheets (CSS), and JavaScript. It is these three technologies working in tandem that help the web content to be changeable dynamically.

DHTML is neither a markup language nor a technology by itself and is not a World Wide Web Consortium (W3C) standard. The term "DHTML" is more of a buzzword in the Internet world.

All the page elements in HTML are recognized by a construct called the Document Object Model (DOM). This model describes the structure of a web page by emphasizing each page element and its behavior with a set of properties and methods defined. JavaScript interacts with DOM properties and methods of this model to manipulate the page elements. We'll discuss the structure of DOM later in this hour.

Dynamic HTML was initially introduced by Microsoft in its Internet Explorer 4.0 version. Netscape has also come up with its DHTML support in Navigator 4.0. In this version, Netscape introduced the concept of layers, which was also known as Cascading Style Sheet Positioning. Unfortunately, Microsoft and Netscape do not share a common DOM. There were implementation differences of DOM between these two vendors. The good news is that efforts to standardize DOM are in place and under constant improvement. The latest specification of DOM can be found at www.w3c.org/DOM.

The introduction of DHTML, coupled with the emergence of Cascading Style Sheets, enabled programmers to modify content or style of a loaded page using JavaScript. Before we jump into an example of how to manipulate content using CSS and JavaScript using DOM, let's throw some light on CSS and JavaScript.

What Is CSS?

Cascading Style Sheets define the page-rendering mechanism by setting page-markup definitions that can be applied to an HTML document. This can be done internally in each HTML document of the web site or can reside on the server in a separate .css file and be referenced in each of the HTML documents. Having this as a separate file makes sense, as this can be a centralized point of change for any styles in the web site. Numerous styles can be applied to a file, and what the developer or end user needs to change is the style name of their HTML elements, which is associated in the .css file.

Well, what is CSS? CSS is basically used for styling and positioning an HTML element. This enables the web site manager to extend formatting features to be presented to the viewer.

One of the major drawbacks of CSS is that it is not compatible with all browsers. If JavaScript is disabled in your web browser or is incompatible across the browsers (even with different versions of the same vendor), the content formatting or styles would not be applied to the HTML elements. They would simply be ignored and would be reverted to the standard HTML.

The idea of implementing DHTML (CSS and JavaScript using DOM) would be most appropriate in an intranet world where all the audience implements the same browser. In this way, the incompatibility issues wouldn't come into the picture and greater performance could be achieved.

Did you Know?

Here is how a typical `.css` file looks:

```
.font
{
font-family:Verdana, Arial, Helvetica, sans-serif;
font-size:10px;
color:#003366;
}
.heading
{
font-family:Verdana, Arial, Helvetica, sans-serif;
font-size:14px;
font-weight:bold;
color:#003366;
}
.subheading
{
font-family:Verdana, Arial, Helvetica, sans-serif;
font-size:12px;
font-weight:bold;
color:#E15438;
}
```

In the preceding content, you find several attributes bundled inside the braces with a name. This is represented as a class in CSS jargon. So, font, heading, and sub-heading are all classes in the sense that they act as formatters when applied to an HTML element in a page. Let's say our web site has standard heading and subhead-ings for several sections spread across all the pages. Instead of setting all these attributes to the HTML tag wherever a heading is present, we can directly associate this class to that tag, as shown next:

```
<div id="divHeading" class="heading">
        Learning Cascading Style Sheets !
</div>
```

By the Way

> When style sheet classes are used in your HTML tags, remember to reference the .css file in each of your HTML pages, as follows:
>
> ```
> <link type="text/css" rel="stylesheet" href="styles.css">
> ```
>
> Here, the name of the .css file is styles.css. It is recommended to place the Link tag in between the <Head> starting and closing tags.

So far, we've discussed content display using CSS. The next important thing to know is positioning the content dynamically. Positioning a block of content certainly requires specifying the Style properties. Table 4.1 displays the various Style properties available.

TABLE 4.1   **Style Properties**

Position	This is used to specify where the block is to be placed relative to other page elements. These values can be one of the following:
	"position:absolute;"
	"position:relative;"
	"position:static;"
Width	This is used to specify the width in pixels or percentage at which the content of the block should wrap.
	Examples: "width:25px;" or "width:25%;"
Height	This is used to specify the height of the block in pixels or percentage.
	Examples: "height:25px;" or "height:25%;"
Left	This is used to specify the relative offset of the left edge of the block. If you specify positive values, it implies offset toward the right; negative values imply offset toward the left.
	Examples: "left:10px;" or "left:-10px;"
Top	This is used to specify the offset from the top edge of the block relative to the *position* attribute. As usual, +ve values imply toward the bottom and –ve values imply toward the top of the block.
	Examples: "top:10px;" or "top:-10px;"
Clip	This is used to specify the visible rectangular portion of the block. You can use this to show a specific portion of the block only to the user.
	Syntax: clip:rect(*top right bottom left*)

TABLE 4.1 Continued

visibility	This is used to indicate whether the block should or should not be visible.
z-index	This is used to specify the z-index or the "stacking order" of blocks.
	Example: *"z-index:5;"*
background-color	This is used to specify the background color of a block.
	Example: *"background-color:blue;"*
background-image	This is used to specify the background image of a block.
	Example: *"background-image:url('images/joydip-sriram.jpg');"*

> To position a block of content dynamically, Netscape uses <LAYER> tag or style sheet syntax. On the contrary, Microsoft's IE supports the style sheet syntax only.

By the Way

Here is an example of a <DIV> tag, which holds a hyperlink to redirect it to a details page:

```
<DIV ID="details" STYLE="position:absolute; width:auto; height:auto; left:300px;
top:100px; background-color:white">
        <a href="Details.aspx">Show Details</a>
</DIV>
```

We've used CSS positioning for the preceding <DIV> tag by using the Style property. Table 4.1 describes the various attributes of the Style property. In the preceding snippet, we've referred to the following attributes: position, width, height, left, top, and background color.

The CSS positioning is fine, but how do we make this dynamic, or what could be the different cases to make this dynamic? Let's say we want to make this block invisible or change the background color. This is where JavaScript comes in. This scripting language is used to modify the properties of the <DIV> tag. Now you can change the background color, or make it visible or invisible, with the help of events like onmouseover, onmouseout, onclick, and so on, which we discuss later in this hour.

Now how does JavaScript access the properties of the <DIV> tag? The contents of the <DIV> tag are exposed as a property by the Document Object Model (DOM). These properties act as objects, which, in turn, have properties inside them. STYLE is a property of the <DIV> tag. But STYLE, in turn, has several properties, such as position, width, height, and so on. Therefore, STYLE can be treated as an object in itself that contains several properties.

You can use JavaScript statements to set or get the properties of an object. You can even use JavaScript to access the style sheet properties of a block by following the object and property specifications of DOM. However, as said earlier, Netscape and Microsoft do not share a common DOM. Each of these has a specification of its own. Like in the example we've seen previously, the `<DIV>` block takes the form of a Layer object in Netscape's DOM; Microsoft exposes this as a `<DIV>` object that has STYLE as an object, which in turn has several properties.

For example, to refer to the background color of the content block in Microsoft's Internet Explorer, you can use the following:

```
document.all[Details].style.backgroundColor = red;
```

In Netscape, the same can be represented as follows:

```
document.layers[Details].bgcolor = red;
```

To refer to height property, use the following:

```
document.all[Details].style.height = 10; //In Internet Explorer
document.layers[Details].height = 10; //In Netscape Navigator
```

There can be several other uses of dynamic positioning apart from what we've seen in the preceding examples. The most common in our day-to-day applications is having a drop-down menu that is categorized, well structured, and organized, which helps in navigating the entire web site with ease. When placed on a menu item that has several subitems under it, a block of content would be visible to navigate to any of its subitems. You can achieve this using JavaScript and DOM. Its properties make it easier to modify the block of content and then swap it at different positions on the page.

Event Handling with JavaScript

The dynamic content or style modifications happen when the user triggers an action on a web page. This is achieved through events on the HTML elements. Many events can occur on a web page—for example, when you are moving the mouse over an HTML element, an `onmouseover` event is fired. When a button is clicked, an `onclick` event is fired. You can have these events handled through JavaScript code. The good thing is all the basic events are handled quite similarly among different browsers. Here is a small example showcasing the `onclick` event and its handler:

```
<input type=button id=btnDisplay value=Display
onclick=alert('Button click event is fired !');/>
```

The HTML button `btnDisplay` has an attribute, `onclick`, which is an event fired whenever the button is clicked. Note that you can write your JavaScript code inline—that is, by placing the code directly inside the `onClick` attribute of a button or, even in a function, referred to as an event handler because it is associated with a particular event. But, what are event handlers? An event is associated with its corresponding event handler—a function that is triggered when the event is fired. As an example, you can associate an event handler to the `onClick` event that actually does some processing, such as form validations, calculations, and so on. Table 4.2 lists all the common event handlers.

TABLE 4.2   Event Handlers

Event	Description
onClick	Occurs when you click an element
onSubmit	Occurs when you submit a form and prior to the same being processed
onReset	Occurs when you reset a form
onFocus	Occurs when you bring an element to focus
onBlur	Occurs when the focus on an element is lost
onMouseOver	Occurs when you move the mouse over an element
onMouseOut	Occurs when you mouse off an element
onMouseMove	Occurs when you move the mouse
onChange	Occurs when you change the value in a text, a text area, or a select field
onSelect	Occurs when you select a portion of text in a text or a text area element
onResize	Occurs when you resize the browser window or the frame
onMove	Occurs when you move the browser window or the frame
onLoad	Occurs when the page has finished loading
onUnload	Occurs when you exit off a page
onError	Occurs when an error has occurred due to a fault in loading an image or a document
onAbort	Occurs when you stop an image while it is loading
Onkeydown	Occurs when you press a key
Onkeyup	Occurs when you release a key
Onkeypress	Occurs when the onkeydown event is followed by the onkeyup event

> Not every event is applicable to every HTML element. This varies among different browsers. For a complete reference of events and event handlers, refer to the following resources:
>
> http://msdn.microsoft.com/workshop/author/dhtml/reference/events.asp
>
> http://developer.netscape.com/docs/manuals/communicator/jsref/evnt.htm

JavaScript and the Document Object Model

JavaScript is a client-side scripting language brought out by Netscape. It is an interpreted language that comes along with the browser. Today every browser in the market supports JavaScript language. Keep in mind, however, that it is in no way connected to the language Java. The syntax is similar to C language and is dynamically typed. In this hour, we discuss the major concepts related to JavaScript to obtain a basic understanding of client-side scripting using JavaScript.

JavaScript is an ECMAScript-based language that makes use of the Document Object Model (DOM). ECMAScript is the innovation of the European Computer Manufacturers Association and is said to be the standardized version of JavaScript. ECMAScript is a general standard for many other scripting languages.

What is Document Object Model (DOM)? The DOM is a set of objects, methods, and properties that allow JavaScript to read and modify an HTML or XHTML document. XHTML is the newer version of HTML, which states that all the tags should be well formed (as in the case of XML).

JavaScript is based on objects and its properties and methods. A few of the JavaScript objects include the Window object, the Array object, the Object object, the Document object, and so on. The DOM represents the tree structure of a document, where the nodes of this tree can be accessed using the JavaScript programming language. Figure 4.1 shows the representation of the DOM tree.

There are different types of nodes in the tree shown in Figure 4.1: elements, attributes, and text nodes. The root node is called the document element. The example of an attribute node is href in the anchor tag. The relationships that exist in this tree are parent, children, and siblings. Each node has a parent except the root. An attribute's parent is the element, and an element's parent is the element that contains it. Here, href is an attribute of the <a> (anchor) element, which, in turn, is an element of the <p> element. The children of a node are the ones that come out of a parent. In Figure 4.1, the two p elements are children of the body element. Elements also have siblings. The preceding two p elements are siblings to each other. Tables 4.3 and 4.4 show the Node object properties and methods, respectively.

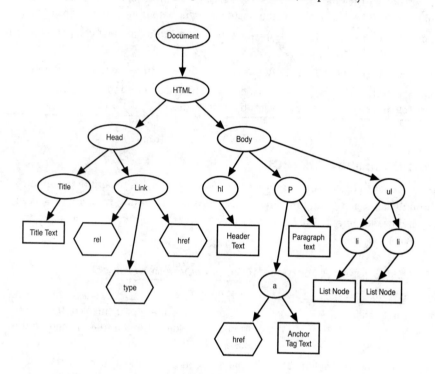

FIGURE 4.1
Representation of a DOM tree

TABLE 4.3 Node Object Properties

Node Property	Description
nodeName	The name of the node.
nodeType	The type of the node, such as element, attribute, text, and so on.
nodeValue	The value of the node (applicable to text nodes).
parentNode	Reference to the parent node of the current node.
childNodes	List of child nodes (array).
firstChild	First child of a node.
lastChild	Last child of a node.
previousSibling	Refers to the previous sibling node. This occurs when multiple child nodes belong to the same parent.
nextSibling	Refers to the following sibling node. This occurs when multiple child nodes belong to the same parent.

TABLE 4.4 Node Object Methods

Node Method	Description
insertBefore(newChild, currentChild)	Inserts a new node referenced by the newChild into the document right before the currentChild node
appendChild(newChild)	Appends the newChild as the last child of the document
removeChild(currentChild)	Removes the currentChild from the document
replaceChild(newNode, nodeToReplace)	Replaces the child node referred by nodeToReplace with the newNode

The Document Object

The Document object is the primary object of DOM. It holds the entire document through its properties and methods. This is accessed through JavaScript as document or window.document. The key properties and methods of the Document object are listed in Table 4.5.

TABLE 4.5 Key Properties/Methods of Document Object

Property/Method	Description
documentElement	This property is the root element of the document. html element is the root element in the case of HTML/XHTML documents.
getElementById(elementID)	This is the most commonly used method in JavaScript. This method searches the entire document to find the element mentioned in the elementID attribute. If found, it returns that element.
getElementsByTagName(tagName)	This method returns a collection of nodes (array) of all the elements in the Document object that match the tagName attribute.
createElement(element)	This method creates a new element in the Document object with the element mentioned in the attribute element. For example, document.createElement("div"); creates a div element. This element does not appear in the document until it has been added with the appendChild or insertBefore methods in the document.

TABLE 4.5   Continued

Property/Method	Description
createTextNode(textNode)	This method creates a text node mentioned in the attribute textNode in the Document object. This element does not appear in the document until it has been added with the appendChild or insertBefore methods in the document.

The Element **Object**

Elements are nothing but the tags in a HTML document. All of these tags create an element in the Document object. For example, the <p> tag creates a p element in the Document object. All the methods mentioned earlier for the Node object are applicable to the Element object. Some of the other key methods are listed in Table 4.6.

TABLE 4.6   Key Methods of the Element **Object**

Property/Method	Description
getAttribute(attributeName)	This method returns an element's attribute, attributeName, in the form of a string.
setAttribute(attributeName)	This method sets an element's attribute, attributeName.
getElementsByTagName(tagName)	This method returns a collection of nodes (array) of all the elements that are the descendants of an Element object that match the tagName attribute. This method is quite similar to the Document object's methods except that this fetches all the elements under this element.

Implementing Client-Side Scripting

In the last section, we witnessed how the DOM is structured with a collection of methods and properties. We will go ahead and work with the creation of an HTML table dynamically and traverse through its rows and columns, which demonstrates the usage of DOM with JavaScript. The DOM methods presented in the example also apply for XML apart from HTML/XHTML. The following is the code snippet in an HTML page for creating an HTML table dynamically. This HTML table displays a multiplication table from 1–10 in the web page after execution.

```
<html>
<head>
<title>Working with JavaScript and DOM</title>
<script>
    function createTable() {
        // get the reference for the body element
        var body = document.getElementsByTagName("body")[0];
        var prg = document.createElement("p");
        prg.data = "Example demonstrating the creation of HTML Table
dynamically";
        body.appendChild(prg);
        // creates a <table> element and a <tbody> element
        var table     = document.createElement("table");
        var tableBody = document.createElement("tbody");
        // creating all cells
        for (var i = 1; i <= 10; i++) {
            // creating a table row
            var row = document.createElement("tr");
            for (var j = 1; j <= 10; j++) {
                // Creating a <td> element, associating text node with it,
                // and appending at the end of the table row
                var cell = document.createElement("td");
                var cellText = document.createTextNode(i*j);
                cell.appendChild(cellText);
                row.appendChild(cell);

            }
            // adding the row to the end of the table body
            tableBody.appendChild(row);
        }
        // appending <tbody> in the <table>
        table.appendChild(tableBody);
        // appending <table> into <body>
        body.appendChild(table);
        // setting the border attribute of table to 1;
        table.setAttribute("border", "1");
    }
</script>
</head>
<body onload="createTable()">
</body>
</html>
```

Did you Know?

JavaScript is a case-sensitive language. For example, the variable names myVar and MyVar are different. However, HTML is not case-sensitive. For example, the HTML onclick event handler is generally specified as OnClick or onClick in HTML, but in JavaScript, this must be referred as onclick.

The following sequence of steps discusses how this application works:

1. The onload event of the <body> is fired. The function createTable() is executed.

2. In this method, first the <body> element is searched in the document with the method getElementsByTagName and assigned to the variable body using the following statement:

```
var body = document.getElementsByTagName("body")[0];
```

3. Create a paragraph element using the createElement method of the Document object and assign text to it through the data property, adding the paragraph element to the <body> using the appendChild method:

```
var prg = document.createElement("p");
prg.data = "Example demonstrating the creation of HTML Table dynamically";
body.appendChild(prg);
```

4. Create the elements table and tbody, which are required to hold the table rows:

```
var table = document.createElement("table");
var tableBody = document.createElement("tbody");
```

5. This is the most important part of the code—the logic to create a set of rows and columns for a table. This logic is to create a table that holds the results of a multiplication table. The first for loop creates rows (<tr>), and the internal for loop creates cells (<td>); the multiplied value of the first loop index and the second loop index is associated as text to a cell. The createTextNode method does this job of associated text value to a cell. After the internal or the second loop is done, all the cells are appended to the row using the appendChild method of the corresponding row. When each row is iterated, it is appended to the <tbody> element. At the end of the main loop, a 10×10 multiplication matrix is created in the form of an HTML table.

```
for (var i = 1; i <= 10; i++) {
        var row = document.createElement("tr");
        for (var j = 1; j <= 10; j++) {
            // Creating a <td> element, associating text node with it,
            // and appending at the end of the table row
            var cell = document.createElement("td");
            var cellText = document.createTextNode(i*j);
            cell.appendChild(cellText);
            row.appendChild(cell);
        }
        // adding the row to the end of the table body
        tableBody.appendChild(row);
    }
```

6. Now the <tbody> is appended to the <table>, and the <table>, in turn, is appended to the <body> element.

```
table.appendChild(tableBody);
// appending <table> into <body>
body.appendChild(table);
```

7. This is an optional step to demonstrate the setting of attributes to an element. Here, an attribute called border with a value of 1 is set to the <table> element:

```
table.setAttribute("border", "1");
```

Copy and paste the preceding code in an HTML page and execute it in the IE web browser.

We are done! When you execute the application, the output is similar to what is shown in Figure 4.2. The next hour focuses on the different data formats that can be used in the client-server communication.

FIGURE 4.2
Displaying a
multiplication
table

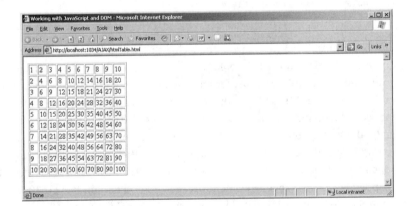

Summary

In this hour, we had a bird's-eye view of client-side scripting. It discussed exactly what constitutes client-side activities, which includes DHTML and its components. DHTML constitutes HTML/XHTML, CSS, and JavaScript. These technologies integrate together and, working in tandem, give you dynamic behavior. To write scripts in JavaScript, however, we need to understand the DOM as it acts as an API for providing different methods, as well as the properties where JavaScript would use it to program HTML elements. All of this has been demonstrated in this hour with the help of hands-on examples to give you an understanding of client-side scripting. In the next hour, we will discuss how data communication takes place between the server and the client.

Workshop

Quiz

1. What is dynamic HTML?

2. What is a class in Cascading Style Sheets?

3. True or False: An onLoad event is called while the page is loading.

4. True or False: JavaScript is not a case-sensitive language.

5. What property and attribute of an element is to be used, when an element's visibility has to be changed?

6. Write a JavaScript snippet to search for an element called btnDisplay in your HTML page.

7. How do you create and add a new element in the HTML document?

8. What is DOM?

Answers

1. Dynamic HTML is a combination of the three technologies—Hypertext Markup Language (HTML), Cascading Style Sheets (CSS), and JavaScript—that work together in tandem to make the web content to be changeable dynamically.

2. A class in Cascading Style Sheets is a collection of properties and attributes of HTML elements represented by a single name. It helps in formatting the HTML elements of a page and can be used throughout the web site for standardization and easy maintainability.

3. False. An onLoad event is called after the page is loaded onto the browser.

4. False. JavaScript is a case-sensitive language.

5. The Style property with the attribute `Visibility`. This attribute has several values: `hidden`, `visible` (in the case of IE), `hide`, and `show` (in the case of Netscape).

6. The following code snippet shows how you can search for an element called `btnDisplay`:

```
document.getElementById(btnDisplay)
```

7. To create an HTML element:

```
var divNode = document.createElement(div);
```

To find a body element in the document:

```
var body = document.getElementByTagName(body)[0];
```

To add the element to body:

```
body.appendChild(divNode);
```

8. The Document Object Model—or DOM, as it is popularly called—is a set of objects, methods, and properties that allow JavaScript to read and modify an HTML or XHTML document. It is an API provided by the browser's vendor. The DOM versions differ slightly between Microsoft's and Netscape's browsers.

HOUR 5

Data Communication with the Server

What You'll Learn in This Hour:

▶ Different data interchange formats between client and server
▶ An introduction to JSON
▶ Working with JSON

In Hour 2, "Understanding the ASP.NET Ajax Architecture," we looked at the architecture of ASP.NET Ajax, which gave us a glimpse of the components in the Microsoft Ajax Client Library and the ASP.NET server extensions. One of the layers in the Client Library included the Component Layer, which comprises a set of nonvisual components providing support for asynchronous communication, XML, and JSON serialization. The ASP.NET server framework communicates with the Client Library with the help of the Component Layer in the Client Library. This hour throws light on JSON—JavaScript Object Notation, pronounced "Jason"—apart from covering XML and string formats.

The Request and Response Cycle

Before we delve into the discussion of data interchange formats in ASP.NET Ajax, let's look at the difference between how a traditional web application model and an Ajax-based web application model works. In traditional web applications, when a form is submitted, a request is sent to the web server. The web server acts upon this and sends back the response in the form of a web page. In this process, a lot of bandwidth is consumed, as the entire page has to be submitted, and either the same page or a new page has to be sent back as a response. More often than not, during this postback, much of the HTML of the first page is present in the second page. This is the case for every user interaction that happens on the client browser. The result is higher response times from the server, which thus affect the overall performance and create a rich user experience.

On the other hand, when an Ajax-based web application sends requests to the web server, the web server in return sends only the data that is requested. This is usually done in SOAP, HTML, XML, plain text, or JSON, and using JavaScript on the client to process the response. In this process, the amount of data interchange between the server and client is greatly reduced, thus improving the responsiveness of the application. This enhances rich user experience as the web server saves a lot of time by processing only the data that is required.

Figure 5.1 compares a traditional web application model to an Ajax-based web application model.

FIGURE 5.1
Traditional web application model versus Ajax-based web application model

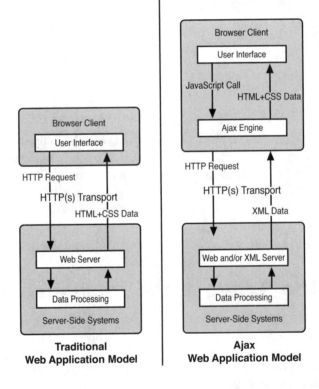

Traditional
Web Application Model

Ajax
Web Application Model

Understanding the Data Interchange Formats

As discussed in the earlier section, the emphasis in Ajax-based applications is more on data than on content being sent across the web browser. Therefore, we shall discuss more on the available data interchange formats. Based on the need of the application, different data interchange formats can be used. The following are some examples of these different formats:

- ▶ HTML content
- ▶ Plain text or string format
- ▶ XML (Extensible Markup Language)
- ▶ JSON (JavaScript Object Notation)

We now discuss each of these formats in the sections that follow.

HTML Content

One of the more common data interchange formats is the normal HTML content being transferred from server to client. When the server sends the HTML content as a response to a request, this content can be accessed by JavaScript and can be placed in any element using the innerHTML property or related methods. In our example of the Items list, the HTML content that would be sent to the browser is as follows:

```
<div><span>HP</span><span>5446 A</span>
<span>2007</span><span>$ 896.00</span></div>
<div><span>Compaq</span><span>654AN</span>
<span>2006</span><span>$ 655.00</span></div>
<div><span> DELL </span><span>34543656</span>
<span>2007</span><span>$ 720.00</span></div>
```

This content can be taken as is and inserted as HTML content in any of the elements that have the innerHTML property. Therefore, it is simple to bind, but formatting the HTML received from the server would be a big disadvantage.

The Most Common Plain Text or String Format

Plain text or string format is a simple data interchange format as it does not involve any complexity. The server just returns plain text, and this can be bound to any element in the HTML using properties like value, text, and innerText based on the element chosen for display. We can also go for delimited string values as the response format for related data, although this has some disadvantages. Some of the ASP.NET Ajax server controls we examine later in the book emit delimited string values in their response format. One such control is an `UpdatePanel` control, which emits the response in the following format:

```
Size¦ControlType¦ControlName¦ControlData
```

The preceding string is delimited by "¦" (the pipe symbol). Here, `Size` is in number of bytes, `ControlType` is the type of control (in this case, it is UpdatePanel), and `ControlName` is the name assigned to the control. The last delimited value is `ControlData`, which holds HTML content to be displayed on the browser. The advantage of using this format is the simplicity in coding, but the disadvantage is that if the position of the values is changed, it requires changes in the client code.

XML—The Language of the Web for Data Exchange

XML is a markup language that was designed to describe data. XML stands for EXtensible Markup Language and is a W3C recommendation. XML today is a common standard for exchanging and manipulating data. It is one of the most commonly used data interchange formats in today's web- and windows-based applications, because of its wide acceptance among several software vendors.

The exchange of data in XML is more so between the web server and client browser, as most browsers today implement XML DOM specifications, making it easier for the JavaScript to handle XML. XML does not have any predefined tags, and you must define your own tags to describe data. It uses a Document Type Definition (DTD) or an XML Schema to describe the data. In other words, a DTD or an XML Schema performs a grammar check to ensure its validity. This has gained popularity because of the simplicity in its data representation and its support for hierarchical data. Also, XML is free and extensible.

The following is an example of XML data representation:

```xml
<?xml version="1.0" encoding="utf-8" ?>
<ItemList>
  <Item>
    <Name>HP</Name>
    <Model>5446 A</Model>
    <Make>2007</Make>
    <Price>$ 896.00</Price>
  </Item>
  <Item>
    <Name>Compaq</Name>
    <Model>654AN</Model>
    <Make>2006</Make>
    <Price>$ 655.00</Price>
```

```
    </Item>
    <Item>
      <Name>DELL</Name>
      <Model>34543656</Model>
      <Make>2007</Make>
      <Price>$ 720.00</Price>
    </Item>
</ItemList>
```

The preceding XML data represents Items and its attributes, such as Name, Model, Make, and Price. It is a simple structure that is self-explanatory.

The XML data retrieved from the server can be displayed on the browser in a couple of ways, as follows:

- ► **Use of XML DOM specification**—This API can be used to parse the XML, access it, and transform into HTML content using JavaScript. To know more about the specifications of XML DOM API, go to www.w3.org.

- ► **Use of XSLT to transform the document into HTML**—XSLT is a declarative, XML-based transformation language used to convert an XML document from one form to other. The XSLT processor uses an XSLT style sheet for converting XML document to HTML, plain text, or any other format supported by the processor. XSLT in itself is a huge subject and can take a complete book to cover it. You can refer to the book *Sams Teach Yourself XSLT in 21 Days* by Michiel van Otegem to gain more insight into XSLT.

Introducing JSON

With the advent of XML-based web services around 2004, XML has become the de-facto standard for data transmission. In Ajax-based applications, XML can be accessed by the XMLHttpRequest object in XML format using the responseXML property or in string format using the responseText property.

However, choosing XML as a data exchange format has its downsides, too. It is not suited especially when heavy data has to be exchanged between the server and client. Why? First, it becomes difficult to parse huge XML and access data; second, the XML data format is higher in bytes in what could have been accomplished in a smaller form.

Douglas Crockford has created an alternate format, which is extremely lightweight and string-based for data exchange between server and client. Called JSON, it is an acronym for JavaScript Object Notation—a light-weight data interchange format.

JSON is the data format of choice for exchanging data between the Microsoft Ajax Library and the ASP.NET Ajax Framework. Incidentally, the majority of the data exchange is in JSON—around 80% to be precise; the rest is in XML and string formats.

JSON supports two data structures: objects and arrays. Objects are unordered collections of name/value pairs. This object is enclosed in { and }. Name and value are separated by :, and the name/value pairs are separated by ,.

Arrays are an ordered sequence of values. An array is enclosed in [and], and its values are separated by ,.

The name is a string enclosed in double quotes. Values can be any one of the following data types: String, Number, Boolean [true or false], Object, Array, and null.

JSON is flexible in the sense that it can represent any data structure as is, and it provides the flexibility to add any new field to an existing structure without making the existing programs obsolete. The big advantage of JSON is that it's more compact and a lot easier to parse than XML. All we need to do is to pass the JSON string to the eval of JavaScript. The eval function of JavaScript evaluates the input string and assigns the output to the HTML elements. It should be noted, however, that usage of the eval function hampers performance. You might have to think of a different option, but only when the data is huge—converting huge strings on the client side might cause delays to the end user. But the best part of JSON is that you can have this parsing in a .js file and can include it in any page. Also, JSON has no version number because the specification is declared stable forever. There are several JSON parsers that support most of the programming languages; these parsers can be downloaded from www.json.org/.

Most of the ASP.NET Ajax server controls use JSON as a data interchange format. The server controls emit JSON strings, and the Microsoft Ajax Client Library parses this data using the internal .js files and hands the data to the client. This format is preferred because of its size, compactness, and ease of parsing the data. Overall, it helps improve the performance of the ASP.NET Ajax application. Before looking into JSON, it is important to understand the JavaScript array and object literals.

Using Arrays to Store Multiple Ordered Items

What are arrays? Arrays are ordered sequence of values. Arrays are specified by using square brackets ([and]). They can be created using a constructor, or the values can directly be assigned in square brackets ([and]). The following is the array declaration using a constructor:

```
var myItems = new Array();
```

Now, you can add items into the array using square brackets and an index value that indicates the position of the item in the array:

```
myItems[0] = "HP";
myItems[1] = "Compaq";
myItems[2] = "DELL";
```

The same object can be created in a more efficient way using the array literal:

```
var myItems = ["HP", "Compaq", "DELL"];
```

Another way of declaring the preceding is as follows:

```
var myItems = new Array("HP", "Compaq", "DELL");
```

Arrays in JavaScript are not typed. Therefore, we can have different data types stored in a single array.

By the Way

Although an array can be created using a constructor, as shown previously, JSON accepts only the Array Literal Declaration Model:

```
JSON format: ["HP", "Compaq", "DELL"]
```

Using Object Literals to Store Name/Value Pairs

Objects are defined to store name/value pairs. You can create this basically to store a business entity in the form of an object. The name/value pairs are enclosed between curly braces ({ and }). The names and values in each pair are separated by :, and each of the name/value pairs are separated by ,. An example of an Item object is as follows:

```
var objItem = {
        "Name" : "HP",
        "Model" : "5446 A",
        "Make" : "2007",
        "Price" : "$ 896.00"
};
```

The preceding code creates an Item object with the attributes Name, Model, Make, and Price, and values assigned to each of the attributes. Each of these attributes can be accessed using the object name and dot notation, such as the following:

```
objItem.Name //accessing Name property
objItem.Model //accessing Model property
objItem.Make //accessing Make property
objItem.Price //accessing Price property
```

An alternate way of accessing the same properties is as follows:

```
objItem["Name"];
objItem["Model"];
objItem["Make"];
objItem["Price"];
```

What Are the Other Ways?

An object can also be created using the constructor with a new keyword:

```
var objItem = new Object();
```

Now, you can add parameters and assign values, as shown next:

```
objItem.Name = "HP";
objItem.Model = "5446 A";
objItem.Make = "2007";
objItem.Price = "$ 896.00";
```

Properties can also be added in using array syntax, as follows:

```
objItem["Name"] = "HP";
objItem["Model"] = "5446 A";
objItem["Make"] = "2007";
objItem["Price"] = "$ 896.00";
```

An object is represented in JSON as follows:

```
{
    "Name": "HP",
    "Model": "5446 A",
    "Make": "2007",
    "Price": "$ 896.00"
}
```

JSON does not use constructors to define either arrays or objects. It uses only literals.

Understanding JSON

The JSON syntax is a collection of array and object literals, as shown previously. The only difference is it does not have any variables, assignments, or operators. JSON is just a representation of data and is not a language by itself. It is a subset of JavaScript using array and object literals to describe data.

As discussed earlier, the JSON representation of an Item object is similar to what is given next:

```
{
    "Name": "HP",
```

```
    "Model": "5446 A",
    "Make": "2007",
    "Price": "$ 896.00"
}
```

In a typical communication between the server and the client browser, generally, the data in the form of JSON is returned to the browser as a string. To use this string on the client browser, it needs to be converted into an object. This is done by the eval() function. This function parses the string and converts it into a JavaScript object.

Let's assume that the data is retrieved in the variable vItem. The following code snippet shows how to convert this JSON string into an object:

```
var vItem = eval("(" + vItem + ")");
```

Now, the variable vItem holds an Item object retrieved from the server in the form of JSON. The values from the vItem object can be retrieved as shown:

```
alert(vItem.Name); // outputs "HP"
alert(vItem.Model); // outputs "5446 A"
alert(vItem.Make); // outputs "2007"
alert(vItem.Price); // outputs "$ 896.00"
```

The extra brackets are a must when converting a JSON string to an object using eval(), because curly braces({ }) in JavaScript can be identified by an If statement, a for statement, or any other construct. It is a must to enclose the JSON object (bundled in { }) in the extra brackets, as shown in the preceding example.

By the Way

Parsing JSON

The eval() function is a general function used to evaluate or parse any JavaScript data type in it. If you want to use an explicit JSON parser to create objects and arrays from JSON text and vice versa, you can use a JSON parser provided at www.json.org/json.js. This file can be copied and referenced to your page in the head section of the .aspx page:

```
<script type="text/javascript" src="json.js"></script>
```

The parser in the json.js file has two basics functions in it:

```
ParseJSON()
toJSONString()
```

The ParseJSON() function converts the JSON text into a JavaScript object. The toJSONString() function converts the JavaScript objects into a JSON text/string.

After the json.js file is added to your page, the toJSONString() function is added to JavaScript object and array definitions. The following example illustrates the use of this method:

```
<script language="javascript">
var myItem = new Object();
myItem.Name = "HP";
myItem.Model = "5446 A";
myItem.Make = "2007";
myItem.Year = "$ 896.00";
myItem = myItem.toJSONString();
alert("Item Object representation as a JSON string : " + myItem);
</script>
```

When the preceding script is executed, the output is as shown next:

```
Item Object representation as a JSON
string : {"Name": "HP","Model": "5446 A","Make": "2007","Price": "$ 896.00"}
```

Note that when you use ASP.NET server controls for Ajax operations in ASP.NET, such parsing/conversion issues are taken care of internally by the Microsoft Ajax Client Library.

Using JSON with Ajax

In Hour 3, "Working with the XMLHttpRequest Object," we demonstrated the retrieval of XML data and string data with the XMLHttpRequest object. We will now look at how JSON data is retrieved using the XMLHttpRequest object. Because JSON is a text-based format, we have to retrieve the data using the responseText property of the XMLHttpRequest object. We've already seen the implementation of responseText property. The only difference now is that the responseText string holds JSON data.

Let's explore this with the help of the same example in Hour 3, but by retrieving a JSON file on the server instead of an XML file. This example has two buttons on the web page, namely Load Item Names and Load JSON as Text. Initially, when the page is executed, the dropdownlist for Item Names is empty. Clicking the Load Item Names button fetches the Item Names (which is in JSON format) from the Items.txt file on the server and binds it to the dropdownlist asynchronously. Second, clicking the Load JSON as Text button binds the JSON string data in the Items.txt file on to the <div> tag on the browser. A step-by-step execution of this program is given next, and the output in the browser is shown later in Figure 5.2.

Refer to the solution we created in Hour 3. Now, open the same solution again and follow this sequence of steps:

1. Add a new item, the Web Form, and name it FetchJSON.aspx.

2. Create a text file called Items.txt populated with the following sample data:

```
{"Items": [
    {
"Name": "HP",
"Model": "5446 A",
"Make": "2007",
"Price": "$ 896.00"
    },
    {
"Name": "Compaq",
"Model": "654AN",
"Make": "2006",
"Price": "$ 655.00"
    },
    {
    "Name": "DELL",
"Model": "34543656",
"Make": "2007",
"Price": "$ 720.00"
    }
  ]
}
```

3. Add the Items.txt file to the solution.

4. Switch to the FetchJSON.aspx page and paste the following code in the source view:

```
<%@ Page Language="C#" AutoEventWireup="true" CodeFile="FetchJSON.aspx.cs"
Inherits="FetchJSON" %>
<!DOCTYPE html PUBLIC "-//W3C//DTD XHTML 1.0 Transitional//EN"
"http://www.w3.org/TR/xhtml1/DTD/xhtml1-transitional.dtd">
<html xmlns="http://www.w3.org/1999/xhtml">
<head runat="server">
    <title>Example of retrieving JSON</title>
<script language="javascript" type="text/javascript"
src=xmlhttp.js></script>
<script language="javascript" type="text/javascript">
    var xmlHttp = false;
    function LoadItemNames() {
        getXmlHttpRequestObject();
        xmlHttp.open("GET", "Items.txt", true);
        xmlHttp.onreadystatechange = function()
        {
                if (xmlHttp.readyState == 4) {
                    //If the Http Status code is 200, i.e., if the
►request is ok.
                    if (xmlHttp.status == 200) {
                        var sJson = xmlHttp.responseText;
```

```
                        sJson = eval("(" + sJson + ")");
                        //Fetching the reference of the <select> tag -
➥ddlItems
                        var ddlItems = document.getElementById("ddlItems");
                        for(var i = 0; i < sJson.Items.length; i++) {
                            //creating new <option> tag
                            var newOption =
document.createElement('option');
                                //assigning value and text to the new option tag.
                                newOption.value = sJson.Items[i].Name;
                                newOption.text = sJson.Items[i].Name;
                                //adding new item in the <select> tag ddlItems.
                                ddlItems.options.add(newOption);
                        }
                    }
                }
            xmlHttp.send(null);
        }
            function LoadItemText() {
            getXmlHttpRequestObject();
            xmlHttp.open("GET", "Items.txt", true);
            xmlHttp.onreadystatechange = function()
            {
                    if (xmlHttp.readyState == 4) {
                        //If the Http Status code is 200, i.e, if the
➥request is ok.
                        if (xmlHttp.status == 200) {
                            document.getElementById("lblText").innerText =
➥xmlHttp.responseText;
                        }
                    }
            }
            xmlHttp.send(null);
        }
        </script>
</head>
<body>
    <form id="form1" runat="server">
        <input type="button" id="btnLoadItemNames"
value="Load Item Names"
onclick="LoadItemNames();" /> 
<span id="spnItemNames">Items</span>
        <select id="ddlItems">
            <option value="">— — — — — -</option>
        </select><br /><br />
        <input type="button" id="btnLoadItemText"
value="Load JSON as Text"
onclick="LoadItemText();" /> 
        <div id="lblText"></div>
    </form>
</body>
</html>
```

5. Now that the entire infrastructure is in place, we'll go ahead with executing the application to see the results. Set this as the start-up page and execute the application by pressing the function key F5. If debugging is set to false in the web.config file, you'll be prompted to enable it to true. After this is done, the application opens up in a browser, as shown in Figure 5.2.

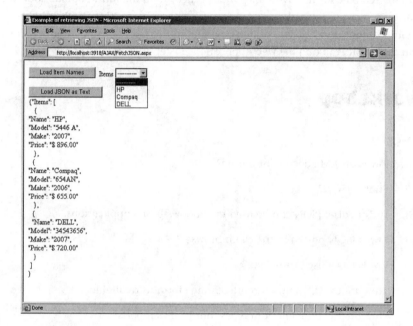

FIGURE 5.2
The
FetchJSON.aspx
page in the
browser

The only change in the preceding example is having the responseText (which holds JSON data) in a variable instead of having the XML documentElement object, as was the case in Hour 3. Now, the sJson variable holds the data in Items.txt as a string and is evaluated by JavaScript's eval() function to convert this into a JavaScript object:

```
var sJson = xmlHttp.responseText;
sJson = eval("(" + sJson + ")");
```

The data in the sJson object can be fetched through the Items collections, as follows:

```
sJson.Items[i].Name; //Fetching the value of the Name property.
//i is the index in the loop.
```

Summary

In this hour, we looked at the different data interchange formats used in the request and response cycles of a web page. The most popular data exchange formats are XML, plain text/string format, HTML, and JSON. Among these, JSON is the newest data interchange format available, and it is becoming the most popular data interchange format used in web applications. In comparison to XML, JSON is lightweight, compact, and easy to understand and maintain. It carries fewer bytes of data than XML, making the web applications faster and more responsive.

Workshop

Quiz

1. How is an XML document parsed?

2. What is JSON?

3. True or False: JSON can be used in windows-based applications.

4. How is JSON parsed in the client browser?

5. How is JSON used with Ajax?

6. What are the different data interchange formats available?

7. What are the different data types that JSON supports?

Answers

1. An XML document should be well formed to be parsed and requires an XML Schema in the form of a DTD (Document Type Definition) or XSD (XML Schema Definition) to be properly validated.

2. JSON, an acronym for JavaScript Object Notation, is a lightweight data interchange format that is a subset of JavaScript. It supports two data structures of JavaScript: object literals and array literals.

3. False. Because JSON is a format derived from JavaScript, its parsing is done only by a JavaScript engine in the browser. Therefore, JSON is not a format for windows-based applications.

4. JSON is received as a string from the response object. This is parsed by an `eval()` function in JavaScript. The `eval()` function converts the JSON string into a JavaScript object for perusal.

5. The JSON string can be retrieved using the XMLHttpRequest object in Ajax. The `responseText` property of the XMLHttpRequest object holds this data.

6. The different data interchange formats available are as follows:

    a. HTML content

    b. Plain text/string delimiters

    c. XML

    d. JSON

These are the most popular ones. There might be several other formats available.

7. JSON supports the following data types:

    a. String

    b. Number

    c. Boolean

    d. Array

    e. Object

    f. Null

HOUR 6

Working with the Microsoft Ajax Client Library

What You'll Learn in This Hour:

▶ Introducing the Microsoft Ajax Client Library
▶ Goals of the Microsoft Ajax Client Library
▶ Inside the Microsoft Ajax Client Library namespaces
▶ The building blocks of the Microsoft Ajax Client-Side Library

An Ajax Library is an API that enables you to design and implement Ajax-enabled web applications. We have had a brief overview of the most widely used Ajax libraries earlier in this book. The Microsoft Ajax Library is one such library that is freely available and is comprised of a JavaScript Client Library and a collection of server-side ASP.NET controls. The JavaScript Client Library provides object-oriented extensions to the JavaScript scripting language. The Microsoft Ajax Client Library ships along with the ASP.NET Ajax extensions. You can use this Library to call server-side methods and even web services. You can download the Library from this link: http://ajax.asp.net/downloads/default.aspx.

In this hour, we look at the Microsoft Ajax Client Library, including its namespaces, classes, and so on, as well as their applicability.

Introducing the Microsoft Ajax Client Library

Before we discuss the classes and the namespaces that comprise the Microsoft Ajax Client Library, here's an overview of what this Library actually is and what its goals are.

The Microsoft Ajax client framework is comprised of a collection of JavaScript classes with object-oriented programming support; these classes form together an engine that wraps up the client components, the controls, and their behavior.

The Microsoft Ajax Client Library is written entirely using the JavaScript scripting language. It is comprised of a collection of object-oriented JavaScript classes and their members in the form of `.js` files, and it is wrapped inside the `System.Web.Extensions.dll` assembly.

> Because the Microsoft Ajax Client Library is based on JavaScript, a cross-browser scripting language, it is not tied to ASP.NET; rather, it is compatible with any web development platform irrespective of the application server in use.

Goals of the Microsoft Ajax Client Library

The basic goal of the Microsoft Ajax Client Library is to provide a client-side framework that is simple and rich—one that would enable you to design and implement your Ajax-enabled dynamic web applications seamlessly. Moreover, you can use the Microsoft Ajax Client Library to achieve asynchronous communication between the server and the client.

Here is a list of the major goals of Microsoft Ajax Client Library in a nutshell:

▶ Invoke the server-side methods and web service methods using asynchronous calls

▶ Perform serialization and deserialization using JSON

▶ Provide an interface that facilitates the communication between an ASP.NET client application and an ASP.NET server application

By the Way

> JavaScript is an object-based scripting language; it is not an object-oriented language because it lacks support for inheritance, one of the most important properties that an object-oriented language should possess.

In the sections that follow, we look at the namespaces, classes, and enumerations that comprise the Microsoft Ajax Client Library.

Inside the Microsoft Ajax Client Library Namespaces

The following is the complete list of the namespaces contained inside the Microsoft Ajax Client Library:

- Global namespace
- Sys
- Sys.Net
- Sys.Serialization
- Sys.Services
- Sys.UI
- Sys.WebForms

By the Way

The Microsoft Ajax Client Library, a 100% pure JavaScript library, includes the following files:

MicrosoftAjax.js

MicrosoftAjaxTimer.js

MicrosoftAjaxWebForms.js

Note that these files are available in both debug and release versions. While the debug versions have a .debug.js extension, the release versions have only .js extensions.

In the following sections, we look at each of these namespaces and learn what each of them relates to.

The Global Namespace—Extending JavaScript

As its name suggests, the global namespace provides extensions to the JavaScript scripting language. It houses types that are actually extensions to the JavaScript types, such as String, Array, Number, and so on. The global namespace is mainly comprised of these extensions and the Type class.

The Type class, one of the most important of all the classes in this Library, is comprised of a collection of global methods and provides many features. These features include the following:

- Registration of the namespaces, classes, interfaces, and enumerations
- Typing and type-reflection

In order to register a namespace, you can use the static method of the Type class called registerNamespace(). Apart from this, the Type class contains other register methods, such as registerBaseMethod(), registerClass(), registerInterface(), registerNamespace(), and the registerEnum() method. We will learn more about the Type class and how we can use it in your applications as we move further ahead through the sections in this hour.

The Sys Namespace—The Root of All Namespaces

The Sys namespace is the root of all the namespaces in the Microsoft Ajax Client Library and is comprised of a collection of classes and types.

The classes in the Sys namespace include the following:

- ▶ Sys._Application class
- ▶ ApplicationLoadEventArgs class
- ▶ Browser class
- ▶ CancelEventArgs class
- ▶ Component class
- ▶ CultureInfo class
- ▶ Debug class
- ▶ EventArgs class
- ▶ EventHandlerList class
- ▶ The IContainer interface
- ▶ The IDisposable interface
- ▶ The INotifyDisposing interface
- ▶ The INotifyPropertyChange interface
- ▶ The PropertyChangedEventArgs class
- ▶ The ScriptLoader class
- ▶ The ScriptLoaderTask class
- ▶ The StringBuilder class

The `Sys.Net` **Namespace**

The `Sys.Net` namespace contains classes and types that facilitate the communication between an ASP.NET Ajax-enabled client application and an ASP.NET server application or web services using asynchronous calls. The classes in the `Sys.Net` namespace include the `Sys.Net.NetworkRequestEventArgs` class, the `Sys.Net.WebRequest` class, the `Sys.Net.WebRequestExecutor` class, the `Sys.Net.WebRequestManager` class, and the `Sys.Net.XmlHttpExecutor` class.

The `Sys.Serialization` **Namespace**

The `Sys.Serialization` namespace contains types that facilitate serialization and deserialization of data in Ajax-enabled applications. You have only one class in this namespace: `Sys.Serialization.JavaScriptSerializer`.

The `Sys.Services` **Namespace**

The `Sys.Services` namespace is comprised of types and classes that can be used to invoke the ASP.NET application services using client-side scripts. The classes inside the `Sys.Services` namespace include the `AuthenticationService`, the `ProfileService`, and the `ProfileGroup` class.

The `Sys.UI` **Namespace**

As the name suggests, the `Sys.UI` namespace is comprised of classes and types that provide you with a rich set of controls to build awesome user interfaces.

The classes in this namespace include the `Sys.UI.Behavior` class, `Sys.UI.Bounds` class, `Sys.UI.Control` class, `Sys.UI.Key` class, `Sys.UI.MouseButton` enumeration, `Sys.UI.Point` class, and `Sys.UI.VisibilityMode` enumeration.

The `Sys.WebForms` **Namespace—Enabling Partial Rendering**

The `Sys.WebForms` namespace consists of classes and types that help in partial rendering of the web pages in your Ajax-enabled ASP.NET applications. The classes in this namespace include the following:

- ► `BeginRequestEventArgs` class

- ► `EndRequestEventArgs` class

- ► `InitializeRequestEventArgs` class

- ► `PageLoadedEventArgs` class

▶ PageLoadingEventArgs class

▶ PageRequestManager class

The JavaScript extensions framework of the Microsoft Ajax Library provides extensions to JavaScript types, such as Array, Boolean, Date, Error, Number, Object, RegExp, and String.

As discussed earlier in this section, the ASP.NET Ajax Client Library is comprised of three components, namely the core framework, the UI framework, and the JavaScript extensions framework. In the section that follows, we plunge into the most important classes and namespaces that comprise these three components and discuss each of those classes and their applicability. We also delve into some code where necessary to illustrate how you can use these classes and namespaces in your applications.

The Building Blocks of the Microsoft Ajax Client Library

In this section, we discuss the building blocks of the ASP.NET Ajax Client-Side Library. We examine the classes and the namespaces that make up these blocks and what each of these blocks relates to.

In essence, the Microsoft Ajax Client-Side Library is comprised of the following components:

▶ The user interface (UI) framework

▶ The core framework

▶ The JavaScript extensions framework

Although the UI framework consists of the System.UI namespace, the core framework of this Library is comprised of the Sys.Net, Sys.Serialization, Sys.Services, and Sys.WebForms namespaces.

Figure 6.1 depicts the building blocks and the namespaces of the Microsoft Ajax Client Library diagrammatically.

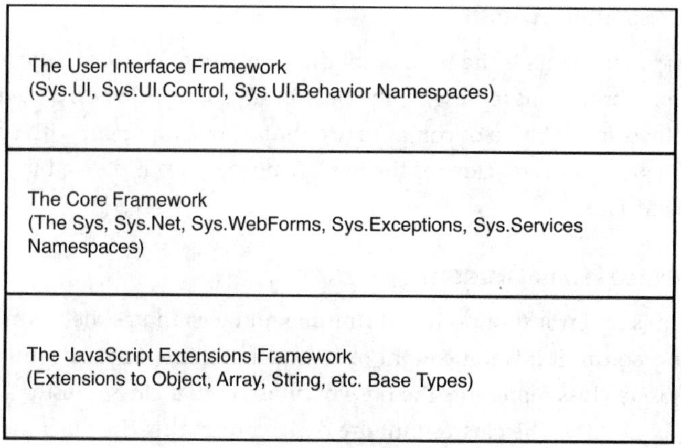

FIGURE 6.1
Components of
the Microsoft
Ajax Client Side
Library

```
┌─────────────────────────────────────────────────┐
│                                                   │
│  The User Interface Framework                     │
│  (Sys.UI, Sys.UI.Control, Sys.UI.Behavior Namespaces) │
│                                                   │
├─────────────────────────────────────────────────┤
│                                                   │
│  The Core Framework                               │
│  (The Sys, Sys.Net, Sys.WebForms, Sys.Exceptions, Sys.Services │
│  Namespaces)                                       │
│                                                   │
├─────────────────────────────────────────────────┤
│                                                   │
│  The JavaScript Extensions Framework              │
│  (Extensions to Object, Array, String, etc. Base Types) │
│                                                   │
└─────────────────────────────────────────────────┘
```

Components of the Microsoft Ajax Client Side Library

What's Inside the Core Framework?

In this section, we look at the major classes that make up the core framework of the Microsoft ASP.NET Ajax Client Library.

The Sys._Application Class

The Application class within the Sys namespace is one of the most important classes in the entire Microsoft ASP.NET Ajax Library. Note that most of the classes of the Microsoft ASP.NET Ajax base framework are housed inside the Sys namespace. The Sys.Application object provides an instance much the same as the Page class in ASP.NET. The Sys.Application instance is actually the ASP.NET Ajax application object or the controller that controls the overall execution of an ASP.NET Ajax web page.

The first time an Ajax-enabled ASP.NET web page loads, the runtime instantiates the Sys._Application class and assigns this instance to the Sys.Application object, as shown in the following code snippet:

```
Sys.Application = new Sys._Application();
```

Microsoft's official site on ASP.NET Ajax (www.asp.net/ajax) states the following on the Sys._Application class: "Provides a run-time object that exposes client events and manages client components that are registered with the application. The members of this object are available globally after the client application has been initialized. The members can be invoked without creating an instance of the class."

The Sys.Component Class

The Sys.Component class is the base of all the component classes in the Microsoft ASP.NET Ajax Library and represents the base of all control classes. Note that a control is actually a special type of component—that is, a component with some added behavior. The Sys.Control class of the Sys.UI namespace is derived from the Sys.Component class.

The Sys.Exceptions Class

An exception is an error that occurs at runtime and terminates the normal flow of control of a program if it is not caught or handled properly in your source code. The Sys.Exceptions class represents the base of all exception classes in the Microsoft ASP.NET Ajax Library. The classes that are derived from this class include the following:

- ▶ Sys.InvalidOperationException
- ▶ Sys.NotImplementedException
- ▶ Sys.ScriptLoadFailedException
- ▶ Sys.ParameterCountException
- ▶ Sys.ArgumentNullException
- ▶ Sys.ArgumentOutOfRangeException
- ▶ Sys.ArgumentTypeException
- ▶ Sys.ArgumentException
- ▶ Sys.ArgumentUndefinedException

The Sys.Net.WebRequest Class

The Sys.Net.WebRequest class provides a client-side script API that is used to make a web request using client-side scripts in the Microsoft ASP.NET Ajax client framework. You can use this class to access remote data—that is, an XML document or a web service. The Sys.Net.WebRequest class can be instantiated as shown in the following code snippet:

```
var webRequestInstance = new Sys.Net.WebRequest();
```

The Sys.WebForms.PageRequestManager Class

The Sys.WebForms.PageRequestManager class is responsible for managing the partial web page updates of the updatable panels—that is, UpdatePanel controls. It also contains a set of methods and properties that can be used to customize a web page of an ASP.NET Ajax-enabled application using client-side scripts.

The `Sys.Net.WebRequestExecutor` Class

The `Sys.Net.WebRequestExecutor` class represents the base of all network executor classes in< the Microsoft ASP.NET Ajax client framework.

The `Sys.Net.XMLHttpExecutor` Class

The `Sys.Net.XMLHttpExecutor` class facilitates asynchronous network calls from client-side script using the `XMLHttpRequest` object. The following code snippet illustrates how you can instantiate the `Sys.Net.XMLHttpExecutor` class:

```
var xmlHttpExecutorInstance = new Sys.Net.XMLHttpExecutor();
```

What's Inside the User Interface Framework?

Let's now take a look at the major classes that are part of the user interface framework in this Library.

The `Sys.UI.Control` Class

The `Sys.UI.Control` class is derived from the `Sys.Component` class and represents the base class for all user interface controls in the Microsoft ASP.NET Ajax client framework. Table 6.1 lists some of the members of this class.

TABLE 6.1   Members of the `Sys.UI.Control` class

Member	Description
The `id` property	This is used to get or set the unique identifier for the control.
The `visible` property	This is used to get or set the visibility of the control.
The `initialize` method	Used to initialize the control.
The `dispose` method	Disposes the control instance and releases the memory occupied by the control and its associated resources.
The `element` property	Used to retrieve the DOM element that this control is associated with.

The `Sys.UI.Behavior` Class

The `Sys.UI.Behavior` class is the base class of all ASP.NET Ajax behavior, and it typically represents the behavior of all the client components that are derived from this class. Table 6.2 lists some of the members of this class.

TABLE 6.2   Members of the Sys.UI.Behavior class

Member	Description
The id property	This is used to get or set the unique identifier for the Behavior instance.
The name property	This is used to get or set the name of the Behavior instance.
The initialize method	Used to initialize the current instance of the Behavior class.
The dispose method	Disposes the control instance and releases the memory occupied by the control and its associated resources.
The element property	Used to retrieve the DOM element that this Behavior instance is associated with.

The System.UI.DomElement Class

The System.UI.DomElement class is derived from JavaScript's Object class and represents a native DOM element. It contains a set of static methods and properties that can typically be used to manipulate such elements. Table 6.3 lists some of the important members of the System.UI.DomElement class.

TABLE 6.3   Members of the Sys.UI.DomElement class

Member	Description
The setLocation method	This is used to position the DOM element.
The getLocation method	This is used to get the absolute position of the DOM element.
The addCssClass method	This is used to add a css class to the DOM element.
The removeCssClass method	This is used to remove a css class from the DOM element.

The System.UI.DomEvent Class

The System.UI.DomEvent class is used to work with the events that are related to the DOM elements, which are represented by the System.UI.DomElement class discussed previously. Table 6.4 lists some of the important members of the System.UI.DomEvent class.

TABLE 6.4 Members of the Sys.UI.DomEvent class

Member	Description
The addHandler method	This is used to add an event handler to the DOM element.
The removeHandler method	This is used to remove the specified event handler from the DOM element.
The target field	This is used to retrieve the instance on which the event occurred.
The type field	This is used to retrieve the name of the event that was raised.

Extending the JavaScript Library with the Microsoft Ajax JavaScript Extensions Framework

The Microsoft Ajax JavaScript base type extensions framework is comprised of a collection of member extensions that actually extend the existing JavaScript base types and classes to provide added features, behavior, and object-oriented programming support. Not only do these extensions facilitate object-oriented programming, but they also are extensions to the existing JavaScript types. These extensions typically include the following:

- Object type extensions
- Number type extensions
- String type extensions
- Array type extensions
- Boolean type extensions
- Date type extensions
- Error type extensions

We discuss each of these extensions briefly in the sections that follow.

The Object Type Extensions

These extensions use reflection to further enhance the base of all JavaScript objects called Object.

The Number Type Extensions

This is an extension to the JavaScript base object called the Number object. As an example, refer to the following code snippet that illustrates how create a number value out of a string using the parseInvariant() extension function:

```
var numberAsString = "10";
var number = Number.parseInvariant(numberAsString);
alert("The value is: "+number);
```

The String Type Extensions

These are extensions that further enhance the JavaScript base object called Array.

As an example, refer to the following code snippet that illustrates how you can trim leading and trailing spaces from a String object in JavaScript using the trim() extension function:

```
var unTrimmedStringInstance = "  Joydip Kanjilal  ";
var trimmedStringInstance = unTrimmedStringInstance.trim();
alert("The trimmed string is: "+trimmedStringInstance);
```

When executed, the preceding code snippet displays the string "Joydip Kanjilal." Note that the leading and trailing spaces are trimmed but not the embedded spaces within the string.

What Are Array Type Extensions?

These extensions comprise a set of static methods that further enhance the JavaScript base object called Array. As an example, you can add elements or remove elements to and from an array or even clear all the elements of an array using the add(), remove(), or clear() extension functions to the JavaScript base Array type. This is illustrated in the following code snippet:

```
var testArray = new Array();
Array.add("Joydip",testArray);
Array.add("Sriram",testArray);
Array.remove(testArray,1);
Array.clear(testArray);
```

The Boolean Type Extensions

This further enhances the JavaScript Boolean object. As an example, you can create a Boolean variable using the following code snippet:

```
var test = new Boolean.parse("true");
```

Similarly, you use the parse method that has been introduced in this Library as an extension to the existing `Boolean` object, as follows:

```
var booleanVariable = Boolean.parse("true");
if(booleanVariable == true)
alert("The value is true");
else
alert("The value is false");
```

The Date **Type Extensions**

These extensions extend the base JavaScript object called the `Date` object. Here is how you can use it:

```
var dt = new Date();
```

The Error **Type Extensions**

These provide extensions that actually enhance the base JavaScript object called the `Error` object. You can use it as shown in the following code snippet:

```
var error = Error.create(message, errorInformation);
```

For a more complete reference to the Microsoft ASP.NET Ajax Client Library, please refer to the following link:

http://asp.net/AJAX/Documentation/Live/ClientReference/default.aspx

Summary

The Microsoft Ajax Client Library, or the Client Library of the Microsoft Ajax framework, is a pure JavaScript library that extends the JavaScript scripting language and provides you with a collection of namespaces, classes, properties, types, events, enumerations, and so on—features that are already part of the Microsoft.NET framework-compliant languages. In this hour, we have provided a ready-guide and a quick reference to the Microsoft Ajax Client Library namespaces and shown how you can use it in your Ajax-enabled web applications. In the next hour we will examine the ASP.NET Ajax Server Extensions framework.

Workshop

Quiz

1. What are the basic goals of the Microsoft Ajax Client Library?

2. True or False: The Microsoft Ajax Client Library can be used from PHP.

3. What are the major building blocks of the Microsoft Ajax Client Library?

4. What are the Microsoft Ajax JavaScript base type extensions?

5. Name the namespaces that the Microsoft Ajax client framework is comprised of.

6. What is the base class of the `Sys.UI.Control` class?

7. Name the classes of the `System.WebForms` namespace.

8. Name the extensions of the Microsoft Ajax JavaScript base type extensions framework.

Answers

1. The basic goals of the Microsoft Ajax Client Library are as follows:

   ▶ Invoke the server-side methods and web service methods using asynchronous calls

   ▶ Perform serialization and de-serialization using JSON

   ▶ Provide an interface that facilitates the communication between an ASP.NET client application and an ASP.NET server application

2. True. It can be used from any server-side language, such as PHP, JSP, and so on, as it is designed entirely in JavaScript.

3. The major blocks of the Microsoft Ajax client framework are as follows:

   ▶ The user interface (UI) framework

   ▶ The core framework

   ▶ The JavaScript extensions framework

4. The Microsoft Ajax JavaScript base type extensions framework is comprised of a collection of member extensions that extend the existing JavaScript base types and classes to provide added features with object-oriented programming support.

5. The Microsoft Ajax Client Library is comprised of the following: the global namespace, and the `Sys`, `Sys.Net`, `Sys.Serialization`, `Sys.Services`, `Sys.UI`, and `Sys.WebForms` namespaces.

6. `Sys.Component`.

7. The `Sys.WebForms` namespace consists of the following classes:

   ▶ The `BeginRequestEventArgs` class

   ▶ The `EndRequestEventArgs` class

   ▶ The `InitializeRequestEventArgs` class

   ▶ The `PageLoadedEventArgs` class

   ▶ The `PageLoadingEventArgs` class

   ▶ The `PageRequestManager` class

8. The Microsoft Ajax JavaScript base type extensions framework includes the following extensions:

   ▶ `Object` type extensions

   ▶ `Number` type extensions

   ▶ `String` type extensions

   ▶ `Array` type extensions

   ▶ `Boolean` type extensions

   ▶ `Date` type extensions

   ▶ `Error` type extensions

PART II

Working with Ajax

HOUR 7

Using ASP.NET Ajax Server Extensions

What You'll Learn in This Hour:

▶ The ASP.NET Ajax server extensions framework

▶ Microsoft Ajax server reference

▶ Inside the Microsoft server reference namespaces

You can use Ajax to build applications with rich and interactive user interfaces seamlessly. ASP.NET Ajax basically integrates the Client-Side Libraries with the ASP.NET 2.0 engine running in the server side. In the previous hour, we examined the Microsoft ASP.NET Ajax Client Library. Remember, the Microsoft Ajax Library is freely available and is comprised of a JavaScript Client Library and a collection of server-side ASP.NET controls. In this hour, we will discuss this server-side framework and how we can use it in our applications. Microsoft ASP.NET Ajax server extensions framework, as this is called, is comprised of a set of server controls that enable you to design and implement applications that leverage the awesome power of Ajax and provide you with rich user interfaces.

The ASP.NET Ajax Server Extensions Framework

The ASP.NET Ajax server framework is comprised of a collection of server controls and services that extend the ASP.NET 2.0 core framework and can be used to design and develop applications with rich user interfaces and better response times. These are commonly known as server extensions. Note that the Ajax server extensions provide support for many ASP.NET services. These include the following:

- ▶ Localization
- ▶ Globalization
- ▶ Authentication
- ▶ Debugging
- ▶ Tracing
- ▶ Web services
- ▶ Application services

We will now quickly run through what each of these services imply.

You use localization to make an application adaptable to a specific locale—that is, it may be defined as the process of designing an application such that it can be used with a specific locale. So, what is globalization? Well, it is the process with which you identify the portion of your application that needs to be localized. In other words, it may be defined as the process of identifying the application's localizable resources.

You use authentication for identification and validation of a user's credentials—that is, for checking whether the user has a valid credential to log into the application. Now, once a user has been authenticated, you use authorization to determine what resources this authenticated user can have access to.

Debugging is the process of running through your code to fix errors. Tracing can be defined as the process of debugging your application's code. You can use tracing to analyze the application's performance, record a program's flow and the stack trace information of exceptions that occur in your program.

You can enable tracing at the page and the application levels. To enable tracing at the page level, use the following:

```
<%@ Page Language="C#" Trace="true" %>
```

To do the same at the application level, you can use the following:

```
<system.web>
   <compilation debug="false" />
     <authentication mode="Windows" />
   <trace enabled ="true" pageOutput ="true" />
</system.web>
```

Web services are based on SOAP protocol, and they may be defined as platform-independent software components that comprise a collection of methods that are packaged together for use in a common framework throughout a network. SOAP (Simple Object Access Protocol), is a light-weight, XML-based, cross-platform, cross-language protocol that can be used for exchanging data and information in a distributed environment. Web services are applications that have the ability to expose data and functionality through the use of "web methods."

Application services are the building blocks of ASP.NET 2.0. Actually, ASP.NET 2.0 contains a collection of such blocks or frameworks. The following is a list of some of the most important blocks or services for which ASP.NET 2.0 has support:

- ▶ The Membership API
- ▶ The Profile API
- ▶ The Personalization API

The Membership API

The Membership API in ASP.NET 2.0 enables you to manage the users and roles of an application. In essence, it enables you to store the user's credentials in a secure and declarative way. ASP.NET 2.0 ships in with the `ActiveDirectoryMembershipProvider` and the `SqlMembershipProvider`; you can use these to manage user information efficiently and with much less code.

The Profile API

The ASP.NET 2.0 Profile API can be used to store profile information for both authenticated and anonymous users and make it available to the application for the user's subsequent visits to the application.

The Personalization API

The ASP.NET 2.0 Personalization API enables you to personalize your application seamlessly. You can use this API to customize the user profiles, themes, error pages of your application, etc.

> All the Provider abstract classes in the ASP.NET Provider Model extend the abstract class called ProviderBase present in the System.Configuration. Provider namespace.

Looking at the Components of the ASP.NET Ajax Server Extensions Framework

The ASP.NET Ajax server extensions framework includes the following components:

- ▶ Application services bridge
- ▶ Web services bridge
- ▶ ASP.NET Ajax server controls

Now let's take a look at what each of these components relates to.

The Application Services Bridge

This component is used to provide access to the application services available as part of ASP.NET 2.0 from client-side scripts. The basic services provided by this bridge include, but are not limited to, the following:

- ▶ User authentication using the Membership API
- ▶ Storage of user's data using the Profile API

The Web Services Bridge

The web services bridge is used to consume external web services from the client side in an Ajax-enabled web application. Web services have already been explained in the previous section. The web services bridge makes use of the JSON serializer, JavaScript proxies, and the .asbx files or the bridge files to call the web services.

> You can use the web services bridge to connect to any external or custom web service using the SOAP protocol, irrespective of the technology with which the web service was built.

What Are the ASP.NET Ajax Server Controls?

Let's now take a look at the ASP.NET Ajax server controls available as a part of the ASP.NET Ajax server extensions framework. These server controls include the following:

- ▶ Timer

- ▶ ScriptManager

- ▶ ScriptManagerProxy

- ▶ UpdateProgress

- ▶ UpdatePanel

Let's take a brief look at what each of these controls relates to.

The Timer Control—Setting Intervals

Using the Timer control, you can set a timer for your web page. You can ensure that the web page can post back to the web server after a specified interval of time. You can use the Interval property of this control to set an interval in milliseconds, after which the web page will refresh itself. Once this interval elapses, the control fires a post back to the web server. This is how the mark-up code of a typical Timer control looks:

```
<asp:Timer ID="Timer1" runat="server" Interval="5000"
OnTick="MyMethod" />
```

The Timer control is discussed in detail in Hour 9.

The ScriptManager Control—The Brain of an Ajax-Enabled Web Page

The ScriptManager control is a part of the System.Web.UI namespace and is the brain of an Ajax-enabled ASP.NET web page. As the name implies, it is responsible for managing scripts and registering them as and when required; it is also instrumental in partial web page rendering in your Ajax-enabled ASP.NET web applications. The documentation at the ASP.NET Ajax site states, "Manages Microsoft ASP.NET 2.0 Ajax extensions script libraries and script files, partial-page rendering, and client proxy class generation for web and application services." When there is a need to update the web page, this control would run through all the UpdatePanel controls in your web page, initiate a trigger, and update the required portions of the web page. Awesome, isn't it?

The following code snippet illustrates the source code for this control once you include it in your .aspx page:

```
<asp:ScriptManager ID="MyScriptManager" runat="server" />
```

> **By the Way**
>
> The ScriptManager control is an invisible control, and you should include this control in your web page prior to including any other Ajax-enabled control. Moreover, you can have only one instance of a ScriptManager control in your web page.

The `ScriptManager` control is discussed at length in Hour 9.

The `ScriptManagerProxy` Control—Adding Scripts and Services

The documentation at the ASP.NET Ajax site states, "ScriptManagerProxy control enables you to add scripts and services that are specific to nested components." Note that you can use this control only to add scripts or services that have been predefined by the `ScriptManager` control. However, you cannot remove these scripts using this control. In other words, you can use this control to add scripts and services to your web page, which already has a `ScriptManager` control inside.

The following code snippet illustrates how your source code in the `.aspx` file looks once you include this control in your web page:

```
<asp:ScriptManagerProxy ID="MyScriptManagerProxy"
runat="server" />
```

By the Way

> You should have a `ScriptManager` control in a web page that has a `ScriptManagerProxy` control, or else an `InvalidOperationException` will be thrown when you try to access the `ScriptManagerProxy` control.

Considering that you can't have more than one `ScriptManager` control in a web page, what if you are using master pages in your application and have all your content pages inherited from it, and you want to register some specific scripts in your content pages but not the scripts that are part of the `ScriptManager` control? That's where a `ScriptManagerProxy` control fits in. Here is a code snippet that shows how you can do this:

```
<asp:ScriptManagerProxy ID="ScriptManagerProxy1" runat="server">
        <Services>
        <asp:ServiceReference Path="Test.asmx" InlineScript="false" />
        </Services>
</asp:ScriptManagerProxy>
```

The `UpdateProgress` Control—Displaying Progress Status During Partial Updates

The `UpdateProgress` control can be used to display the progress status when using partial-page rendering in an Ajax-enabled ASP.NET web page. You can use this control, together with the `UpdatePanel` control, to display the status of partial page updates in an asynchronous mode of operation to the user in an Ajax-enabled web application.

The following code snippet illustrates the source code for this control in the .aspx file once you include this control in your web page:

```
<asp:UpdateProgress ID="MyUpdateProgress" runat="server"
...
</asp:UpdateProgress>
```

You can find more detailed discussion on the UpdateProgress control in Hour 8.

The UpdatePanel **Control—Facilitating Partial Page Updates**

The UpdatePanel control included as a part of the Ajax server extensions framework is used to update only a specified portion of the web page. This feature is what is commonly known as partial-web page rendering. In other words, you can eliminate the need to refresh the entire web page using this feature for improved performance and better responsiveness.

Fine, but what is this partial-web page rendering all about? Well, partial-web page rendering is a feature that allows you to specify portions of your web page that would be updated to eliminate the need for the entire page being posted back to the web server, and thus boost the application's performance. With this feature, you can easily define the "updatable" portions of your web page and make way for asynchronous calls. According to the ASP.NET Ajax web site's documentation, "Partial-page rendering removes the need for the whole page to be refreshed as the result of a postback. Instead, only individual regions of the page that have changed are updated. As a result, users do not see the whole page reload with every postback, which makes user interaction with the web page more seamless. Microsoft ASP.NET Ajax enables you to add partial-page rendering to new or existing ASP.NET web pages without writing client script."

You can use an UpdatePanel control to ensure that these controls and the controls contained in them are updated incrementally without the need of a postback to the web server. There is no absolutely no need for an entire page to be posted back to the web server.

This is how your source code in the .aspx file looks once this control has been included in your web page:

```
<asp:UpdatePanel ID="GenrePanel" runat="server"
...
</asp:UpdatePanel>
```

You can find more detailed discussion on the UpdatePanel control in Hour 8.

We have had a brief look at each of the controls included as part of the Ajax server extensions framework. We will discuss more on these controls and how we can use them in the Ajax-enabled ASP.NET web applications in the hours that follow.

We will now take a look at the namespaces and classes that comprise the Microsoft Server Reference Library.

In ASP.NET Ajax, you have support for both web services and partial-page rendering—features that allow you to update portions of your user interface as and when they are needed.

A Quick Look at the Microsoft Ajax Server Reference Library

The ASP.NET Ajax server reference consists of the following namespaces:

- ▶ System.Web.UI
- ▶ System.Web.UI.Design
- ▶ System.Web.Configuration
- ▶ System.Web.Handlers
- ▶ System.Web.Script.Serialization
- ▶ System.Web.Script.Services

Let's now discuss each of these namespaces briefly.

The System.Web.UI Namespace

The System.Web.UI namespace consists of classes that provide you with a rich user interface while working with the ASP.NET Ajax server extensions framework. The classes and interfaces included as part of this namespace are the following:

- ▶ The IExtenderControl interface
- ▶ The AsyncPostBackErrorEventArgs class
- ▶ The AsyncPostBackTrigger class
- ▶ The AuthenticationServiceManager class
- ▶ The TargetControlTypeAttribute class
- ▶ The Timer class
- ▶ The UpdatePanel class
- ▶ The UpdatePanelControlTrigger class
- ▶ The UpdatePanelRenderMode enumeration
- ▶ The UpdatePanelTrigger class

- The `UpdatePanelTriggerCollection` class
- The `UpdatePanelUpdateMode` enumeration
- The `UpdateProgress` class
- The `ExtenderControl` class
- The `IScriptControl` interface
- The `PostBackTrigger` class
- The `ProfileServiceManager` class
- The `ScriptBehaviorDescriptor` class
- The `ScriptComponentDescriptor` class
- The `ScriptControl` class
- The `ScriptControlDescriptor` class
- The `ScriptDescriptor` class
- The `ScriptManager` class
- The `ScriptManagerProxy` class
- The `ScriptMode` enumeration
- The `ScriptReference` class
- The `ScriptReferenceCollection` class
- The `ScriptReferenceEventArgs` class
- The `ScriptResourceAttribute` class
- The `ServiceReference` class
- The `ServiceReferenceCollection` class

The `System.Web.UI.Design` Namespace

The `System.Web.UI.Design` namespace is comprised of a collection of extensible classes that you can use to extend the behavior of the user interface while working with ASP.NET server extensions framework. The following lists the classes that are part of this namespace:

- The `AsyncPostBackTriggerControlIDConverter` class
- The `AsyncPostBackTriggerEventNameConverter` class
- The `CollectionEditorBase` class

- ▶ The `TimerDesigner` class

- ▶ The `PostBackTriggerControlIDConverter` class

- ▶ The `UpdatePanelDesigner` class

- ▶ The `UpdateProgressDesigner` class

- ▶ The `UpdatePanelTriggerCollectionEditor` class

- ▶ The `UpdateProgressAssociatedUpdatePanelIDConverter` class

- ▶ The `ExtenderControlDesigner` class

- ▶ The `ScriptManagerDesigner` class

- ▶ The `ScriptManagerProxyDesigner` class

The `System.Web.Configuration` Namespace

The `System.Web.Configuration` namespace is comprised of a collection of classes that can be used to work with the configuration data of the Microsoft ASP.NET Ajax server extensions. The classes and interfaces that comprise this namespace include the following:

- ▶ The `Converter` class

- ▶ The `ConvertersCollection` class

- ▶ The `SystemWebExtensionsSectionGroup` class

- ▶ The `ScriptingWebServicesSectionGroup` class

- ▶ The `ScriptingProfileServiceSection` class

- ▶ The `ScriptingScriptResourceHandlerSection` class

- ▶ The `ScriptingAuthenticationServiceSection` class

- ▶ The `ScriptingJsonSerializationSection` class

- ▶ The `ScriptingSectionGroup` class

The `System.Web.Handlers` Namespace

The `System.Web.Handlers` namespace, as its name suggests, is comprised of a set of Http Handlers that can be used to process the HTTP requests sent to the web server. This namespace is comprised of two classes. These are as follows:

- ▶ The `ScriptModule` class

- ▶ The `ScriptResourceHandler` class

The `System.Web.Script` Namespace

The `System.Web.Script.Serialization` namespace contains a collection of classes that facilitate using JSON for object serialization and deserialization in Ajax-enabled applications in ASP.NET. The classes that comprise this namespace include the following:

- The `SimpleTypeResolver` class
- The `ScriptIgnoreAttribute` class
- The `JavaScriptConverter` class
- The `JavaScriptSerializer` class
- The `JavaScriptTypeResolver` class

The `System.Web.Script.Services` Namespace

The `System.Web.Script.Services` namespace is comprised of a collection of classes that can be used to customize the web services that you can use while working with the ASP.NET server extensions framework. The classes and interfaces included in this namespace are the following:

- The `ScriptMethodAttribute` class
- The `ScriptServiceAttribute` class
- The `GenerateScriptTypeAttribute` class

Summary

In this hour, we have had a detailed look at the Microsoft ASP.NET Ajax server extensions framework—including the namespaces, classes, and interfaces that this framework is comprised of—and illustrated how you can use it in your Ajax-enabled ASP.NET web applications. Within this framework, you have a collection of controls that you can use to Ajax enable your web applications seamlessly. In the hour that follows, we will take a look at how we can work with the `UpdatePanel` and the `UpdateProgress` controls in our Ajax-enabled ASP.NET web applications.

Workshop

Quiz

1. What are the components of the Microsoft Ajax server extensions framework?

2. Name the ASP.NET services that are provided by the Ajax server extensions framework.

3. What are the namespaces contained as part of Ajax server framework?

4. What is the `ScriptManager` control, and what is it used for?

5. Name the server controls that are included within the ASP.NET Ajax server extensions framework.

6. What are web services and application services bridges?

7. What is partial-page rendering?

8. What is the purpose of the `UpdatePanel` control?

9. What is the purpose of the `ScriptManagerProxy` control?

10. What is the purpose of the `System.Web.UI` namespace in the Microsoft Ajax Server Reference library? Name some important classes in this namespace.

Answers

1. The ASP.NET Ajax server extensions framework includes the following components:

   ▶ Application services bridge

   ▶ Web services bridge

   ▶ ASP.NET Ajax server controls

2. The ASP.NET Ajax server extensions framework provides support for these ASP.NET services:

   ▶ Localization

   ▶ Globalization

   ▶ Authentication

   ▶ Debugging

- ▶ Tracing
- ▶ Web services
- ▶ Application services

3. The ASP.NET Ajax server reference consists of the following namespaces:

- ▶ `System.Web.UI`
- ▶ `System.Web.UI.Design`
- ▶ `System.Web.Configuration`
- ▶ `System.Web.Script.Serialization`
- ▶ `System.Web.Handlers`
- ▶ `System.Web.Script.Services`

4. The `ScriptManager` control is a part of the `System.Web.UI` namespace and is the brain of an Ajax-enabled ASP.NET web page. As the name implies, it is responsible for managing scripts and registering them as and when required; it is also instrumental in partial-web page rendering in your Ajax-enabled ASP.NET web applications.

5. The server controls included as part of the ASP.NET Ajax server extensions framework are as follows:

- ▶ Timer
- ▶ ScriptManager
- ▶ ScriptManagerProxy
- ▶ UpdateProgress
- ▶ UpdatePanel

6. The application services bridge is used to provide access to the application services available as part of ASP.NET 2.0 from client-side scripts. The web services bridge is used to consume external web services from the client side in an Ajax-enabled web application. It makes use of JSON serializer, JavaScript proxies, and the `.asbx` files or the bridge files to call the web services.

7. Partial-web page rendering is a feature that allows you to specify portions of your web page that would be updated to eliminate the need for the entire page to be posted back to the web server and thus boost the application's performance. With this feature, you can easily define the "updatable" portions of your web page and make way for asynchronous calls.

8. The UpdatePanel control is included as a part of the Ajax server extensions framework and is used to update only a specified portion of the web page, thus eliminating the need to refresh the entire web page for improved performance and responsiveness.

9. The ScriptManagerProxy control is one that can be used to add scripts or services that have been pre-defined by the ScriptManager control—that is, you use the ScriptManagerProxy control to add scripts and services to your web page, which already has a ScriptManager control inside.

10. The System.Web.UI namespace in the Microsoft Ajax Server Reference library comprises of a collection of classes that facilitate design of rich and responsive user interfaces. Here is a list of some of the classes of this namespace.

- ▶ Timer class

- ▶ UpdatePanel class

- ▶ UpdatePanelControlTrigger class

- ▶ UpdatePanelTrigger class

- ▶ UpdateProgress class

- ▶ ExtenderControl class

- ▶ PostBackTrigger class

- ▶ ProfileServiceManager class

- ▶ ScriptBehaviorDescriptor class

- ▶ ScriptControl class

- ▶ ScriptDescriptor class

- ▶ ScriptManager class

- ▶ ScriptManagerProxy class

- ▶ ScriptResourceAttribute class

- ▶ ServiceReference class

- ▶ ServiceReferenceCollection class

HOUR 8

Working with the `UpdatePanel` and `UpdateProgress` Controls

What You'll Learn in This Hour:

▶ An introduction to partial-page rendering

▶ The `UpdatePanel` control and its usage

▶ The `UpdateProgress` control and its usage

In the previous hour, we discussed the ASP.NET Ajax server extensions framework that includes the new ASP.NET Ajax server controls—the `UpdatePanel`, `UpdateProgress`, ScriptManager, and Timer controls. In this hour, we discuss how we can use the `UpdatePanel` and `UpdateProgress` controls for implementing partial-page rendering in an ASP.NET Ajax application.

What Is Partial-Page Rendering?

Typically, web pages with the ASP.NET server controls perform a postback to the server when there is an action performed by the user on a control. The server renders all the controls into a page in response. It even renders the controls where its state has not been changed between postbacks. The new ASP.NET Ajax server controls render only a portion of the web page to enrich user experience and performance. Partial-page rendering is a concept of rendering only a portion of a web page to avoid complete page refreshes and improve the user experience. It can be achieved using Microsoft ASP.NET Ajax without writing any client scripts. It is actually made possible through the interaction of the server controls with the Microsoft Ajax Client Library. The page updates are taken care of automatically by the client code injected into the server controls.

The new server controls that ship with the ASP.NET Ajax server extensions framework include the `UpdatePanel` control, which is responsible for implementing the partial-page rendering behavior in your web applications. This new control helps in eliminating the page refresh during a postback just by writing a few lines of code and without any client script.

The communication between the server controls and the Microsoft Ajax Library for asynchronous postback is taken care of internally by the server control. In addition, the server controls invoke the appropriate client code that corresponds to a specific type of a browser with the help of the Microsoft Ajax Library, thus solving the compatibility issues with the client browser.

> The ASP.NET Ajax server controls automatically provide support for partial-page rendering, but you can also manually use the Client Library exposed in the Microsoft Ajax Library to achieve the same.

Why Use Partial-Page Rendering?

Now that we know what partial-page rendering is, let's discuss why this feature is required. The following lists some of the benefits that this feature has to offer:

▶ Improves user experience with web pages that behave more like a traditional client application

▶ Improves the responsiveness upon user actions on a web page

▶ Reduces complete page refreshes and makes only portions of the web page post back to avoid page flickering

▶ Enables client-server communication without writing client scripts

▶ Eliminates writing browser-compatible code

Looking Back in Time

We will discuss how we can implement this feature using the `UpdatePanel` and `UpdateProgress` controls in this hour. But before we do so, let's walk through the earlier approaches that were followed to accomplish partial-page rendering in web applications.

The `IFrame` Technique

`IFrame` stands for Inline Frame. It is an HTML element that acts as a container to hold other HTML documents. This supports the concept of partial-page rendering because the whole web page is not refreshed at one time—only the content of the `IFrame` control is posted back to the server. This improves the user experience a bit, but is not the best solution. Why?

First, this is a synchronous operation that causes the portion of the page to reload and flicker. And second, the client-side script needs to be written for hiding or showing the `IFrame`, when dynamic loading of a portion of the page is to be handled on an event. Thus, we may say that `IFrame` does not provide the best solution for partial-page rendering.

The `XMLHttpRequest` Approach

The next alternative—a better one—is the Ajax approach in the form of the `XMLHttpRequest` object. This object is used to make requests to the server, and the response updates portions of the web page using the client script (JavaScript). This approach isn't the best, as the logic has to be moved from the server to client. Also, the browser incompatibility issues come into the picture when using the `XMLHttp` protocol. But with the help of a generic client library for `XMLHttp`, this is quite a reliable solution. The best bet for the partial-page rendering comes with the ASP.NET Ajax server control—the `UpdatePanel`. In the coming sections, let's explore this control in more detail.

The `UpdatePanel` Server Control—Your Companion for Implementing Partial Updates

The `UpdatePanel` control is a new server control shipped with the ASP.NET Ajax server extensions framework. This control is responsible for enabling partial-page rendering in a web page, thus enhancing the richness of the user interface and improving the performance and responsiveness. In this section, we will learn how this control can be used in your applications.

Here is a simple example that illustrates how we can display the current date of the server on a `Label` control when you click on a `Button` control in the web page. To do this, follow the steps outlined next:

1. Open Visual Studio and create a new Ajax-enabled web site.

2. Create a new ASPX page and switch to design view mode.

3. Drag and drop a `Label` and a `Button` control in design view of the web page.

4. In the `Page Load` event of this web page, assign the current date to the `Label` control that we just created.

   Note that the name of the `Label` control in our example is `Label1`. Refer to the following code snippet:

```
protected void Page_Load(object sender, EventArgs e)
  {
      this.Label1.Text = DateTime.Now.ToString();
  }
```

5. Next, in the button click event, assign the current date to the `Label` control, as shown in the following code snippet:

```
protected void Button1_Click(object sender, EventArgs e)
    {
      this.Label1.Text = DateTime.Now.ToString();
  }
```

When you execute this application in the web browser, the current date and time are displayed. Upon the button click, the page is posted back to the server, and the latest date and time are rendered to the Label control.

In the preceding example, we have demonstrated a traditional ASP.NET page behavior—that is, you have the entire web page being posted back. Let's now learn how the use of the `UpdatePanel` control can make things simpler for you.

Refer to the web page created earlier. In the same web page, drag and drop an `UpdatePanel` control from the toolbox. Now, include a `Label` and `Button` control inside this `UpdatePanel` control, and have the same code in the page load and button click events, as demonstrated earlier.

Figure 8.1 illustrates the `UpdatePanel` control in design time with a `Label` and `Button` control placed in it.

FIGURE 8.1
The
UpdatePanel
control at
design time

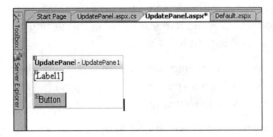

Here is the declarative markup of the UpdatePanel control:

```
<body>
    <form id="form1" runat="server">
    <div>
          <asp:ScriptManager ID="ScriptManager1" runat="server">
        </asp:ScriptManager>
        <br />
        <br />
         <asp:UpdatePanel ID="UpdatePanel1" runat="server">
            <ContentTemplate>
                <asp:Label ID="Label1" runat="server" Text="Label"></asp:Label>
<br />
                <br />
                <asp:Button ID="Button1" runat="server" OnClick="Button1_Click"
Text="Button" />
            </ContentTemplate>
        </asp:UpdatePanel>
    </div>
    </form>
</body>
```

Note that in the preceding markup, apart from the UpdatePanel control, a
ScriptManager control also has been placed. This is done to support partial-page
rendering. The ScriptManager control keeps track of all the UpdatePanel controls
on the page and its triggers. Also it determines the portions of the page that have to
be rendered as a result of an asynchronous postback operation. We'll learn more
about triggers as we progress through this hour.

After the preceding code is executed, the browser shows the initial output, which is
similar to what is depicted in Figure 8.2.

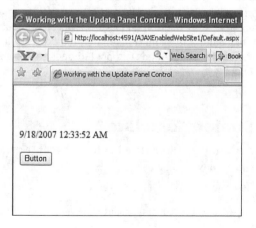

FIGURE 8.2
The
UpdatePanel
control at work!

When the Button control is clicked, all you find is an updated date and time rendered on the page without any postback at all! Amazing, isn't it? The Label control holds the updated date and time of the server, as shown in Figure 8.3.

FIGURE 8.3
Date and time updated without postbacks!

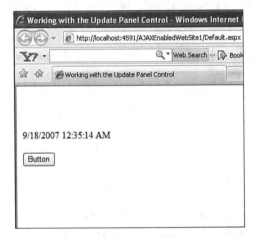

During the execution of the button click event, you will find that the entire page is not posted back. Rather, only the portion of the page holding the UpdatePanel is posted back without any flickering. This is the power of the UpdatePanel—with just a drag and drop of the control, and with no client-side scripting, partial-page rendering can be accomplished.

By the Way

> There is a misconception about the UpdatePanel control. You may think that when using the UpdatePanel control, no postback occurs because the user does not find any flickering when the event happens on the browser. In fact, the portion of the page that holds the UpdatePanel is posted back to the server but is posted back asynchronously.

What Is a ContentTemplate?

The content of the UpdatePanel is declared in the ContentTemplate tag of the UpdatePanel, as shown next:

```
<asp:UpdatePanel ID="UpdatePanel1" runat="server">
        <ContentTemplate>
            <asp:Label ID="Label1" runat="server" Text="Label"></asp:Label>
➡<br />
            <br />
```

```
                    <asp:Button ID="Button1" runat="server" OnClick="Button1_Click"
Text="Button" />
                </ContentTemplate>
            </asp:UpdatePanel>
```

Any content defined in this tag will be posted back to the server asynchronously. In the preceding example, we have a Label and a Button control placed inside it at design time. In fact, this can even be done programmatically. All the controls inside the ContentTemplate tag are considered to be child controls.

The UpdatePanel works on an asynchronous postback operation, which the ScriptManager control intercepts by replacing the traditional postback. Internally during the postback operation, the page updates are governed by injecting JavaScript on the UpdatePanel control automatically.

Let's now illustrate this concept with a simple example, as follows:

```
public partial class UpdatePanel : System.Web.UI.Page
{
    private Label Label1;
    protected void Page_Load(object sender, EventArgs e)
    {
        UpdatePanel uPanel = new UpdatePanel();
        uPanel.ID = "UpdatePanel1";
        // create the label
        Label1 = new Label();
        Label1.ID = "Label1";
            Label1.Text = DateTime.Now.ToString();
        //create the button
        Button button1 = new Button();
        button1.ID = "Button1";
        button1.Click += new EventHandler(Button1_Click);
        // create a literals
        LiteralControl literal = new LiteralControl("<br><br>");
        // embed the controls to the UpdatePanel
        uPanel.ContentTemplateContainer.Controls.Add(Label1);
        uPanel.ContentTemplateContainer.Controls.Add(literal);
        uPanel.ContentTemplateContainer.Controls.Add(button1);
        // Add the UpdatePanel to the form
            this.Form.Controls.Add(uPanel);
    }
    protected void Button1_Click(object sender, EventArgs e)
    {
        this.Label1.Text = DateTime.Now.ToString();
    }
}
```

In the preceding code, we've created a Label, a Button, and a Literal control dynamically and added them to the UpdatePanel control. The ContentTemplateContainer is a property of the UpdatePanel control, which acts as a container that holds the control collection along with the content.

The Render Modes of the `UpdatePanel` Control

The content in `UpdatePanel` is rendered to the page in `<div>` or `<span>` tags. The `RenderMode` property determines to which tag the content is rendered. The default setting for this property is `Block`, meaning that it renders to a `<div>` tag. The other option is the `Inline` setting, which renders the content to a `<span>` tag. Let's take a look at an example that demonstrates this. The following is the markup code of a `ScriptManager` control together with two `UpdatePanel` controls that we will use in this example:

```
<asp:ScriptManager ID="ScriptManager1" runat="server">
    </asp:ScriptManager>
    <br />
    <asp:UpdatePanel ID="UpdatePanel1" runat="server" RenderMode="Inline">
        <ContentTemplate>
            <%= DateTime.Now.ToString() %>
        </ContentTemplate>
    </asp:UpdatePanel>
    <br />
    <asp:UpdatePanel ID="UpdatePanel2" runat="server" RenderMode="Block">
        <ContentTemplate>
            <%= DateTime.Now.ToString() %>
        </ContentTemplate>
    </asp:UpdatePanel>
```

Referring to the preceding code snippet, note that there are two `UpdatePanel` controls: one with the `RenderMode` as `Inline` and the second with the `RenderMode` as `Block`. After you execute the web page in the web browser, the output is similar to what is shown in Figure 8.4 below:

FIGURE 8.4
The `UpdatePanel` control in action with `Inline` and `Block` render modes

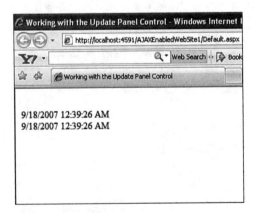

When you open the source of the web page, you can see that the content of an `UpdatePanel` control with its render mode set as `Inline` is rendered inside an HTML

<span> element, whereas the one with its render mode property set as `Block` is rendered inside an HTML <div> element:

```
<br />
 <span id="UpdatePanel1">
              11-06-2008 23:35:07
   </span>
          <br />
<div id="UpdatePanel2">
              11-06-2008 23:35:07
</div>
```

The Event Model of the UpdatePanel Control

In this section, we discuss the Event model of the `UpdatePanel` control. Note that the `UpdatePanel` control is inherited from the base `control` class. Therefore, it supports the events that are common in the ASP.NET server controls. The `UpdatePanel` actions for the page life cycle events are shown in Table 8.1.

TABLE 8.1   The Page Life Cycle Events of the UpdatePanel Control

Page Event	What Happens?
Init	All the UpdatePanel controls on the page are registered with the ScriptManager control.
Load	Initializes all the triggers for each of the UpdatePanel controls in an asynchronous postback.
PreRender	Checks for the correct settings of the UpdatePanel. For example, if the ChildrenAsTriggers property is set to true, then the UpdateMode property should be set to Conditional.
Unload	The user brings focus to an element either via mouse click or by using the Tab key on the keyboard.

In the next section, we discuss the `UpdateMode` property of the `UpdatePanel` control.

Specifying Update Modes Using the UpdateMode Property

The `UpdateMode` property defines whether the rendering of the `UpdatePanel` should be set to `Always` or `Conditional`. By default, it is set to `Always`, meaning that whenever the page is posted back, the contents of the `UpdatePanel` are rendered. When it is set to `Conditional`, the `UpdatePanel` renders under the following circumstances:

1. A child control of the `UpdatePanel` invokes the postback.

2. A trigger is associated with the `UpdatePanel`. (We discuss triggers in the next section.)

3. The `Update` method of the `UpdatePanel` is called during a postback.

The following code demonstrates the UpdatePanel with the two UpdateModes available. The first UpdatePanel in the code is Always (which is by default), and the second UpdatePanel has its UpdateMode set to Conditional. Here the child control in it invokes the postback. Figure 8.5 illustrates the following example.

```
<asp:ScriptManager ID="ScriptManager1" runat="server" />
        <asp:UpdatePanel ID="UpdatePanel1" runat="server">
            <ContentTemplate>
                <div>
                    Date and Time:
                    <%= DateTime.Now.ToString() %>
                </div>
                <div>
                    <asp:Button ID="Button1" runat="server" Text="Update" />
                </div>
            </ContentTemplate>
        </asp:UpdatePanel>
        <hr />
        <asp:UpdatePanel ID="UpdatePanel2" runat="server"
➥UpdateMode="Conditional">
            <ContentTemplate>
                <div>
                    Date and Time:
                    <%= DateTime.Now.ToString() %>
                </div>
                <div>
                    <asp:Button ID="Button2" runat="server" Text="Update" />
                </div>
            </ContentTemplate>
        </asp:UpdatePanel>
```

FIGURE 8.5
Illustrating conditional
UpdateMode
property of the
UpdatePanel
control

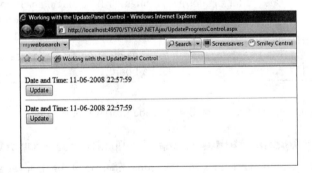

> Setting the UpdateMode property to Conditional is advisable because it improves the performance of the web page considerably by sending only the data that is to be updated in the page.

Now when you click on the first button, you can see that the date and time of the first div has changed, but not the second (see Figure 8.6).

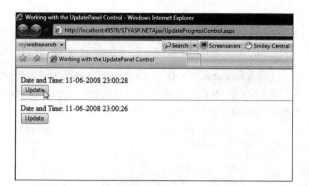

FIGURE 8.6
Date and time changed using UpdateMode property set as Update

On the contrary, when you click on the Button control on the other div, that is, the second div, you can notice that the date and time changes in both cases, as shown in Figure 8.7.

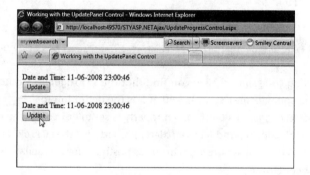

FIGURE 8.7
Date and time changed in both cases

We now discuss how you can work with events when using the UpdatePanel control in the section that follows.

What Are Triggers?

A trigger is an event that causes the UpdatePanel to refresh its content. This event can be generated by any control in the form. There are two types of triggers: AsyncPostBackTrigger and PostBackTrigger.

The AsyncPostBackTrigger fires an asynchronous postback event on the UpdatePanel control. The child control's postback of the UpdatePanel by default fires this trigger. This also invokes asynchronous postback for any other UpdatePanel controls on the form that the UpdateMode property set to Always.

Note that all the child controls implicitly post back asynchronously with this trigger. However, you can prevent this by setting the ChildrenAsTriggers property to false. After this is set, the postbacks coming from these controls are ignored.

There are two attributes associated with the AsyncPostBackTrigger: ControlID and EventName. This can be defined either declaratively or programmatically. The following is an example of this trigger in declarative markup:

```
<asp:UpdatePanel ID="UpdatePanel1" runat="server" UpdateMode="Conditional">
            <ContentTemplate>
                <div>
                    Date and Time:
                    <%= DateTime.Now.ToString() %>
                </div>
                <div>
                    <asp:Button ID="Button1" runat="server" Text="Update" />
                </div>
            </ContentTemplate>
            <Triggers>
                <asp:AsyncPostBackTrigger ControlID="Button2"
➡EventName="Click" />
            </Triggers>
        </asp:UpdatePanel>
        <hr />
        <asp:Button ID="Button2" runat="server" Text="Update" />
```

In the preceding code snippet, you can find that the <Triggers> tag has been defined in the UpdatePanel control, which has the definition for AsyncPostBackTrigger. Its ControlD property is set to Button2, which is outside the UpdatePanel control, and its EventName property is set to Click. Now when Button2 is clicked, it causes an asynchronous postback for the UpdatePanel, thus refreshing its content.

You can also add the same trigger programmatically, as shown in the following code snippet:

```
protected override void OnInit(EventArgs e)
    {
        base.OnInit(e);
        AsyncPostBackTrigger asyncTrigger = new AsyncPostBackTrigger();
        asyncTrigger.ControlID = "Button2";
        asyncTrigger.EventName = "Click";
        UpdatePanel1.Triggers.Add(asyncTrigger);
    }
```

If you observe the preceding snippet of code, the AsyncPostBackTrigger is created in the Init event, as this is the event where the UpdatePanel is registered with the ScriptManager control. As you can see in the code snippet, the AsyncPostBackTrigger instance is created. Then its ControlID and EventName properties are set. Finally, the same is added to the `Triggers` collection of the `UpdatePanel` control.

The second type of trigger, the `PostBackTrigger`, fires a traditional postback event on the page. This causes referenced controls inside the `UpdatePanel` to perform regular postbacks. By default, all the child controls in an `UpdatePanel` control operate with the `AsyncPostBackTrigger`. However, there might be situations where a button is clicked in an UpdatePane, and it requires the entire web page to be posted back. In such scenarios, we can go ahead with the `PostBackTrigger`. This trigger does not have an `EventName` property.

Here is the declarative markup of `PostBackTrigger`:

```
<asp:UpdatePanel ID="UpdatePanel1" runat="server" UpdateMode="Always">
        <ContentTemplate>
            <%= DateTime.Now.ToString() %>
            <asp:Button ID="Button1" runat="server" Text="Update" />
        </ContentTemplate>
        <Triggers>
            <asp:PostBackTrigger ControlID="Button2" />
        </Triggers>
    </asp:UpdatePanel>
```

You can also do the same programmatically, as shown in the following code snippet:

```
protected override void OnInit(EventArgs e)
    {
        base.OnInit(e);
        PostBackTrigger trigger = new PostBackTrigger();
        trigger.ControlID = "Button1";
        UpdatePanel1.Triggers.Add(trigger);
    }
```

We are done with our discussion on the `UpdatePanel` control. We now need to provide a visual display to the user regarding the progress of an asynchronous operation in an Ajax-enabled ASP.NET web application. This is where an `UpdateProgress` control fits in. In the section that follows, we discuss this control and how we can use it in our web applications.

Looking at the UpdateProgress Control

The `UpdateProgress` control of the ASP.NET Ajax extensions framework library can be used to display the progress status of one or more `UpdatePanel` controls when using partial-page rendering in an Ajax-enabled ASP.NET web page. You can use this control, together with the `UpdatePanel` control, to provide a visual feedback to the user, such as displaying the progress status of partial-page updates in an asynchronous mode of operation in an Ajax-enabled web application. You can even use your own template to display the progress status on such an operation in your user interface.

The following code snippet illustrates the source code for this control in the .aspx file once you include this control in your web page:

```
<asp:UpdateProgress ID="MyUpdateProgress" runat="server"
...
</asp:UpdateProgress>
```

You can have more than one UpdateProgress control in your web page, and each of them can be associated with a specific UpdatePanel control using the AssociatedUpdatePanelID property. Alternatively, you can also have one UpdateProgress control in your Ajax-enabled ASPNET web page and then associate this control with all the UpdatePanel controls in your web page. However, in order for you to work with UpdatePanel and UpdateProgress controls, you have to have a ScriptManager control in your web page.

Here is the complete code listing for a web page that contains UpdateProgress and UpdatePanel controls:

```
<form id="myForm" runat="server">
        <asp:ScriptManager ID="MyScriptManager" runat="server" />
        <asp:UpdateProgress runat="server" id="MyUpdateProgress"
➥AssociatedUpdatePanelID="MyPanel" DisplayAfter="0">
            <ProgressTemplate>
                The Page is being loaded.  Please wait...
            </ProgressTemplate>
        </asp:UpdateProgress>
        <asp:UpdatePanel runat="server" id="MyPanel">
            <ContentTemplate>
                <asp:Button runat="server" id="MyButton" onclick="ShowProgress"
➥text="LoadPage" />
            </ContentTemplate>
        </asp:UpdatePanel>
    </form>
```

And here is the code that you need to write for the ShowProgress event handler:

```
protected void ShowProgress(object sender, EventArgs e)
    {
        System.Threading.Thread.Sleep(2000);
    }
```

When you execute the preceding program, the output is similar to what is shown in Figure 8.8.

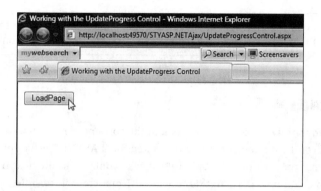

FIGURE 8.8
Working with the UpdateProgres s control

Now, when you click on the Button control, the text message within the ProgressTemplate tag is displayed, as shown in Figure 8.9.

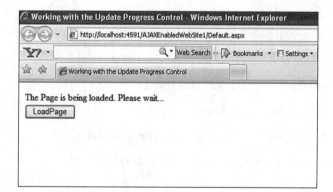

FIGURE 8.9
The UpdateProgres s control at work!

If you look at the preceding code snippet, you will find that we have used two properties: DisplayAfter and AssociatedUpdatePanelID. Although the former is used to specify the time in milliseconds, after which the UpdateProgress control will be displayed, the latter is used to associate the UpdateProgress control with one or more UpdatePanels. Moreover, it ensures that the UpdateProgress control is displayed when an asynchronous operation occurs due to a post-back event that is raised by one or more UpdatePanel controls or any of their child controls in your Ajax-enabled web page. In the ShowProgress event, we have made a call to the Thread.Sleep() method to put the current thread in sleeping state. This will ensure that the text within the ProgressTemplate section is displayed after the interval we have specified in the Thread.Sleep() method. In our case, we have put the current thread to sleep for two seconds—that is, the text gets displayed after two seconds elapse from the time the Button control is clicked by the user.

By the Way

> You should define the `ProgressTemplate` section in an `UpdateProgress` control to specify the content for the `UpdateProgress` control to avoid a runtime error.

Summary

In this hour, we have had a detailed look at the concept of partial-page rendering and how it can be implemented in our Ajax-enabled ASP.NET web applications using the `UpdatePanel` and the `UpdateProgress` controls. In the next hour, we'll examine in detail how the ScriptManager and Timer controls operate.

Workshop

Quiz

1. What is partial-page rendering, and what are its benefits?

2. What is the purpose of the ScriptManager control?

3. How does the `UpdatePanel` control work?

4. What is the `ContentTemplate` tag used for?

5. What is the purpose of an `UpdateProgress` control?

6. What are the basic purposes of the `DisplayAfter` and `AssociatedUpdatePanelID` properties of the `UpdateProgress` control?

7. What is the `ProgressTemplate` in an `UpdateProgress` control used for?

Answers

1. Partial-page rendering is a feature that allows you to specify portions of your web page that would be updated to eliminate the need for the entire page to be posted back to the web server. Partial-page rendering offers many benefits, such as the following:

   ▶ Reduced server hits

   ▶ Improved response

2. The `ScriptManager` control is the brain of an Ajax-enabled ASP.NET web page and keeps track of all the `UpdatePanel` controls on the page and its triggers. Further, it determines the portions of the page to render as a result of an asynchronous postback operation.

3. The `UpdatePanel` works with an asynchronous postback operation, which the ScriptManager control intercepts by replacing the traditional postback. Whenever a postback occurs, the page updates are governed by automatically injecting JavaScript on the `UpdatePanel` control. In fact, the portion of the page that holds the `UpdatePanel` is posted back to the server but is posted back asynchronously.

4. The `ContentTemplate` tag is used to define the content in your Ajax-enabled ASP.NET web page that would be posted back asynchronously to the web server.

5. The `UpdateProgress` control can be used to display the progress to the user when one or more `UpdatePanel` controls in your web page is being updated. You can use it to depict the progress status of an asynchronous operation.

6. The `DisplayAfter` property is used to specify the time in milliseconds after which the `UpdateProgress` control will be displayed. The `AssociatedUpdatePanelID` control is used to associate the `UpdateProgress` control with one or more `UpdatePanels`.

7. The `ProgressTemplate` section in an `UpdateProgress` control is used to specify the content for the `UpdateProgress` control.

HOUR 9

Working with the
ScriptManager **and** Timer
Controls

What You'll Learn in This Hour:

▸ The ScriptManager control

▸ The Timer control

▸ How to implement partial page updates using the UpdatePanel and the Timer controls in Ajax-enabled web applications

As we have learned in previous hours, Ajax is awesome in its ability to eliminate postbacks or server hits and still provide the information that the application demands. In this hour, we explore the ScriptManager and the Timer controls and discuss why they are required and how they can be used in your Ajax-enabled web applications.

An Overview of the ScriptManager Control

The ScriptManager control is an invisible control and is the heart of an Ajax-enabled web page. The ScriptManager is the most important control for an Ajax-enabled web page and performs functions in more ways than one. Nikhil Kothari says, "It provides functionality to both the page developer and the control developer (for those writing Atlas-enabled controls), and it orchestrates partial refreshes, incremental updates, and will do even more in the future."

This control allows for partial-page rendering of your Ajax-enabled web page using the UpdatePanel control, and provides access to web services. It also enables loading and registering the scripts. The ScriptManager control is great in enabling the partial-page rendering feature in your web applications. It can update your content stored within the

UpdatePanel control. The control's EnablePartialPageRendering property is a Boolean property that is set to true by default and determines whether or not this feature is required by the web page.

There can be one and only one ScriptManager control in your Ajax-enabled web page. You can place the ScriptManager control in the master page(s) of your application and inherit all context pages from it.

The following are some of the useful features provided by the ScriptManager control:

▶ Client-side scripting

▶ Access to web services using JavaScript proxy classes

▶ Partial-page rendering

▶ Error handling during processing of the asynchronous requests

So what are the prerequisites for partial-page rendering in your web page? Well, you need to have a ScriptManager control and at least one UpdatePanel control, and also ensure that the SupportsPartialPageRendering and the EnablePartialPageRendering properties are set to true. Note that both of these properties are set to true by default.

To use the ScriptManager control, simply drag and drop the control from the Ajax extensions in the toolbox, as shown in Figure 9.1.

FIGURE 9.1
The ScriptManager control

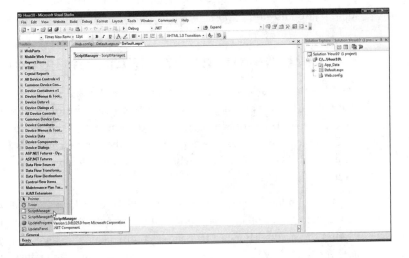

The markup code that gets generated is as follows:

```
<asp:ScriptManager ID="ScriptManager1" runat="server" />
```

You can also write the same code shown previously directly in your web page to use this control programmatically:

```
<form id="form1" runat="server">
    <asp:ScriptManager ID="ScriptManager1" runat="server" />
    <div>
        <asp:UpdatePanel ID="UpdatePanel1" runat="server">
        </asp:UpdatePanel>
    </div>
</form>
```

By the Way

If you add more than one ScriptManager control in your web page, an InvalidOperationException is thrown at runtime, with the message, "System. InvalidOperationException: Only one instance of a ScriptManager can be added to the page."

Error Handling Using Ajax

We now use the ScriptManager and UpdatePanel controls to implement an error handling mechanism that is efficient and devoid of annoying JavaScript alerts. So, let's get started!

To implement this application, follow these steps:

1. Click File, New, New Web Site to create a new web site and save it with a name.

2. In the Default.aspx file that gets created by default, place the following code:

```
<body>
    <form id="form1" runat="server">
    <div>
        <asp:ScriptManager ID="ScriptManager1" runat="server" />
        <asp:UpdatePanel runat="server" ID="UpdatePanel1">
          <ContentTemplate>
            <asp:Button runat="server" ID="Button1"
              Text="Click Me" OnClick="Button1_OnClick" />
          </ContentTemplate>
        </asp:UpdatePanel>
    </div>
    <br />
    <br />
    <div id="Message" style="visibility: hidden;">
        <asp:HyperLink ID="HyperLink1"  Font-Bold="true" Text="Error
➥Occurred..." Font-Italic="true" ForeColor="red" runat="server">
➥</asp:HyperLink>
    </div>
    </form>
</body>
```

You can see in the previous code that we have a ScriptManager control, an UpdatePanel control, and a Button control inside the ContentTemplate tag of the UpdatePanel control. Further, we have a HyperLink control inside a div tag that we will use to display messages to the user. The Button control has in its OnClick event a handler associated called Button1_Click. So when you click on the Button control, this event handler is invoked. Here is the code for this event handler:

```
protected void Button1_OnClick(object sender, EventArgs e)
    {
        throw new Exception();
    }
```

What are we doing here? We are throwing an exception in the previous event handler.

3. Now, create a script file called ErrorhandlingScript.js and place in it the following code:

```
Sys.Application.add_load(pageLoad);

function pageLoad()
{
    Sys.WebForms.PageRequestManager.getInstance().add_beginRequest
➥(BeginRequestHandler);
    Sys.WebForms.PageRequestManager.getInstance().add_endRequest
➥(EndRequestHandler);
}

function BeginRequestHandler(sender, args)
{
    $get('HyperLink1').style.visibility = "hidden";
}

function EndRequestHandler(sender, args)
{

}
```

When you execute the application, the output is similar to Figure 9.2.

4. Now let's write some code to handle this exception using Ajax. Here is the changed code in the script file:

```
Sys.Application.add_load(pageLoad);

function pageLoad()
{
    Sys.WebForms.PageRequestManager.getInstance().add_beginRequest
➥(BeginRequestHandler);
    Sys.WebForms.PageRequestManager.getInstance().add_endRequest
➥(EndRequestHandler);
}
```

```
function BeginRequestHandler(sender, args)
{
  $get('HyperLink1').style.visibility = "hidden";
}

function EndRequestHandler(sender, args)
{
 if (args.get_error() != undefined)
  {
    $get('HyperLink1').style.visibility = "visible";
    args.set_errorHandled(true);
  }
}
```

FIGURE 9.2
System.
Exception
thrown

Notice the use of the BeginRequestHandler and the EndRequestHandler methods. We have made a call to the set_errorHandler method in the EndRequestHandler method to suppress the error. Prior to this, we have displayed the message using the HyperLink control.

We are done! When you execute the application again, the output is similar to Figure 9.3.

Note that the message "Error Occurred..." is displayed in the HyperLink control and without a postback!

We now learn how we can use the Timer control to display the current time, which changes every second to display the current time to the user. In the section that follows, we will explore the Timer control and examine how we can use it to achieve the output that we just discussed.

FIGURE 9.3
Error handled
using Ajax

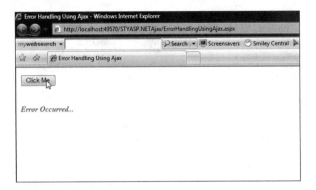

You can load a script in debug mode as shown in the following code:

```
<asp:ScriptManager ID="ScriptManager1" runat="server">
        <Scripts>
            <asp:ScriptReference Path="ErrorHandlingScript.js"
            ScriptMode="Debug" />
        </Scripts>
</asp:ScriptManager>
```

And here is how you can load a script in the release mode:

```
<asp:ScriptManager ID="ScriptManager1" runat="server">
        <Scripts>
            <asp:ScriptReference Path="ErrorHandlingScript.js"
            ScriptMode="Release" />
        </Scripts>
</asp:ScriptManager>
```

Working with the Timer Control

A Timer control is typically used to create a client-side timer so that the page can refresh data at specified intervals of time. In other words, you use the Timer control for updating the content in your web page periodically. It raises an event at periodic intervals of time (in milliseconds) that you need to pre-define using the Interval property of this control. So if you want to use an UpdatePanel control (the content of which needs to be updated periodically), this is the control that you need to use. Awesome, isn't it?

To use the Timer control, simply go to the design view mode of your web page and drag and drop the control from the Ajax extensions group of the toolbox. You can also write your code to create the control programmatically using markup code in your .aspx file. In either case, here is how the markup code in your web page looks after you have placed a Timer control inside it:

```
<asp:Timer ID="Timer1" runat="server" Interval="5000"
OnTick="UpdateTime" />
```

You can use the UpdatePanel and the Timer controls, to achieve partial updates for a web page at specific intervals of time. This implies that a specific portion of the web page—that is, the portion of the web page contained inside one or more UpdatePanel controls—will be updated periodically at specified intervals of time without the need for postbacks; this will improve the performance and the responsiveness of your web applications, which leverages the benefits of Ajax. The Timer control will actually cause the UpdatePanel's load event to be invoked at specified intervals of time.

This comes in handy particularly in situations where you want to update data for your required controls periodically to ensure that the data stored in the underlying data store is in sync with the data being displayed by the data control. We will discuss this in the next section.

Let's now make use of the Timer control to display the current time dynamic—the current time will be updated every second so as to display the most recent time to the user.

You can write the code for creating a Timer control directly in the .aspx; the markup code is as follows:

```
<asp:Timer ID="Timer1" runat="server" Interval="1000" OnTick="UpdateTime" />
```

Every 1000 milliseconds, the Timer control initiates a postback, which in turn causes the load event of the UpdatePanel to be called again, and the current time is updated. Done!

Note that you can use the Timer control inside or outside the UpdatePanel control. When you place the Timer control inside the UpdatePanel control, the JavaScript timing component will be re-created once the postback is complete in its entirety. Therefore, if the timing interval that you have set using the Interval property has a value of 5000 milliseconds, and the postbacks require 5 milliseconds, the next postback of the web page will happen after 1000 + 5—that is, 1005 milliseconds.

This is in contrast to what happens if you place the JavaScript timing component outside the UpdatePanel control. In this case, the timing component will continue its execution even when the postback operation is being performed. Thus, in this case, the next postback to the server will happen after 1000 milliseconds only. So the user will see that the data is being updated every 1000 – 5 or 995 milliseconds.

Implementing Partial Page Updates Using the UpdatePanel **and the** Timer **Controls**

In this section, we learn how to use the concepts that we have discussed so far to implement a simple application that displays the most recent data in a GridView control from the database.

Consider a table called Sales that contains the sales data of some inventory items. The table gets updated often based on the sales of those items. The intent is that we need to display the most recent data from this table to the end user—that is, the data displayed should always be in sync with the data stored in the database table. How do we achieve this?

To do this, follow these steps:

1. Create a database table called Sales. Here is the table script:

```
CREATE TABLE [dbo].[Sales](
        [SalesID] [int] NOT NULL,
        [SalesmanName] [varchar](50) COLLATE Latin1_General_CI_AI NOT NULL,
        [ItemName] [varchar](50) COLLATE Latin1_General_CI_AI NOT NULL,
        [NoOfItems] [smallint] NOT NULL
) ON [PRIMARY]
```

2. Store some sample records in your table.

3. Next, go to the design view mode and create a SqlDataSource control and configure it so that it refers to the Sales table we have just created.

4. Switch to the Ajax extensions group in your toolbox in the design view mode of your web page.

5. Now, simply drag and drop a GridView control and a Timer control in your web page.

6. Associate the GridView control with the SqlDataSource control by setting the DataSourceID property of the control to the ID of the SqlDataSource control.

   Note that the GridView control is placed inside an UpdatePanel control.

   Here is the complete markup code in your .aspx file:

```
        <asp:ScriptManager ID="ScriptManager1" runat="server"
➥EnablePageMethods="true" />
        <asp:UpdatePanel runat="server" ID="UpdatePanel1"
➥UpdateMode="Conditional">
            <ContentTemplate>
                <asp:GridView ID="GridView1" runat="server"
➥Font-Size="Medium" GridLines="None" Width="600px"
                    AutoGenerateColumns="false" BorderStyle="Solid"
➥AllowSorting="true" DataSourceID="SqlDataSource1"
                    OnRowDataBound="GridView1_RowDataBound"
➥HeaderStyle-BackColor="Blue" HeaderStyle-ForeColor="White"
```

```
                        HeaderStyle-Font-Names="Verdana" HeaderStyle-Font-
Size="10pt"
➥RowStyle-ForeColor="Black"
                        RowStyle-BackColor="DeepSkyBlue" RowStyle-Font-
Names="Verdana"
➥RowStyle-Font-Size="10pt">
                        <AlternatingRowStyle BackColor="AliceBlue" />
                        <HeaderStyle HorizontalAlign="Left" />
                        <Columns>
                            <asp:BoundField DataField="SalesID" HeaderText=
➥"Sales ID" />
                            <asp:BoundField DataField="SalesmanName"
HeaderText=
➥"Salesman Name" />
                            <asp:BoundField DataField="ItemName" HeaderText=
➥"Name of Sold Item" />
                            <asp:BoundField DataField="NoOfItems" HeaderText=
➥"Number of Sold Items" />
                        </Columns>
                    </asp:GridView>
                    <asp:Timer ID="Timer1" runat="server" Interval="5000"
➥ OnTick="UpdateData" />
                </ContentTemplate>
            </asp:UpdatePanel>
            <asp:SqlDataSource ID="SqlDataSource1" runat="server"
DataSourceMode=
➥"DataSet" ConnectionString="<%$ ConnectionStrings:DBConnectionString %>"
                SelectCommand="SELECT * FROM [Sales]"></asp:SqlDataSource>
```

Note the use of the connection string to connect to the database. Consider that this connection string is stored in your config file.

We have used a Timer control to achieve periodic updates to the data being displayed in the GridView control. Here is the markup code for the event handler:

```
<asp:Timer ID="Timer1" runat="server" Interval="5000" OnTick="UpdateData"
/>
```

We have specified the interval of the Timer control using its Interval property and the event handler to be triggered periodically using the OnTick property of the control.

The UpdateData event handler that gets executed every five seconds is as follows:

```
public void UpdateData(object sender, EventArgs args)
    {
        GridView1.DataBind();
    }
```

7. Press the F5 key to execute the application.

When you execute the application, the output is similar to Figure 9.4.

FIGURE 9.4
The
ScriptManager
control at work!

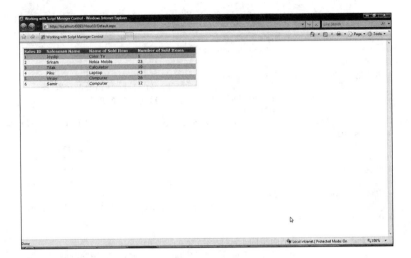

Note that the contents of the `GridView` control will be refreshed after every five seconds. Now insert a record in the Sales table manually using the Query Editor of the Sql Server Management Studio or whatever is preferable for you to use. Here is the insert statement that inserts a record in the Sales table:

```
INSERT INTO [Test].[dbo].[Sales]
        ([SalesID]
        ,[SalesmanName]
        ,[ItemName]
        ,[NoOfItems])
    VALUES
        (7,'Rama','Washing Machine',201)
```

When you execute the application, the output is similar to what is shown in Figure 9.5.

So, as is evident from Figure 9.5, the data displayed by the `GridView` control has been updated with the most recent data contained in the Sales table. The record that we just inserted in the Sales table is displayed in the `GridView`, and without a postback! This concludes our discussion on how we can update data contained in a data control (we used the `GridView` control in our example) using the `Timer` control.

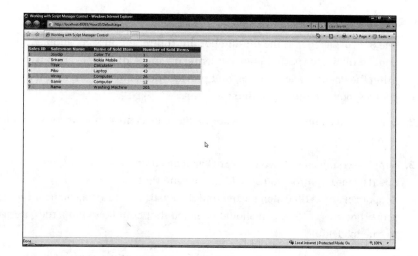

FIGURE 9.5
Data updated
without
postbacks!

Summary

In this hour, we learned how we can use the `ScriptManager` and `Timer` controls and why they are so important. We also implemented a sample application that illustrated how we can achieve partial updates in web applications by making use of the `Timer` and `UpdatePanel` controls. In the next hour, we will take a look at the ASP.NET Ajax control toolkit.

Workshop

Quiz

1. What is the purpose of a `ScriptManager` control?

2. How many `ScriptManager` controls can you have for your Ajax-enabled web page?

3. I need to have partial-page rendering in my web page; what am I required to do?

4. What is the `Timer` control used for?

5. What are partial-page updates?

Answers

1. The ScriptManager is the most important control for an Ajax-enabled web page. It allows for partial-page rendering of your Ajax-enabled web page using the UpdatePanel control, and provides access to web services. It also enables loading and registering the scripts

2. You can have one and only one ScriptManager control in your Ajax-enabled web page.

3. Simple—you need to have a ScriptManager control and at least one UpdatePanel control; you should also ensure that the SupportsPartialPageRendering and the EnablePartialPageRendering properties are set to true. It should be noted that both these properties are set to true by default.

4. The Timer control is used for updating the content in your web page periodically. It raises an event at periodic intervals of time (in milliseconds), which you need to predefine using the Interval property of this control.

5. Partial page update is a feature that allows you to periodically update the data contained in one or more UpdatePanel controls at specified intervals of time. This is done without the need of postbacks to improve the performance and responsiveness of your Ajax-enabled web applications.

HOUR 10

Working with the Ajax Control Toolkit—Part I

What You'll Learn in This Hour:

▶ The introduction to ASP.NET Ajax Control Toolkit
▶ How Ajax-enabled controls are built
▶ The Control Toolkit developed by Microsoft and the community

We have examined the salient controls shipped with the ASP.NET Ajax server extensions in the earlier hours. Note that the server controls `ScriptManager`, `UpdatePanel`, `UpdateProgress`, and `Timer` are part of the ASP.NET Ajax server extensions. In this hour, we look at how the ASP.NET server controls are extended to get an Ajax-like behavior and also examine the Ajax Control Toolkit API. This is comprised of a collection of different extenders and script controls developed using the Microsoft Ajax Library. Moreover, this Toolkit acts as a server API for developing Ajax-enabled controls.

Looking back in time, the ASP.NET Ajax Control Toolkit was initially started by Microsoft and was released with the first version of ASP.NET Ajax in early January 2006. Later it was made available to the community with contributions to extend it further. Now this Toolkit includes controls developed by non-Microsoft programmers as well!

Introducing the Control Toolkit

The Ajax Control Toolkit is an open source project introduced by Microsoft to leverage the power of Ajax-enabled controls into ASP.NET applications. The Toolkit is available online at its official site hosted by Microsoft at http://ajax.asp.net/. The project is available with source code, is hosted at www.codeplex.com, and can be freely downloaded. The project contains several samples and components that provide extenders and script controls packaged into an assembly. This enables the developer to create Ajax-enabled controls and custom extenders using ASP.NET. The features of all these controls can be seen at www.asp.net/ajax/ajaxcontroltoolkit/.

You can find the latest release of the project inclusive of the source code at the following:

www.codeplex.com/Release/ProjectReleases.aspx?ProjectName=Atlascontroltoolkit

After you download the project, include the Control Toolkit assembly in your ASP.NET Ajax-enabled web site to use its functionality. Before we delve into the working of the controls in the Toolkit, we need to discuss extenders and script controls and learn how the Ajax-enabled controls are built in order to leverage its power in ASP.NET applications. This hour gives us insight into the building of Ajax-enabled controls and kick-starts the usage of the Control Toolkit in ASP.NET applications.

What Are Ajax-Enabled Controls?

Ajax-enabled controls are ASP.NET server controls built by wiring the client components to the ASP.NET server controls. The client components are built using the Microsoft Ajax Library. Ajax-enabled controls are built either by script controls or extenders. *Extenders* are external objects that are wired with ASP.NET server controls to get the Ajax behavior, and *script controls* are server controls created as Ajax-enabled controls that specifiy both the server and client capabilities at the same place.

The Ajax-enabled controls render HTML code that generates $Create statements based on the client components it wants to instantiate. These $Create statements are used by the respective client components of the Microsoft Ajax Library to instantiate the control. *Script descriptor* takes care of generating the $Create statements programmatically. Apart from this, the Ajax-enabled controls load the necessary script files in the page, and this is done with the help of the ScriptReference object. In essence, every Ajax-enabled control returns script descriptors and script references to the client components for achieving Ajax-like behavior.

A *script descriptor* is an object that generates $Create statements programmatically. This $Create statement is automatically injected into the JavaScript code block and executed during the init stage of the client page life cycle to instantiate the client behavior and client control for usage. ScriptDescriptor is a base abstract class under the System.web.UI namespace, which is a part of the System.Web. Extensions assembly. During the Render phase of the server page life cycle, the

ScriptManager control queries the server control for a list of script descriptors. These script descriptors collected are used to render $Create statements in the HTML code generated and sent to the browser. The client components of the Microsoft Ajax Library identify this statement and instantiate the corresponding control for perusal.

A *script reference* is an object that loads script files in the page. It exposes the properties needed to load a script file. This script file can be located in a folder on the web server or can be located as a web resource (embedded in assembly). Again, the ScriptManager control can be used to load the script files needed by a page. This is done by declaring the ScriptReference elements in the script section of the ScriptManager control.

Therefore, script descriptors and script references are the objects needed to build Ajax-enabled controls.

Building Ajax-Enabled Controls

As discussed previously, the client components instantiate the Ajax-enabled control. The client components are part of the Microsoft Ajax Library, and these components expect a $Create statement that is rendered to the client browser to instantiate the control.

The objects responsible for generating $Create statements are the script descriptor and script reference. The following outlines the activities that illustrate the building of an Ajax-enabled control:

1. To make use of client components, an ASP.NET server control must implement one of the interfaces, extender or script control. By implementing one of the interfaces, the server control provides a list of script descriptors and script references for client components to instantiate client behavior and control.

2. The Ajax-enabled control should register itself with the ScriptManager control during the PreRender phase of the server page life cycle. This indicates that the ScriptManager is willing to instantiate client components.

3. The Ajax-enabled control should register script descriptors with the ScriptManager control during the Render phase of the server page life cycle. During this phase, the ScriptManager queries a list of script descriptors and script references.

4. Finally, the returned objects from the ScriptManager—that is, script descriptors and script references—are used to render the script tags and $Create statements in the web page.

The entire registration process is automated by deriving the base classes for creating an Ajax-enabled control and implementing the methods that return the list of script descriptors and references. Figure 10.1 illustrates this process.

FIGURE 10.1
Registration process of Ajax-enabled controls

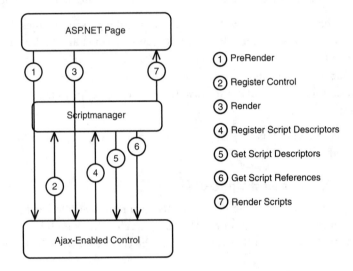

Let's discuss the two kinds of interfaces in the next section.

Extender

An extender is a kind of Ajax-enabled control to provide a list of script descriptors and script references. The purpose of an extender is to wire a client component to an existing server control. An extender acts as an external object and attaches itself to a server control. This can also be done alternatively by deriving from a base class. Let's think of a simple client component that does an auto-complete functionality similar to that of Google Suggest and wire this to a TextBox server control. All we have to do is create a class AutoComplete with script descriptors and script references and derive it from the TextBox class. But the simple way is to use an external object and wire to the server control. Figure 10.2 displays the model of an extender generating script descriptors and script references.

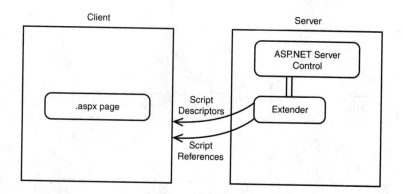

Client

Server

FIGURE 10.2
The extender
model

How Do You Build an Extender Control?

An extender is built by declaring a class that inherits from the base class ExtenderControl. This class should implement the interface IExtenderControl. Doing this registers the extender with the ScriptManager control. Also, this class should override the methods of the IExtenderControl interface.

The registration of an extender is done automatically by the ExtenderControl class, as a new extender is always created by deriving this class. But internally, the registration is done by calling the RegisterExtenderControl method of the ScriptManager control during the PreRender phase by passing the instance of the extender and the extended control as arguments. And during the Render phase, the RegisterScriptDescriptors method of the ScriptManager control should be called by passing the extender as an argument.

Script Control

The goal of a script control is the same as that of the extender—that is, to provide a list of script descriptors and script references—but here, the client and server capabilities should be present at the same place. This does not need an external object. The class AutoComplete, deriving from the TextBox class (which we discussed in an earlier section), is a classic candidate for a script control.

To choose a script control or an extender depends on the requirement. If you want to plug the client functionality to a server control without creating a new control and are thinking in terms of reusing it for different server controls, then an extender is the right choice. However, if you want to have complete control over its capabilities on both the server and client, then a script control would be the right choice. Figure 10.3 displays the model of a script control generating script descriptors and script references.

FIGURE 10.3
The script control model

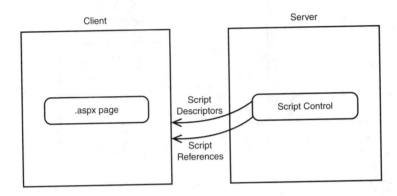

How Do You Build a Script Control?

A script control is built by declaring a class that inherits from the base class ScriptControl. This class should implement the interface IScriptControl. Doing this registers the script control with the ScriptManager control. Also this class should override the methods of the IScriptControl interface.

The registration of a script control is done automatically by the ScriptControl class, as a new script control is always created by deriving this class. But internally, the registration is done by calling the RegisterScriptControl method of the ScriptManager control during the PreRender phase by passing the current instance of the script control as an argument. And during the Render phase, the RegisterScriptDescriptors method of the ScriptManager control should be called by passing the current instance of the script control as an argument.

Working with the Control Toolkit

As discussed earlier, the Control Toolkit is an open source project initiated by Microsoft. There are several extenders that come with the Toolkit, which can be used in our ASP.NET Ajax-based application. One of the most useful extenders is the AutoComplete extender. We'll see its working functionality in the upcoming section.

Once an extender is associated with a server control, it inherits a set of properties for configuring the client-side functionality. The Toolkit consists of several extenders that are all built on top of a custom API provided by the ASP.NET Ajax to build Ajax-enabled controls.

The AutoComplete Extender

One of the simple examples to demonstrate Ajax capabilities is the AutoComplete extender. `AutoComplete` is an ASP.NET Ajax extender that can be wired to any `TextBox` control, to display a suggested list of words in a pop-up panel with the prefix typed into the text box. This is similar to the one in Google Suggest, which suggests a list of words as the user types.

Ajax makes this task simpler, as things happen on-the-fly in the background, and the end user does not know what actually is happening. Without Ajax, all the possible suggestions will be embedded in a web page and sent back to the browser. If the data list is huge, this could mean megabytes of data being transferred to the browser. But with Ajax, we can filter the possible suggestions on the server in real time when the user is typing.

The client component `AutoCompleteBehavior` is used to perform the client-side functionality through the `AutoComplete` extender. The `AutoCompleteBehavior` is attached to the ASP.NET `TextBox` through the AutoComplete extender to achieve the auto-complete functionality. The step-by-step process of creation and execution is discussed next.

The first step is to create an Ajax-enabled web site through Visual Studio 2005. The prerequisites in this regard involve having the ASP.NET Ajax extensions installed. Also the `AJAXControlToolkit.dll` assembly must be referenced or manually added to your web site's bin folder.

After you create a new Ajax-enabled web site, create a new page called `AutoCompleteDemo.aspx`.

Next, switch to the design mode and drag a `TextBox` control onto the designer and give it the name Items. Drag the `AutoComplete` extender from the toolkit listed in the toolbox and place it near the `TextBox` control.

Now, if the toolkit is not listed in the toolbox, just right-click the toolbox, click Choose Items, browse to the `AjaxControlToolkit.dll` assembly, and select it. This lists all the extenders in the toolbox, as shown in Figure 10.4.

The following is the `@Register` directive added to the page after placing the AutoComplete extender on the designer:

```
<%@ Register Assembly="AjaxControlToolkit"
Namespace="AjaxControlToolkit"
TagPrefix="ajaxToolkit" %>
```

FIGURE 10.4
The list of controls in Ajax Control Toolkit

By default, the tag prefix would be cc1 after we drop the control on the page. We have renamed this to ajaxToolkit in the preceding markup.

Now go to the design view and drag the AutoComplete extender onto the designer. Open the source view, and you'll find the following markup:

```
<ajaxToolkit:AutoCompleteExtender ID="AutoCompleteExtender1" runat="server">
        </ajaxToolkit:AutoCompleteExtender>
```

There are two main properties to be set for the AutoComplete extender to work. They are TargetControlID and ServiceMethod. The TargetControlID specifies the control to which this extender has to bind to, and the ServiceMethod attribute specifies the web method that needs to be invoked to fetch the data.

By the Way

There is an issue with the extenders provided in the Control Toolkit, when its properties are to be viewed from the design view. Some of the properties are not visible in the Properties window when viewed from the design view. Go to the source view, and you can now view these properties by pressing Ctrl+Space (using IntelliSense). In the AutoComplete extender markup, you cannot find properties such as ServiceMethod, ServicePath, ContextKey, and so on from the design view, but these properties can be seen from the source view.

Now, replace the previous markup with the following AutoComplete extender markup:

```
<asp:ScriptManager ID="ScriptManager1" runat="server">
</asp:ScriptManager>
<asp:TextBox runat="server" ID="txtItems" />
<ajaxToolkit:AutoCompleteExtender ID="AutoCompleteExtender1" runat="server"
          TargetControlID="txtItems"
          ServiceMethod="GetItemList"
          CompletionSetCount="10"
          MinimumPrefixLength="1"
          EnableCaching="true" />
```

If you observe the preceding code snippet, the TargetControlID property is set to the TextBox control txtItems, and the ServiceMethod property is set to GetItemList. This is a web method that fetches the countries list from the Countries.xml file on the server. This list is bound to the TextBox txtItems. The rest of the properties in this extender are optional.

Table 10.1 lists the complete set of properties for the AutoComplete extender.

TABLE 10.1 Properties of the AutoComplete Extender Control

Property	Description
TargetControlID	The TextBox control where the user types content.
ServiceMethod	The web method to be called.
ServicePath	The URL or path of the web service to pull data from the server.
ContextKey	User/page- specific context provided to an optional overload of the web method described by ServiceMethod/ServicePath. If the context key is used, it should have the same signature with an additional parameter named CcontextKey of type string.
UseContextKey	Whether to use the ContextKey property or not. This will be automatically enabled if the ContextKey property is ever set (on either the client or the server). If the context key is used, it should have the same signature with an additional parameter named CcontextKey of type string.
MinimumPrefixLength	Minimum number of characters that must be entered before getting suggestions from the web service.

TABLE 10.1   Continued

Property	Description
CompletionInterval	Time in milliseconds when the timer kicks in the web service call.
EnableCaching	Whether client-side caching is enabled or not.
CompletionSetCount	Number of suggestions to be retrieved from the web service.
CompletionListCssClass	Css class to style the completion list.
CompletionListItemCssClass	Css class to style an item in the completion list.
CompletionListHighlightedItemCssClass	Css class to style the highlighted item in the completion list.
DelimiterCharacters	Specifies one or more character(s) used to separate words. The text in the AutoComplete text box is tokenized using these characters, and the web service completes the last token.
FirstRowSelected	Determines if the first option in the AutoComplete list will be selected by default.
Animations	Generic animations for the AutoComplete extender.
	OnShow—The OnShow animation will be played each time the AutoComplete completion list is displayed. The completion list will be positioned correctly but will be hidden. The animation can use <HideAction Visible="true" /> to display the completion list, along with any other visual effects.
	OnHide—The OnHide animation will be played each time the AutoComplete completion list is hidden.

Now create the web method in the code-behind of the AutoCompleteDemo.aspx page with the name GetItemList and paste the following code in the method:

```
[WebMethod]
public static string[] GetItemList(string prefixText, int
count)
```

```
    {
        List<string> suggestions = new List<string>();
        using (XmlTextReader reader = new
        XmlTextReader(HttpContext.Current.Server
        .MapPath("~/Countries.xml")))
        {
            while (reader.Read())
            {
                if (reader.NodeType == XmlNodeType.Element &&
                reader.Name == "Item")
                {
                    string itemName = reader.ReadInnerXml();
                    if (itemName.StartsWith(prefixText,
                    StringComparison.InvariantCultureIgnoreCase))
                    {
                        suggestions.Add(itemName);
                        if (suggestions.Count == count) break;
                    }
                }
            }
        }
        return suggestions.ToArray();
    }
```

Also add the following namespaces in the AutoCompleteDemo.aspx.cs code-behind file:

```
using System.Web.Services;
using System.Web.Script.Services;
using System.Xml;
using System.Collections.Generic;
```

The classes used in the GetItemList web method use the preceding namespaces. This web method performs the task of preparing the list of suggestions to be returned to the client. The method reads the XML file called Countries.xml. Here are the file contents:

```
<?xml version="1.0" encoding="utf-8" ?>
<Items>
  <Item>Argentina</Item>
  <Item>Australia</Item>
  <Item>Austria</Item>
  <Item>Germany</Item>
  <Item>Iceland</Item>
  <Item>India</Item>
  <Item>Italy</Item>
  <Item>United States of America</Item>
</Items>
```

The Read() method of the XmlTextReader reads data until all the xml tags have been read. When Item's prefix value matches the input prefix value, it is added to an ArrayList. After the entire xml is read, the list of suggestions is returned to the client in the form of string[].

Figure 10.5 displays the output of the program on execution.

FIGURE 10.5
Auto complete
demo

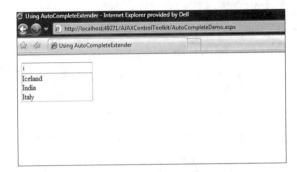

This is how simply the extenders are wired to server controls to achieve Ajax behavior in our ASP.NET applications. In the next hour, we'll discuss a few more controls and their usage.

Summary

This hour introduced the ASP.NET Ajax Control Toolkit, which is a repository of controls that can be used to attach themselves with server controls to make Ajax-enabled controls. We discussed the two kinds of Ajax-enabled controls, script controls, and extenders and how they are built; we also examined how they return script descriptors and references, which the client components of the Microsoft Ajax Library understand and parse the logic to achieve client behavior and control. In addition, we discussed how the AutoComplete extender works. In the next hour, we will look at several other controls in the Toolkit.

Workshop

Quiz

1. What are Ajax-enabled controls?

2. What is a client component?

3. What is an extender?

4. What is a script control?

5. True or False: Ajax Control Toolkit is a licensed release from Microsoft.

6. What is the client component used for an `AutoComplete` extender?

7. Name the key attributes required for an `AutoComplete` extender.

Answers

1. Ajax-enabled controls are ASP.NET server controls built by wiring the client components to the ASP.NET server controls.

2. Client components are part of the Microsoft Ajax Library. They act on the script descriptors and references generated by the Ajax-enabled controls from the server side. There are basically two types of client components: client behavior and client control.

3. An extender is an Ajax-enabled control to provide a list of script descriptors and script references. The goal of an extender is to wire a client component to an existing server control. An extender acts as an external object and attaches itself to a server control.

4. A script control is also an Ajax-enabled control to provide a list of script descriptors and script references, but here, the client and server capabilities should be present at the same place. This does not need an external object.

5. False. The Ajax Control Toolkit is an open source project initiated by Microsoft, and there are several contributions in it from the community as well.

6. The `AutoCompleteBehavior` component. This component is used to attach itself to the server control through an `AutoComplete` extender.

7. The key attributes for an `AutoComplete` extender are as follows:

- **ID**—Name given the extender.

- **TargetControlID**—The server control ID to which this has to be attached.

- **ServicePath**—The web service URL to fetch the list of suggestions.

- **ServiceMethod**—The web method name in the web service to fetch the list of suggestions as the user types.

HOUR 11

Working with the Ajax Control Toolkit—Part II

What You'll Learn in This Hour:

▶ **Some interesting controls in the Ajax Toolkit**
  - ▶ ConfirmButton
  - ▶ DropDown

In the last hour, we learned how we can work with the AutoComplete extender from the Ajax Control Toolkit. In this hour, we explore two more extender controls. The Ajax Control Toolkit has been contributed to by Microsoft and the open source community and has a wealth of controls in its Toolkit today. It is not possible to cover all its controls in this hour, as there are more than 40 controls. Instead, we demonstrate the working of two extenders in this hour. To learn about all the other controls, check out the wonderful "How Do I" videos presented by Microsoft's Joe Stagner at http://www.asp.net/learn/ajax-videos/.

The ConfirmButton Extender

The ConfirmButton extender is an ASP.NET extender that is wired to a server control-like button or any type derived from a button, which prompts the user with an alert before submitting the page. This generates the JavaScript window.confirm dialog box. If the OK button is clicked, the page is submitted to the server; if the Cancel button is clicked, no action takes place. Let's take a look at a sample demonstrating the ConfirmButton extender. The sample is about binding data from an XML file to a GridView control. The last column in each of the records in the GridView control displays a Delete link. This LinkButton is associated with the ConfirmButton extender. When the Delete button of any record is clicked, the ConfirmButton extender catches the click and prompts the user with an OK and Cancel button in an alert box. Clicking OK deletes a record from the

GridView and updates the XML file on the server about the change. Clicking Cancel does not perform any action, and the original state of the GridView before clicking is restored. Let's take a step-by-step approach toward achieving this functionality.

First, open Visual Studio and then open the Ajax-enabled web site already created in the previous hour for the AutoComplete extender. The prerequisite for developing and running this application is the Ajax Control Toolkit assembly. Make sure this assembly is in the Bin folder of your current application.

Create a new ASPX page called ConfirmButtonExtender.aspx. Then, go to the toolbox; in the Data tab, find the GridView control and drag it onto the page in design view. The primary objective is to bind the XML data to the GridView control. The following XML file is used to bind the data. This file contains the ItemList of three records:

```xml
<?xml version="1.0" standalone="yes"?>
<ItemList>
  <Item>
    <ID>0</ID>
    <Name>HP</Name>
    <Model>5446 A</Model>
    <Make>2007</Make>
    <Price>$ 896.00</Price>
    <Active>Y</Active>
  </Item>
  <Item>
    <ID>1</ID>
    <Name>Compaq</Name>
    <Model>654AN</Model>
    <Make>2006</Make>
    <Price>$ 655.00</Price>
    <Active>Y</Active>
  </Item>
  <Item>
    <ID>2</ID>
    <Name>DELL</Name>
    <Model>34543656</Model>
    <Make>2007</Make>
    <Price>$ 720.00</Price>
    <Active>Y</Active>
  </Item>
</ItemList>
```

After placing the GridView control on the page, go to the HTML source view and replace the existing GridView markup with the declarative markup of the GridView control. This markup declares the TemplateFields of the XML file.

> A TemplateField represents a column that can be used to customize its presentation.

The TemplateFields are Name, Model, Make, Price, and Active. The last TemplateField is the one that we are interested in and is of high importance in this example. This field contains two controls—one is a LinkButton btnDelete, and the second is the ConfirmButton extender used to wire up for the btnDelete control. The markup of this GridView control is as follows:

```
<asp:GridView ID="gvItems" runat="server" AutoGenerateColumns="false"
➥OnRowDataBound="gvItemsOnRowDataBound" OnRowCommand="OnRowCommand">
        <Columns>
            <asp:TemplateField HeaderText="Name">
                <ItemTemplate>
                    <asp:Label ID="lblName" runat="server"
➥Text='<%#Eval("Name")%>'></asp:Label>
                </ItemTemplate>
            </asp:TemplateField>
            <asp:TemplateField HeaderText="Model">
                <ItemTemplate>
                    <asp:Label ID="lblModel" runat="server"
➥Text='<%#Eval("Model")%>'></asp:Label>
                </ItemTemplate>
            </asp:TemplateField>
            <asp:TemplateField HeaderText="Make">
                <ItemTemplate>
                    <asp:Label ID="lblMake" runat="server"
➥Text='<%#Eval("Make")%>'></asp:Label>
                </ItemTemplate>
            </asp:TemplateField>
            <asp:TemplateField HeaderText="Price">
                <ItemTemplate>
                    <asp:Label ID="lblPrice" runat="server"
➥Text='<%#Eval("Price")%>'></asp:Label>
                </ItemTemplate>
            </asp:TemplateField>
            <asp:TemplateField HeaderText="Active ?">
                <ItemTemplate>
                    <asp:Label ID="lblActive" runat="server"
➥Text='<%#Eval("Active")%>'></asp:Label>
                </ItemTemplate>
            </asp:TemplateField>
            <asp:TemplateField>
                <ItemTemplate>
                    <asp:LinkButton ID="btnDelete" runat="server"
➥Text="Delete" CommandName="OnRowDelete" CommandArgument='
➥<%#Eval("ID") %>'></asp:LinkButton>
                    <cc1:ConfirmButtonExtender ID="ConfirmButtonExtender2"
➥runat="server" ConfirmText="Are you sure you want to delete
➥this record ?">
                    </cc1:ConfirmButtonExtender>
                </ItemTemplate>
            </asp:TemplateField>
        </Columns>
</asp:GridView>
```

> Because no control can be dragged inside the GridView control in the design view, we are placing the ConfirmButton extender control from the HTML source view. In the preceding markup pasted in the source view, the ConfirmButton extender is placed in the last TemplateField.

The ConfirmButton extender primarily has to mention the target control ID it has to act upon and the confirmation text to be presented in the alert box when the target control is clicked, as follows:

```
<cc1:ConfirmButtonExtender ID="ConfirmButtonExtender2" runat="server"
➡ConfirmText="Are you sure you want to delete this record ?">
                    </cc1:ConfirmButtonExtender>
```

If you observe the preceding HTML markup of the ConfirmButton extender, we have not mentioned the TargetControlID attribute as the target control btnDelete repeats itself for each row bound to the GridView control. Therefore, this control is wired up at runtime when each row is bound to the GridView. This is done in the event OnRowDataBound of the GridView control. The following is the OnRowDataBound event in the code-behind file:

```
protected void gvItemsOnRowDataBound(object sender, GridViewRowEventArgs e)
    {
        if (e.Row.RowType == DataControlRowType.DataRow)
        {
((ConfirmButtonExtender)e.Row.FindControl("ConfirmButtonExtender2")).
➡TargetControlID = ((LinkButton)e.Row.FindControl("btnDelete")).ID;
        }
    }
```

The preceding event is fired for each row bound to the GridView control. In this event, we first are finding the control ConfirmButtonExtender2 through the FindControl function of the row property and setting its TargetControlID property to the ID of the btnDelete control. So in essence, if there are three records bound to the GridView control, there would be three ConfirmButton extender controls wiring themselves to three different Delete controls.

Table 11.1 lists the complete set of properties for the ConfirmButton extender.

TABLE 11.1   Properties of the `ConfirmButton` Extender

Property	Description
TargetControlID	The TextBox control where the user types content.
ConfirmText	The text that is displayed when you want to confirm the click. Any HTML entities can be used here, such as \n, \t, and so on.
OnClientCancel	The client-side script to be executed when the Cancel button is clicked.
ConfirmOnFormSubmit	Set to true if this is submitted after all the client validations (if any) are done—that is, the confirm dialog box should wait until any ASP.NET validators are passed.

> **By the Way**
>
> As discussed in the last hour, there is an issue with the extenders provided in the Control Toolkit, when its properties are to be viewed from the design view. Some of the properties are not visible in the Properties window when viewed from the design view. Go to the source view, and you can view these properties by pressing Ctrl+Space (using Intellisense).

The client component `ConfirmButtonBehavior` is used to perform the client-side functionality through the `ConfirmButton` extender. The `ConfirmButtonBehavior` is attached to the ASP.NET `LinkButton` through the `ConfirmButton` extender to achieve the functionality.

Let's now look at the code to bind the `GridView` and delete the record in the GridView:

```
static DataSet ds;
    protected void Page_Load(object sender, EventArgs e)
    {
        if (!Page.IsPostBack)
        {
            ds = new DataSet();
            this.BindGrid();
        }
    }
    private void BindGrid()
    {
        ds.Clear();
        ds.ReadXml(Request.PhysicalApplicationPath + @"\Items.xml");
        DataView dv = ds.Tables[0].DefaultView;
        dv.RowFilter = "Active = 'Y'";
        gvItems.DataSource = dv;
        gvItems.DataBind();
    }
```

```
protected void OnRowCommand(object sender, GridViewCommandEventArgs e)
    {
        if (e.CommandName == "OnRowDelete")
        {
            int i = int.Parse(e.CommandArgument.ToString());
            ds.Tables[0].Rows[i]["Active"] = "N";
            ds.WriteXml(Request.PhysicalApplicationPath + @"\Items.xml");
            this.BindGrid();
        }
    }
```

The load event in the preceding code handles the binding of the GridView control
with an XML file, as described earlier in the hour. The XML file described previously
has an attribute called Active. This attribute defines whether this item is currently
active or not and dictates whether or not a record has to be displayed in the
GridView control. If the value in the attribute is Y, then its item is displayed—or else
it is not displayed in the GridView control. Therefore, in the preceding code, you can
find that after reading the XML file, we've used a DataView to filter out the rows
and fetch only those items that are active. Let's now execute the page in the browser. The output is shown in Figure 11.1.

FIGURE 11.1
List of items in
a GridView
control

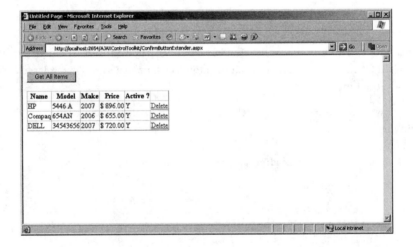

Right now, all three records in the XML file are displayed. If you check the view
source of the ASPX page after it is rendered on the browser, you'll find the script references and the $create statements generated by the Ajax-enabled control
ConfirmButton extender. The following is a $create statement generated for one of
the Delete controls:

```
Sys.Application.add_init(function() {
    $create(AjaxControlToolkit.ConfirmButtonBehavior, {"ConfirmText":"Are you
➥sure you want to delete this record ?",
```

```
➥"id":"gvItems_ctl02_ConfirmButtonExtender2"}, null, null,
➥$get("gvItems_ctl02_btnDelete"));
});
```

The $create statement instantiates the control ConfirmButtonBehavior to get the
Ajax behavior and executes the confirm dialog box with the confirmText mentioned. The Microsoft Ajax Library takes care of this internal script generation and
execution.

Now that the page is loaded on the browser, let's delete a record.

Before we delete a record, let's examine the code for deleting this record. In the
HTML markup, we have mentioned CommandName and CommandArgument attributes
for the LinkButton btnDelete, as follows:

```
<asp:TemplateField>
                    <ItemTemplate>
                        <asp:LinkButton ID="btnDelete" runat="server"
Text="Delete"
➥CommandName="OnRowDelete" CommandArgument='<%#Eval("ID") %>'>
➥</asp:LinkButton>
                        <cc1:ConfirmButtonExtender ID="ConfirmButtonExtender2"
➥ runat="server" ConfirmText="Are you sure you want to delete
➥this record ?">
                        </cc1:ConfirmButtonExtender>
                    </ItemTemplate>
                </asp:TemplateField>
```

The CommandName attribute has a value OnRowDelete, and the CommandArgument
attribute has a value <%#Eval("ID") %>, which after rendering will have an ID
value for each record from the XML file. When any operation is performed on a
GridView control, the OnRowCommand event is fired. In the GridView's markup, we've
mentioned the value OnRowCommand for the attribute OnRowCommand, which is the
method call for this event. This is the method where the delete functionality is written. Let's get into the details of what's happening inside this code:

```
protected void OnRowCommand(object sender, GridViewCommandEventArgs e)
    {
        if (e.CommandName == "OnRowDelete")
        {
            int i = int.Parse(e.CommandArgument.ToString());
            ds.Tables[0].Rows[i]["Active"] = "N";
            ds.WriteXml(Request.PhysicalApplicationPath + @"\Items.xml");
            this.BindGrid();
        }
    }
```

Run the application now. Figure 11.2 shows the confirm dialog being displayed after
clicking the Delete button on one of the records.

FIGURE 11.2
Confirm dialog
box after click-
ing the Delete
button

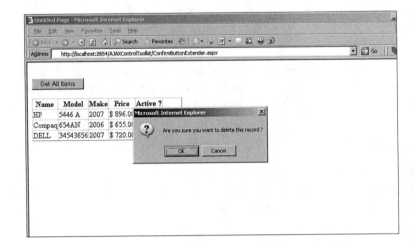

Here, we are fetching the ID of the record through the CommandArgument and updating the XML file with the Active flag set to N for this record. When we are binding
the XML file again to the GridView, we only bind those records that have the
Active flag set to Y. Therefore, we are indirectly deleting this record. Figure 11.3
shows that the second record has been deleted and the GridView has been bound
with the first and third records.

FIGURE 11.3
GridView control
displaying first
and third
records after
deleting the
second record

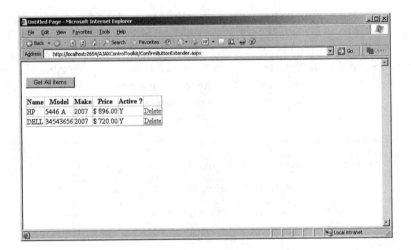

In order to fetch back all the records again, we've provided a button called Get All Items that updates all the Active flag values to Y in the XML file and binds them to the GridView control. The following is the code that does this:

```
protected void btnGetAllItems_Click(object sender, EventArgs e)
    {
        ds.Clear();
        ds.ReadXml(Request.PhysicalApplicationPath + @"\Items.xml");
        foreach (DataRow dr in ds.Tables[0].Rows)
        {
            dr["Active"] = "Y";
        }
        ds.WriteXml(Request.PhysicalApplicationPath + @"\Items.xml");
        this.BindGrid();
    }
```

Figure 11.4 displays all the records again after clicking the Get All Items button.

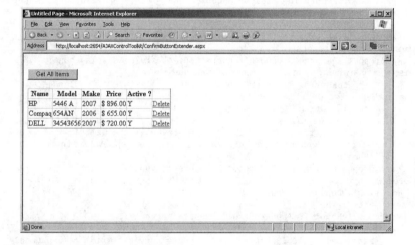

FIGURE 11.4
All the records displayed back in the GridView control

The DropDown **Extender**

The DropDown extender is another ASP.NET extender that wires up with server controls, Label and Panel, to provide a drop-down menu, which is similar to the drop-down style in SharePoint. Let's quickly demonstrate how this drop-down menu is built using the DropDown extender. As usual, let's open our Visual Studio development environment, open the existing Ajax Control Toolkit solution, and create a new web page called DropDownExtender.aspx.

All we are trying to do in this page is to place the following: a Label control; a Panel control consisting of several LinkButtons as menu items; a DropDown extender, attaching it to the Label and Panel controls; and an UpdatePanel, consisting of a Label for displaying content when any LinkButton in the Panel is clicked. An UpdatePanel is used here so that the entire page does not post back, and only this region is updated asynchronously. So in essence, the user does not find any postback at all.

Now go to the source view mode and first drag a Label control inside the <div> tag and give it the name LabelText. Immediately after it is placed, drag a Panel control, give it the name PanelDropDown, and add the attributes Style and CssClass, as mentioned in the HTML source that follows. Now, place three LinkButton controls inside the panel panelDropDown. Each LinkButton here is representing an item in the DropDown. We've added these items in design mode. We can also add the items dynamically from an XML file or a database. The following is the markup for achieving our functionality:

```
<form id="form1" runat="server">
    <asp:ScriptManager ID="ScriptManager1" runat="server"></asp:ScriptManager>
    <div>
    <br />
    <asp:Label ID="LabelText" runat="server" Text="Select an item."
➥Width="161px"></asp:Label>
    <asp:Panel ID="panelDropDown" runat="server" style="display:none;
➥visibility:hidden;" CssClass="ContextMenuPanel">
        <asp:LinkButton ID="btnHp" runat="server" Text="HP" CssClass="
➥ContextMenuItem" OnClick=" OnItemSelect "></asp:LinkButton>
        <asp:LinkButton ID="btnCompaq" runat="server" Text="Compaq"
➥CssClass="ContextMenuItem" OnClick=" OnItemSelect "></asp:LinkButton>
        <asp:LinkButton ID="btnDell" runat="server" Text="Dell"
➥CssClass="ContextMenuItem" OnClick="OnItemSelect"></asp:LinkButton>
    </asp:Panel>
    <cc1:DropDownExtender ID="DropDownExtender1" runat="server"
➥TargetControlID="LabelText" DropDownControlID="PanelDropDown">
        </cc1:DropDownExtender>
    <br /><br /><br />
    <asp:UpdatePanel ID="UpdatePanel1" runat="server">
    <ContentTemplate>
        <asp:Label ID="lblSelectedValue" runat="server" Text=""></asp:Label>
    </ContentTemplate>
    <Triggers>
        <asp:AsyncPostBackTrigger ControlID="btnHp" EventName="Click" />
        <asp:AsyncPostBackTrigger ControlID="btnCompaq" EventName="Click" />
        <asp:AsyncPostBackTrigger ControlID="btnDell" EventName="Click" />
    </Triggers>
    </asp:UpdatePanel>

    </div>
    </form>
```

In the preceding markup, each of the LinkButtons in the panel has the OnClick attribute set to OnItemSelect. This is a method that is fired on the click event of the corresponding LinkButton. After the panel is ready, it's time for the DropDown extender to be placed and associate its attributes TargetControlID to LabelText, and `DropDownControlID` to `panelDropDown`, as mentioned in the preceding markup. Now we are actually ready with the `DropDown` functionality, but we need to display the content when an item in the `DropDown` is clicked. We achieve this by having a `Label` whose value is set in the `OnItemSelect` method, which is fired on the click event of the `LinkButton`. The code-behind for this method is as follows:

```
protected void OnItemSelect(object sender, System.EventArgs e)
    {
        lblSelectedValue.Text = "You have selected <b>" +
➡((LinkButton)sender).Text + "</b>";
    }
```

In the preceding code, we are capturing the sender's text—that is, `LinkButton`'s text, which is an option in our drop-down menu—and displaying this in a label `lblSelectedValue`. This label is placed inside an `UpdatePanel` to get this task done asynchronously. Therefore, if you have observed the markup, we have associated `AsyncPostBackTrigger`'s to each of the `LinkButtons` we've mentioned in the panel. Now let's execute this program and see the output in the browser, as shown in Figure 11.5.

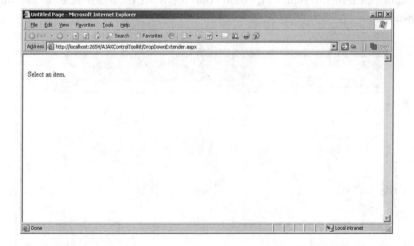

FIGURE 11.5
DropdownExtender at work!

Figure 11.5 shows the text "Select an item." When the cursor is placed on it, and it is either left-clicked or right-clicked, it displays a drop-down menu of items. Figure 11.6 illustrates this.

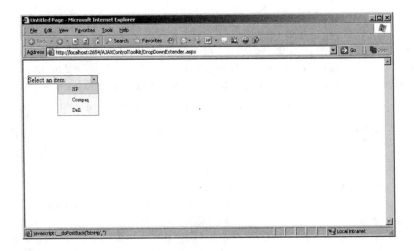

After an item is clicked, an asynchronous postback occurs, courtesy of the
UpdatePanel, and the label lblSelectedValue is updated to the value selected in
the drop-down menu. Figure 11.7 shows that the value HP was selected in the drop-
down menu.

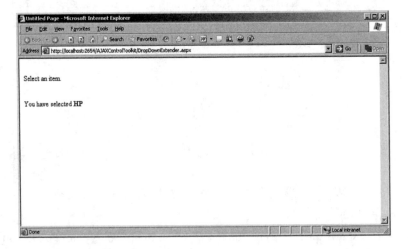

So this is as easy as it gets in demonstrating the ASP.NET Ajax extenders in the Ajax
Control Toolkit. There are many other interesting controls in the Toolkit, but all of
them cannot be explained in this hour. As mentioned at the beginning of this hour,
Microsoft's Joe Stagner has made it easy for all of us to have a glance at all the controls in the Toolkit in his "How Do I" videos presented at
http://www.asp.net/learn/ajax-videos/.

The most appealing part of the `DropDown` extender control is that the panel that is being attached to it can hold any server control, apart from the `LinkButton`. We can have a button, a drop-down list, or even a `DataGrid` for that matter—or any kind of server control inside it—and we can make these dynamic. What we've seen in this section is a simple example demonstrating the `DropDown` extender control. There are a few more extenders demonstrated in the last three hours of the book while building a sample e-commerce application.

Summary

This hour focused on the Ajax Control Toolkit in action. We've explored two extenders: the `ConfirmButton` extender and the `DropDown` extender. The `ConfirmButton` extender is used to attach itself to a `Button` control or any type derived from it, which prompts the user with a confirm dialog before submitting the page to the server. The `DropDown` extender attaches itself to a `Label` and `Panel` control to get a drop-down menu. The advantage of having this extender is that the `Panel` to which we are wiring up the extender can hold any type of server controls and not only link buttons. This provides the option to innovate with this extender. In the next hour, we'll link up what we've seen with the ASP.NET Ajax controls and extenders with the ASP.NET web parts.

Workshop

Quiz

1. What is the property `TargetControlID` in an extender?

2. What are the client behaviors invoked by Microsoft Ajax Library for the `ConfirmButton` extender and `DropDown` extender?

3. True or False: Only a button or a `LinkButton` can be placed inside the Panel wired with the `DropDown` extender.

4. What is the `DisplayModalPopupID` property in the `ConfirmButton` extender?

5. What is the use of the property `DropDownControlID` in the `DropDown` extender?

Answers

1. `TargetControlID` is a property of an extender that indicates to which server control the extender has to attach itself.

2. The client behavior invoked by the Microsoft Ajax Library for the `ConfirmButton` extender is `ConfirmButtonBehavior`, and for the `DropDown` extender, it is DropDownBehavior.

3. False. Any server control can be placed in a panel that is attached to the `DropDown` extender.

4. The property `DisplayModalPopupID` specifies the ID of a `ModalPopup` control to use for displaying the confirmation dialog instead of displaying a `window.confirm`.

5. The `DropDownControlID` property of the `DropDown` extender associates the ID of the `Panel` control, which holds several server controls in the form of a drop-down menu.

HOUR 12

ASP.NET Ajax and Web Parts

What You'll Learn in This Hour:

▶ An overview of web parts in ASP.NET 2.0
▶ Building blocks of web parts
▶ Working example of web parts
▶ Introducing Ajax into web parts

The web revolution is under constant change in terms of look and feel, data transfer technology, improved performance and response times, and presentation. Today's web development is more portal-centric in the sense that the data display in the sites is grouped under several categories, which can be displayed in different sections on the page. These sections can be configured by each user of the site according to his/her preferences. This concept of grouping data to one's preferences is known as *personalization*. One such site is Yahoo!'s MyYahoo!, which gathers information from your Yahoo! account credentials, and as soon as you log in, several settings are applied based on your location. You can find sections like a weather report, local news, maps surrounding your location, stock quotes, and so on. These sites allow you to personalize these components in any way you want.

This hour focuses on creating such web components and including them in your site. These web components are called *web parts*, as introduced by ASP.NET 2.0. After we are done with a working example on web parts, we'll add Ajax into these web parts to make the site more interactive and dynamic in nature. Web parts are a huge concept in ASP.NET 2.0, and we are not covering them in detail here. What we'll cover is an introduction to the concept and its basic building blocks; we'll then come to a position where we are comfortable creating web parts, and later implementing Ajax in it. Figure 12.1 shows the author's personalization in MyYahoo!. You can drag each of these sections and re-arrange them according to your preferences.

FIGURE 12.1
My personaliza-
tion in *MyYahoo*

Introducing Web Parts

Web parts are a set of server controls that are available in ASP.NET 2.0 that allow you to componentize your page into manageable sections. You can edit, move around holding the web part, change its settings at runtime, and can completely personalize your web page. When we say personalize, this refers to setting your preferences in the web page. Let's say, for example, that an application displays a home page, which has several sections such as a weather report, local map information, stock quotes, and your email section. You can have the weather report at the bottom-right of the web page, or you may choose not to have this web part in your web page at all; another user may prefer to have this web part at the top-right corner of the web page. So, personalization is about setting one's preferences in an application. These settings are saved for each user so that the next time the user logs in, he/she will find the same settings configured by him/her.

The web parts introduced in ASP.NET 2.0 are not a completely new concept. This was first introduced in Microsoft Windows SharePoint Services, which is an application used for collaboration, document management, content management, workflows, reporting, and so on. The web parts in SharePoint offer personalization and customization. The web parts can be extensible in the sense that they can be developed in an enterprise and can be deployed in the portal, where other users of the portal leverage the features of this web part in the portal.

By the Way

Let's go ahead and examine the web parts in ASP.NET 2.0 and discuss how we can leverage them in an application.

Features of Web Parts

We now know that web parts are used to build portal-style applications to facilitate easy navigation, to get a consistent look across the site, and also to modularize the content.

The various features of web parts are as follows:

▶ **Drag and drop**—The basic feature of the web part is its drag-and-drop functionality. It can be easily dragged onto different web part zones in the page, as shown in Figure 12.2. A web part zone is a container holding one or more web parts.

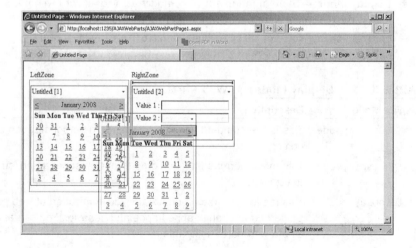

FIGURE 12.2
Dragging and dropping a web part

▶ **Minimize, restore, and close**—Each web part can be minimized, restored, and closed. This feature is available on every web part when it is clicked on the top-right corner of the header, as shown in Figure 12.3.

FIGURE 12.3
The web part in the RightZone displaying the Minimize and Close options

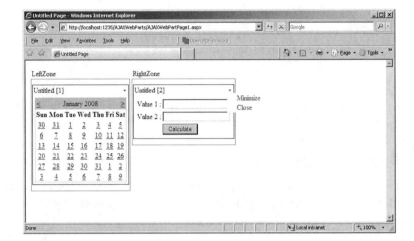

▶ **Customization and personalization**—The web parts can be customized and personalized by each of the users of the site. The changes made to these settings are saved for the corresponding user, and when he/she logs back into the site, the applied settings are loaded.

▶ **Display Modes**—There are many display modes associated with web parts. BrowseDisplayMode is set by default. Other modes available are DesignDisplayMode, EditDisplayMode, ConnectDisplayMode, and CatalogDisplayMode. Table 12.1 briefly describes the role of each mode.

TABLE 12.1   Display Modes in Web Parts

Display Mode	Description
BrowseDisplayMode	This is the standard view mode, where no personalization or editing can be done.
DesignDisplayMode	This mode permits drag-and-drop layout personalization/customization.
EditDisplayMode	This mode permits personalization/customization of web part properties to change appearance and behavior. You can also delete web parts using this mode.
ConnectDisplayMode	This mode permits users to connect web parts together at runtime.
CatalogDisplayMode	This mode permits users to add web parts into web part zones at runtime.

The display mode can be changed at runtime using the following code:

```
WebPartManager1.DisplayMode = WebPartManager.DesignDisplayMode;
```

▶ **Catalog Parts and Zones**—As the name suggests, this view is a catalog of all the available web parts in the site. You can drop in a new collection of web parts here. Also, you can manipulate the web parts to be attached to different zones in this area.

▶ **Editor Parts and Zones**—Editor parts are structured within editor zones that allow user customization. By default, ASP.NET supplies several editor parts. They are shown in the property grid. However, custom editor parts can also be developed.

We will not be concentrating much on catalog and editor parts/zones in this hour because these are huge topics in themselves. To get more details about catalog and editor parts/zones, refer to the book *Web Parts and Custom Controls with ASP.NET 2.0* by Peter Vogel from the Wrox publishers

Creating a Web Part

To create a web part in an ASP.NET page, we need a `WebPartManager` component and web part zones. A `WebPartManager` is the controller of the web part(s) present in the page. There can only be one `WebPartManager` in a web part page. As discussed previously, a web part zone holds web parts.

> A web part page must have a `WebPartManager` and at least one web part zone.

By the Way

Let's go ahead and create a web part in ASP.NET 2.0 using Visual Studio 2005. Open Visual Studio 2005, create a new Ajax-enabled web site named AJAXWebParts. Go to the toolbox, and you'll find a category called WebParts, as shown in Figure 12.4.

Now drag a `WebPartManager` from the toolbox onto the `Default.aspx` designer. Create an HTML table of one row and two columns by going to the source view, aligning the two columns to the top by setting the `valign` attribute of the <td> element to Top, and then dragging two web part zones; name them `LeftWebPartZone` and `RightWebPartZone` in the two columns of the HTML table. Place a calendar control on the `LeftWebPartZone` and a Label and Textbox control in the `RightWebPartZone`. A web part zone denotes one section of the web page. There can be any number of web part zones placed on the page.

FIGURE 12.4
WebParts category in the toolbox

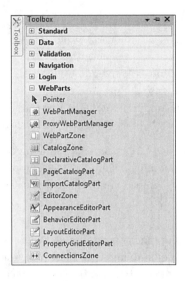

The design view looks similar to Figure 12.5.

FIGURE 12.5
Design view of the web parts—
LeftWebPart
Zone and
RightWebPart
Zone

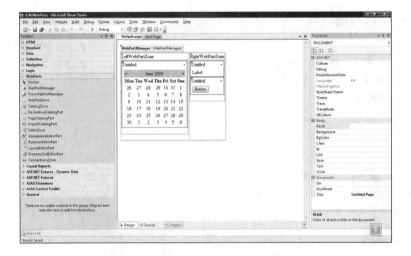

The HTML source view of the web part created is shown next:

```
<form id="form1" runat="server">
        <div>
            <asp:WebPartManager ID="WebPartManager1" runat="server">
            </asp:WebPartManager>
        </div>
        <table>
```

```
        <tr>
            <td valign="top">
                <asp:WebPartZone ID="LeftWebPartZone" runat="server">
                    <ZoneTemplate>
                        <asp:Calendar ID="Calendar1" runat="server">
➭</asp:Calendar>
                    </ZoneTemplate>
                </asp:WebPartZone>
            </td>
            <td valign="top">
                <asp:WebPartZone ID="RightWebPartZone" runat="server">
                    <ZoneTemplate>
                        <asp:Label ID="Label1" runat="server"
➭Text="Label"></asp:Label>
                        <asp:Button ID="Button1" runat="server"
➭Text="Button" />
                    </ZoneTemplate>
                </asp:WebPartZone>
            </td>
        </tr>
    </table>
</form>
```

Next, run the application by setting the Default.aspx as the start page. In Figure 12.6, you can see the web parts LeftWebPartZone and RightWebPartZone in the browser. Also you can find the collapsible symbol on each web part to perform operations such as Minimize, Restore, and Close.

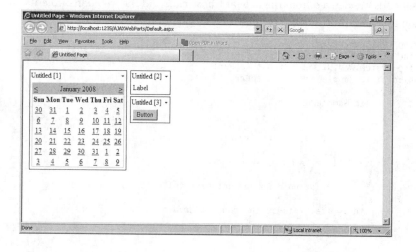

FIGURE 12.6
Output of web parts in browser

The preceding example is a simple one that demonstrates the usage of web parts in ASP.NET 2.0.

> The web part personalization information goes into your local SQL Server Express Edition database by default. Therefore to store the personalized web parts you've designed, you need to have an authenticated client. (The authentication can be of any type—windows, forms, cookie). If you are not an authenticated client, the web parts personalized on the web site would be stored for an anonymous user.

`WebPartManager` is responsible for managing all the web part infrastructure and actions on the web part zones.

Any web part page in ASP.NET 2.0 is designed with the following:

▶ One instance of the `WebPartManager` class

▶ One or more web part zones

▶ Optionally, an editor zone or a catalog zone

A Look into Custom Web Parts

To modularize the content and to offer developer extensibility in the preceding example, creating a custom web part is a good idea. A custom web part can be developed in ASP.NET 2.0 using the Visual Studio 2005 development environment.

Web parts are derived from the `WebPart` base class. All the web parts inherit common functionality. Here is a sample code for a custom web part:

```
using System.Web.UI;
using System.Web.UI.WebControls;
using System.Web.UI.WebControls.WebParts;
public class SampleWebPart : WebPart
{
        public SampleWebPart()
        {
                //
                // TODO: Add constructor logic here
                //
            this.Title = "A Sample Web Part";
        }
    protected override void RenderContents(HtmlTextWriter writer)
    {
        writer.Write("This is the content area of this web part");
    }
}
```

The preceding code can be built in a custom class or a control and embedded into a web part. The `RenderContents` is a method to be overridden in the custom web part class to write the HTML content into the web part zone. All the content for the web part can be built up here. But there will be a case where multiple child controls need to be built up into the same web part. The difficult part here is to write the code for building the HTML content dynamically into the web part.

> All the customization of content in the custom web part needs to be done dynami-cally from the code-behind file. The designer feature for customizing web parts is not available.

Developing Web Parts Using User Controls

An easier way to develop web parts is to build all the content into a user control and add this user control into the web part at design time. This way, you can design the content in the user control and attach events and code to it, in a much easier way than to customize the web part in a custom class.

Web parts can also be developed by having the normal controls dropped into the zone. We can have any number of controls in it. All these controls are implicitly wrapped by the `GenericWebPart` into a single web part control that implements the base class `WebPart`.

> Because you cannot customize the content in the web part from the design view, it is always suggested that you customize all the content of the web part in a user control or a custom control and add this control to the web part.

User controls make a very convenient way to design web parts for the following rea-sons:

- ▶ Full designer support
- ▶ Code-behind file for handling events and logic
- ▶ Need not write custom control

Let's go ahead and create a user control called `MyControl`, which has two `Textbox` controls, a `Button` control, and a `Label` control. Open the AJAXWebParts solution, add the new user control called `MyControl`, and paste the following HTML in the source view of `MyControl`:

```
<%@ Control Language="C#" AutoEventWireup="true" CodeFile="MyControl.ascx.cs"
➥Inherits="MyControl" %>
<table>
    <tr>
        <td>Value 1 : </td>
        <td><asp:TextBox ID="TextBox1" runat="server"></asp:TextBox></td>
    </tr>
```

```
<tr>
    <td>Value 2 :</td>
    <td><asp:TextBox ID="TextBox2" runat="server"></asp:TextBox></td>
</tr>
<tr>
    <td> </td>
    <td><asp:Button ID="btnCalculate" runat="server" Text="Calculate"
➥OnClick="btnCalculate_Click"/>
        <asp:Label ID="lblResult" runat="server"></asp:Label></td>
</tr>
</table>
```

In the Calculate button click event, add the values entered in the two textboxes and display the result in the label lblResult. The following is the code for this event:

```
protected void btnCalculate_Click(object sender, EventArgs e)
    {
        try
        {
            lblResult.Text = Convert.ToString(int.Parse(TextBox1.Text) +
➥int.Parse(TextBox2.Text));
        }
        catch
        {
            lblResult.Text = "Invalid input !";
        }
    }
```

Now create a new web form called AjaxWebPartPage1.aspx, add two web part zones (LeftZone and RightZone), and drop the MyControl user control into the RightZone. The following is the HTML source of this page:

```
<%@ Page Language="C#" AutoEventWireup="true"
CodeFile="AJAXWebPartPage1.aspx.cs"
➥Inherits="AJAXWebPartPage1" %>
<%@ Register Src="MyControl.ascx" TagName="MyControl" TagPrefix="uc1" %>
<!DOCTYPE html PUBLIC "-//W3C//DTD XHTML 1.0 Transitional//EN"
➥"http://www.w3.org/TR/xhtml1/DTD/xhtml1-transitional.dtd">
<html xmlns="http://www.w3.org/1999/xhtml">
<head id="Head1" runat="server">
    <title>Untitled Page</title>
</head>
<body>
    <form id="form1" runat="server">
        <div>
            <asp:WebPartManager ID="WebPartManager1" runat="server">
            </asp:WebPartManager>
        </div>
        <table>
            <tr>
                <td valign="top">
                    <asp:WebPartZone ID="LeftZone" runat="server">
                        <ZoneTemplate>
                            <asp:Calendar ID="Calendar1" runat="server">
```

```
➥</asp:Calendar>
                    </ZoneTemplate>
                </asp:WebPartZone>
            </td>
            <td valign="top">
                <asp:WebPartZone ID="RightZone" runat="server">
                    <ZoneTemplate>
                        <uc1:MyControl ID="MyControl1" runat="server" />
                    </ZoneTemplate>
                </asp:WebPartZone>
            </td>
        </tr>
    </table>
</form>
</body>
</html>
```

Run the application by pressing F5. The browser displays the output shown in Figure 12.7. The preceding HTML source shows the MyControl user control added to the RightZone web part zone in a declarative way. MyControl is automatically added to a GenericWebPart class when it is dropped in the web part zone.

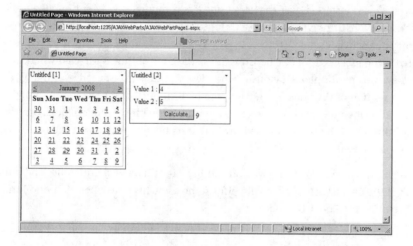

FIGURE 12.7
Output of the addition of two numbers

Now that we are familiar with creating web parts, let's go ahead and introduce Ajax into these web parts to make the user interface more interactive and dynamic.

Introducing Ajax into Web Parts

As we've seen, web parts are a great innovation to personalize and customize portal sites using ASP.NET. We've also learned that Ajax is a technology that can be used to minimize the size of data transfer packets between postbacks. So, one of the interesting innovations is to inject the Ajax technology into the web parts to make the portal site more responsive and interactive to the user's actions. We will discuss an example to illustrate how we can leverage this feature in an application.

In Figure 12.7, you can see information such as a Calendar in the LeftZone and a user control in the RightZone. The MyControl user control performs an addition of two numbers when the Calculate button is clicked. This action triggers a postback, and the entire page is reloaded, along with the result of the addition bound to a Label control. When a complete page postback is done, the server will re-create the entire HTML and send it to the client. This is a time-consuming process and also depends a lot on the underlying internet connection. This page only has one such activity. Let's say there is a page where the user has to perform several activities, and he/she has to spend a lot of time waiting for the page to load, reload, and reload again. This is a typical scenario in any non-Ajax–based application.

However, in an Ajax-based application, pages can be created in a way that requires only small, discrete portions of the page to be posted back. This way, the size of the data that is transferred over the wire is far less compared to the entire page postback, therefore improving response times to the client browser. In our example, when the user clicks the Calculate button, the only control that needs to be rendered is the label lblResult because this is the control that is affected when the click event is performed. Obviously, when lesser data is transferred over the wire and only a portion of the page is rendered, the performance of the page improves drastically. And when all this is happening, the user can perform other actions on the page, thus eliminating dead time in which users have to wait, as in the case of non-Ajax–based applications.

So we'll introduce Ajax in the web part of the RightZone web part zone. The button click of the Calculate button will perform the asynchronous operation and bind the result to the Label lblResult.

This can be done in two ways:

▶ Use an UpdatePanel inside the web part to achieve this functionality.

▶ Use client-side callbacks introduced by Microsoft in ASP.NET 2.0.

Using UpdatePanel

This is the simplest way of injecting Ajax in a web part. Place all the content of the web part inside an UpdatePanel. First, to make the page AjaxWebPartPage1.aspx Ajax-enabled, drop the ScriptManager control onto the page. This control takes care of all the asynchronous operations. Then, in the `RightZone` web part zone, drop an `UpdatePanel` control from the AJAXExtensions toolbox and place the `MyControl` user control inside the `ContentTemplate` tag of the UpdatePanel. As discussed in Hour 8, "Working with the `UpdatePanel` and `UpdateProgress` Controls," the `UpdatePanel` control is used for partial-page rendering, where only the portion of the page under the `UpdatePanel` is posted and rendered back.

The following is the HTML source of the `WebPartZone` `RightZone` after adding `MyControl` user control in an `UpdatePanel`:

```
<asp:WebPartZone ID="RightZone" runat="server">
    <ZoneTemplate>
        <asp:UpdatePanel ID="UpdatePanel1" runat="server">
            <ContentTemplate>
                <uc1:MyControl ID="MyControl1" runat="server" />
            </ContentTemplate>
        </asp:UpdatePanel>
    </ZoneTemplate>
</asp:WebPartZone>
```

Replace the `WebPartZone` `RightZone`'s HTML source in your `AJAXWebPartPage1.aspx` with the preceding code snippet.

Figure 12.8 shows the design mode after `MyControl` is placed in the `UpdatePanel` control.

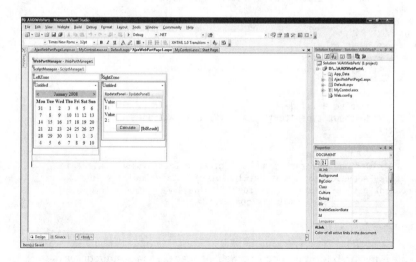

FIGURE 12.8
Design view of the MyControl user control placed in an `UpdatePanel` control

Run the application by pressing F5 and perform the `Calculate` operation after entering the values in the two textboxes provided. You'll find that only the user control is submitted and rendered back to the page. This helps in improving the overall performance of the web page with faster response times and making it more interactive for the user. The other way to inject Ajax into web parts is a feature called *client-side callbacks*, which is more powerful and effective than using an UpdatePanel.

Client-Side Callbacks

Client-side callbacks, a feature introduced by Microsoft in ASP.NET 2.0, allow controls to execute HTTP requests using JavaScript to obtain data on the server without posting the entire page. This is certainly a cool feature to have for performing asynchronous operations on a page without posting the complete page. Let's implement a client-side callback on the Calculate button in the web part of the RightZone in our previous example. Create a new user control called MyControl1. This user control will have the same controls as we had in the earlier user control, MyControl, except that MyControl1 will have all HTML input controls rather than server controls. This is to illustrate that the client callbacks can be done with the plain HTML controls. The following is the source of the MyControl1 user control:

```
<%@ Control Language="C#" AutoEventWireup="true" CodeFile="MyControl1.ascx.cs"
➥Inherits="MyControl1" %>
<script type="text/javascript">
    function ClientCallbackHandler(rValue)
    {
        document.getElementById("result").innerText = rValue;
    }
  </script>
<table>
    <tr>
        <td>Value 1 : </td>
        <td><input type="text" id="txtValue1"/></td>
    </tr>
    <tr>
        <td>Value 2 :</td>
        <td><input type="text" id="txtValue2"/></td>
    </tr>
    <tr>
        <td> </td>
        <td><input type="button" id="btnCalculate" value="Calculate"
➥onclick="AddValues(document.getElementById('txtValue1').value+'¦'+
➥document.getElementById('txtValue2').value)" />
            <span id="result"></span></td>
    </tr>
</table>
```

Create a new web form named AjaxWebPartPage2.aspx and register the MyControl1 user control by dragging and dropping the MyControl1 user control on this page. Now we have the same web part zones as we had in AJAXWebPartPage1.aspx. The only change is to remove the UpdatePanel control, and have the `MyControl1` user control directly in the web part. The following is the source of AJAXWebPartPage2.aspx:

```
<%@ Page Language="C#" AutoEventWireup="true"
CodeFile="AJAXWebPartPage2.aspx.cs"
    Inherits="AJAXWebPartPage2" %>
<%@ Register Src="MyControl1.ascx" TagName="MyControl1" TagPrefix="uc1" %>
<!DOCTYPE html PUBLIC "-//W3C//DTD XHTML 1.0 Transitional//EN"
➥"http://www.w3.org/TR/xhtml1/DTD/xhtml1-transitional.dtd">
<html xmlns="http://www.w3.org/1999/xhtml">
<head id="Head1" runat="server">
    <title>Untitled Page</title>
</head>
<body>
    <form id="form1" runat="server">
        <div>
            <asp:WebPartManager ID="WebPartManager1" runat="server">
            </asp:WebPartManager>
            <asp:ScriptManager ID="ScriptManager1" runat="server">
            </asp:ScriptManager>
        </div>
        <table>
            <tr>
                <td valign="top">
                    <asp:WebPartZone ID="LeftZone" runat="server">
                        <ZoneTemplate>
                            <asp:Calendar ID="Calendar1" runat="server">
➥</asp:Calendar>
                        </ZoneTemplate>
                    </asp:WebPartZone>
                </td>
                <td valign="top">
                    <asp:WebPartZone ID="RightZone" runat="server">
                        <ZoneTemplate>
                            <uc1:MyControl1 ID="MyControl1_1" runat="server" />
                        </ZoneTemplate>
                    </asp:WebPartZone>
                </td>
            </tr>
        </table>
    </form>
</body>
</html>
```

Now that we have the HTML source of the page and the user control ready, let's add logic to implement the client callback on the `Calculate` button. If you observe the HTML source of `MyControl1.ascx`, you can find a JavaScript method called `AddValues` on the click event of the Calculate button.

The idea is when the user clicks the Calculate button, the values in the two textboxes will be sent to the server via a server callback from JavaScript, and the output is updated in the label `lblResult`. All this is done without a full-page postback. This implementation looks fairly simple because all the complexity is abstracted by the

ASP.NET framework. If you notice, the Calculate button calls the JavaScript function AddValues, which does the act of communicating with the web server.

For an Ajax operation to be performed, a control must implement the ICallbackEventHandler interface. This control acts as the handler for performing the asynchronous operation. In our case, the control that is implementing the ICallbackEventHandler is the MyControl1 user control. This interface has two methods, RaiseCallbackEvent and GetCallbackResult, which need to be implemented by MyControl.

The RaiseCallbackEvent is the first method invoked, which processes the results of the callback operation, and the GetCallbackResult method returns the result of the logic performed in the RaiseCallbackEvent method. The following is the code of MyControl1 that implements these two methods:

```
public partial class MyControl1 : System.Web.UI.UserControl,
ICallbackEventHandler
{
    private string _result;
    public string GetCallbackResult()
    {
        return _result;
    }
    public void RaiseCallbackEvent(string eventArgument)
    {
        try
        {
            string[] inputData = eventArgument.Split('|');
            _result = Convert.ToString(int.Parse(inputData[0]) +
➥int.Parse(inputData[1]));
        }
        catch
        {
            _result = "Invalid input !";
        }
    }
    protected void Page_Load(object sender, EventArgs e)
    {
        ClientScriptManager cs = this.Page.ClientScript;
        string callBackFunction = cs.GetCallbackEventReference(this, "arg",
➥"ClientCallbackHandler", "context");
        string clientFunction = "function AddValues(arg, context){ " +
➥callBackFunction + "; }";
        cs.RegisterClientScriptBlock(this.GetType(), "AddValues",
➥clientFunction, true);
    }
}
```

The RaiseCallbackEvent method accepts the input parameter, performs the add operation, and assigns the value to the result variable, which is returned by the GetCallbackResult method. All this is fine, but how is Ajax performed here? The Microsoft Ajax library provides a ClientScript class that exposes a set of

JavaScript methods that help in communicating with the server. One such method is the `GetCallbackEventReference`, which is used to generate the JavaScript function required to invoke the partial-page postback.

In the preceding code, the `GetCallbackEventReference` method generates the JavaScript function and assigns it to the string `callBackFunction`. Now, this string holds the following:

```
WebForm_DoCallback(
'WebPartManager1$gwpMyControl1_1$MyControl1_1',arg,ClientCallbackHandler,
➥context,null,false
);
```

> **By the Way**
>
> After executing the page, you can see the JavaScript function `WebForm_DoCallback` in the HTML generated by the browser by right-clicking on the page and clicking the View Source menu item.

The JavaScript function `WebForm_DoCallback` that is generated is a special ASP.NET JavaScript method used to make the asynchronous callback to the page in the server. This function abstracts the complexity of making the asynchronous request. However, as we've discussed throughout this book, any request to the server asynchronously is done by the `XMLHttpRequest` object. All this is encapsulated in the Microsoft Ajax Library. So in essence, the `WebForm_DoCallback` internally uses this Library to instantiate this object and perform the task.

Now that all the code is ready, we'll go ahead and run the application. Set the `AJAXWebPartPage2.aspx` as the Start page and run the application to see the output in the browser. Enter the two values, **9** and **15**, in the two textboxes provided, and click the `Calculate` button. You can see that the full-page postback is not performed. Figure 12.9 displays the output of this partial-page postback. This example does not return huge data to find the performance difference; in cases where there is considerable real-time data to be displayed in these web parts, which are part of a big content page, you'll find this partial-page postback with the help of Ajax to be very useful. This helps the user perform other actions on the page without waiting for the results to be displayed in this web part.

To choose between implementing the client callbacks or an `UpdatePanel` in a web part is the developer's choice. If only a specific control in an entire web part holding multiple objects is to be affected by an asynchronous operation, then we suggest that you implement the client callback. If the majority of the content in the web part or the entire web part has to be redrawn, you'd be better off with an `UpdatePanel`.

FIGURE 12.9
Output of the
calculation
using a client
callback

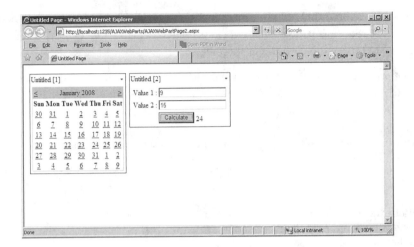

Summary

This hour focused on web parts, their features, and how to build them in ASP.NET
2.0 using Visual Studio 2005. Web parts are designed to build portal-style applications supporting personalization and customization. Web parts were earlier introduced in the SharePoint portal but did not offer developer extensibility. The web
parts in ASP.NET 2.0 support developer extensibility, in the sense that a user of a site
can develop and extend a web part and deploy it in the portal, and other users of
the site can leverage this functionality to personalize their web page. After we
learned how to build web parts, we went through an example to introduce Ajax into
these web parts to make the web page more dynamic and interactive. In the next
hour, we focus on the Ajax Control Toolkit.

Workshop

Quiz

1. What are the components required to run a web part on an ASP.NET page?

2. What is the default display mode of the web parts in a web part page?

3. True or False: There is no need to have an authentication client accessing a
   web part.

4. You have several server controls dropped from the toolbox directly into a web
   part zone. Under which web part class do these controls come from?

5. How do you develop a custom web part?

6. What are the different ways of using Ajax in web parts?

7. What is the interface to be implemented in order to perform client callback on ASP.NET pages?

Answers

1. A `WebPartManager` class and at least one web part zone are required to run web parts in an ASP.NET page.

2. The default Display mode of the web parts in a web part page is `BrowseDisplayMode`.

3. False. You need to authenticate a client to run web parts in pages.

4. `GenericWebPart` class.

5. A custom web part is developed by inhering any class or control from the base web part class.

6. UpdatePanel and HTTP client callbacks.

7. `ICallbackEventHandler`.

HOUR 13

ASP.NET Ajax Client Life Cycle Events

What You'll Learn in This Hour:

▶ An overview of the ASP.NET Ajax client life cycle events

▶ A discussion on the infamous `PageRequestManagerParserErrorException`

Understanding the ASP.NET Ajax Client-Side Event Model

The major difference between how an asynchronous postback and a regular postback works lies in the rendering stage—the rest of the processes are essentially the same. In this section, we examine the client life cycle events in an Ajax-enabled web page.

The client life cycle events in ASP.NET Ajax are triggered by these classes:

▶ `Application`

▶ `PageRequestManager`

Basically, you have two major events in the page processing of a web page for a synchronous postback—these are the `window.load` and `window.unload` DOM events that belong to the window object. However, you won't see any of these events being fired for an asynchronous postback. The `PageRequestManager` class is responsible for managing the sequence of events for an asynchronous postback.

The `PageRequestManager` class belongs to the `Sys.WebForms` namespace. The following are the events of this class:

▶ `initializeRequest`

▶ `beginRequest`

▶ `pageLoading`

▶ `pageLoaded`

▶ `endRequest`

> Out of all the `PageRequestManager` events given previously, when a synchronous postback occurs, only the `pageLoaded` event is fired.

The Application class that is contained in the `Sys` namespace contains these events:

▶ `init`

▶ `load`

▶ `unload`

Here are the sequences of events that occur during an asynchronous postback:

1. `initializeRequest`

2. `beginRequest`

3. `pageLoading`

4. `pageLoaded`

5. `load`

6. `endRequest`

Figure 13.1 illustrates the series of events diagrammatically.

> There are certain situations in which the sequence of events discussed previously may vary. For multiple postbacks, events of the most recent postback are fired. If an asynchronous postback is stopped prematurely, some of the events are not fired. For cancelled postbacks, only the `initializeRequest` event is triggered. For a synchronous postback, when the page is first loaded, or if you refresh the web browser, only the `pageLoaded` event will be fired.

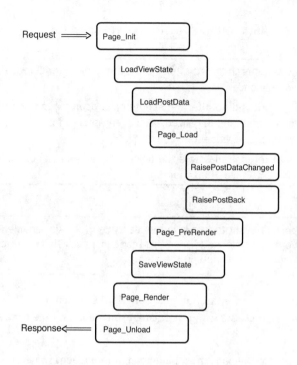

FIGURE 13.1
Asynchronous
postback
events

Table 13.1 summarizes the events of these classes and briefly covers the purposes of each of them.

TABLE 13.1   Events of the `Sys.Webforms.PageRequestManager` Class

Event	Purpose
initializeRequest	This event is fired just before the request for an asynchronous postback is initialized.
beginRequest	This event is fired just before the request is processed or the request data is sent to the server.
pageLoading	This event is fired once the request for the most recent asynchronous postback has been received but before the content of the web page is updated.
pageLoaded	This event is triggered after the page is updated with the most recent postback as a result of either a synchronous or an asynchronous postback.
endRequest	This event is fired after the request processing for an asynchronous postback is complete.

TABLE 13.2   Events of the Sys.Application **Class**

Event	Purpose
init	This event is triggered after the page has been rendered. This event is fired only once.
load	This event is fired after the scripts have been loaded and objects have been created and initialized. This event is fired for both synchronous and asynchronous requests.
unload	This event is fired before the objects have been disposed. You can use this event to clean up your objects.

By the Way

> The most important event triggered in the life cycle of an Ajax-enabled web page is the load event that belongs to the Application class. This event can be used to load other events and scripts in the life cycle.

You can add or remove event handlers of both Application and PageRequestManager classes using their add_eventname and the remove_eventname methods.

To attach handlers to the pageInit, pageLoad, and pageUnload events, you can write this code:

```
Sys.Application.add_init(pageInit);
Sys.Application.add_load(pageLoad);
Sys.Application.add_unload(pageUnload);
```

Here is how you can use the load and unload events of the Application class:

```
function pageLoad()
{
  var instance = Sys.WebForms.PageRequestManager.getInstance();
  //Write your custom code here
}
function pageUnload()
{
  var instance = Sys.WebForms.PageRequestManager.getInstance();
  //Write your custom code here
}
```

How Do I Handle the PageRequest ManagerParserErrorException?

In this section, we discuss a common error called PageRequestManagerParser ErrorException that is encountered in Ajax-enabled ASP.NET web pages. We will learn the cause of this infamous error and its remedies.

Fine, but why does this error occur? When you mix callbacks and postbacks in your Ajax-enabled ASP.NET applications, you might encounter this dreaded error.

You have the following types of exceptions in the `Sys.WebForms` namespace.

- ► `PageRequestManagerParserErrorException`
- ► `PageRequestManagerServerErrorException`
- ► `PageRequestManagerTimeoutErrorException`

You will encounter the `PageRequestManagerParserErrorException` if there is any error when the response is processed. You will encounter the `PageRequestManagerServerErrorException` for all the unhandled errors that occur at the server side. The `PageRequestManagerTimeoutException` can occur if the response is not sent by the server within a specific period of time. You can, however, set the `AsyncPostBackTimeout` property to a higher value in your application's `web.config` file to avoid this error.

This error occurs when the response object is modified due to calls to `Response.Write()` and `Response.Redirect()`, and usage of response filters and `HttpModules`. Actually, this error is a result of mixing postbacks and callbacks in your code. If you want to reproduce this error, you can simply take an `UpdatePanel` control and a `Button` control with it. In the click event of the control, if you make a call to `Server.Transfer` or `Response.Write`, you will see the error.

Here's an example of how the error message will look:

Sys.WebForms.PageRequestManagerParserErrorException: The message received from the server could not be parsed.

Common causes for this error are when the response is modified by calls to `Response.Write()`, response filters and `HttpModules` or when server trace is enabled.

To suppress it, you need to specify the `ScriptModule` in the `web.config` file. There are different measures that you need to adopt for other scenarios. You should ensure that `AutoEventWireup`, `EnableEventValidation`, `ValidateRequest`, and `SmartNavigation` attributes are set to false to avoid this error. You should also disable the caching of cookies in the `RoleManager` in your `web.config` file. Apart from these measures, you should also avoid registering scripts in asynchronous postbacks in your code. Most importantly, calls to `Response.Write()` should be avoided. Rather, if you want to display static text, you can use a Literal control instead.

To attach handlers to the `pageInit`, `pageLoad`, and `pageUnload` events, you can write this code:

```
Sys.WebForms.PageRequestManager.getInstance().add_initializeRequest
(IntializeRequest);
Sys.WebForms.PageRequestManager.getInstance().add_beginRequest
(BeginRequest);
Sys.WebForms.PageRequestManager.getInstance().add_pageLoading
(PageLoading);
Sys.WebForms.PageRequestManager.getInstance().add_pageLoaded
(PageLoaded);
Sys.WebForms.PageRequestManager.getInstance().add_endRequest
(EndRequest);
```

And, here is how you can implement these event handlers:

```
function IntializeRequest(sender,args)
{
    alert("InitializeRequest event called...");
}

function BeginRequest(sender,args)
{
    alert("BeginRequest event called...");
}

function PageLoading(sender, args)
{
    alert("PageLoading event called...");
}

function PageLoaded(sender, args)
{
    alert("PageLoaded event called...");
}


function EndRequest(sender, args)
{
    alert("EndRequest event called...");
}
```

Reproducing the Dreaded `PageRequestManager` `ParserErrorException`

Let us implement a simple example that reproduces the `PageRequestManager` `ParserErrorException`.

To do this, follow these steps:

1. Click File, New, Web Site to create a new web site. Save it with a name.

2. Switch to the design view of the `Default.aspx` file that is created as a default web page.

3. Drag and drop a `ScriptManager` control on to the web form.

4. Drag and drop an `UpdatePanel` control and place it inside the `ScriptManager` control.

5. Now, drag and drop a button control and place it inside the `UpdatePanel` control.

   Here is how the markup code in your ASPX file would now look:

```
<form id="form1" runat="server">
    <asp:ScriptManager ID="ScriptManager1" runat="server" />
    <asp:UpdatePanel ID="UpdatePanel1" runat="server">
      <ContentTemplate>
        <asp:Button ID="Button1" runat="server" Text="Click Here..."
➥OnClick="Button1_Click" />
      </ContentTemplate>
    </asp:UpdatePanel>
</form>
```

6. In the `Click` event of the `Button` control, assign an event handler called `Button1_Click` so that the event handler gets called as and when the button is clicked.

   Here is what the complete mark-up code now looks like:

```
<form id="Form1" runat="server">
    <asp:ScriptManager ID="ScriptManager1" runat="server" />
    <asp:UpdatePanel ID="UpdatePanel1" runat="server">
      <ContentTemplate>
        <asp:Button ID="Button1" runat="server" Text="Click Here..."
➥OnClick="Button1_Click" />
      </ContentTemplate>
    </asp:UpdatePanel>
</form>
```

7. Switch to the code–behind file of the web form and write the following code in the event handler associated with the `Button` control named `Button1`:

```
protected void btnClick_Click(object sender, EventArgs e)
    {
        Response.Write("STY Ajax in 24 Hours");
    }
```

8. Now, right click the `Default.aspx` page in the solution explorer and set it as the start page.

When you execute the application, the output is similar to what is shown in the Figure 13.2.

FIGURE 13.2
The application
at work!

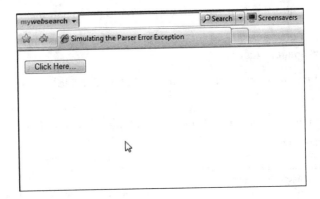

Now, click on the Button control. You can see a message displayed stating that a
PageRequestManagerParserErrorException has occurred. Refer to Figure 13.3.

FIGURE 13.3
The dreaded
PageRequestMa
nagerParserEr
rorException

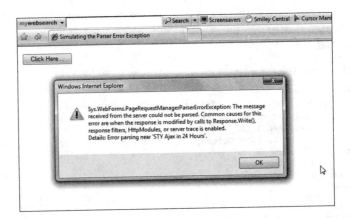

Avoiding the PageRequestManagerParserError Exception

So, how do we fix this? As we have already discussed, you should not use
Response.Write when using partial page updates using the UpdatePanel control.
Now let's take a literal control in lieu of using Response.Write and use it to display
the message we wanted to. Here is the markup code now:

```
<form id="Form1" runat="server">
    <asp:ScriptManager ID="ScriptManager1" runat="server" />
    <asp:UpdatePanel ID="UpdatePanel1" runat="server">
      <ContentTemplate>
        <asp:Literal ID="Literal1" runat="server" Text="" />
        <asp:Button ID="btnClick" runat="server" Text="Click Here..."
➥OnClick="btnClick_Click" />
```

```
        </ContentTemplate>
      </asp:UpdatePanel>
  </form>
```

Now, replace the call to the Response.Write method in the Button1_Click event handler with the one shown here:

```
protected void btnClick_Click(object sender, EventArgs e)
    {
        Response.Write("STY Ajax in 24 Hours");
    }


protected void btnClick_Click(object sender, EventArgs e)
    {
        Literal1.Text = "STY Ajax in 24 Hours";
    }
```

When you execute the application again and click the button, you won't see the error. Rather, the message "STY Ajax in 24 Hours" is displayed. Refer to Figure 13.4.

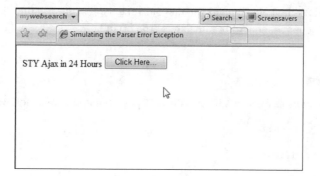

FIGURE 13.4
No parser error this time!

Summary

This hour has examined client-side life cycle events in an Ajax-enabled ASP.NET application. It also discussed the PageRequestManager class and why the dreaded PageRequestManagerParserErrorException occurs when using Ajax and the ways to fix it.

Workshop

Quiz

1. What are the sequences of events executed in the page life cycle of an ASP.NET web page?

2. What are the sequences of events in the client life cycle of an Ajax-enabled web page?

3. What is the purpose of the `PageRequestManager` class?

4. Name the events of the `Application` class.

5. How can you add and remove the `Application` and `PageRequestManager` classes?

6. Why does the `PageRequestManagerParserError` exception occur?

7. Why does the `PageRequestManagerServerErrorException` and the `PageRequestManagerTimeoutException` occur?

Answers

1. The sequences of events in the ASP.NET page life cycle are as follows:

    1. `Page_Init`

    2. `LoadViewState`

    3. `LoadPostData`

    4. `Page_Load`

    5. `RaisePostDataChangedEvent`

    6. `RaisePostBackEvent`

    7. `Page_PreRender`

    8. `SaveViewState`

    9. `Page_Render`

    10. `Page_UnLoad`

2. The sequences of events that are fired during an asynchronous postback are the following:

   ▶ initializeRequest

   ▶ beginRequest

   ▶ pageLoading

   ▶ pageLoaded

   ▶ load

   ▶ endRequest

3. The PageRequestManager class belongs to the Sys.WebForms namespace and is responsible for managing the sequence of events for an asynchronous postback.

4. The Application class belongs to the Sys namespace and contains the following events:

   ▶ init

   ▶ load

   ▶ unload

5. You can add or remove event handlers of both Application and PageRequestManager classes using their add_eventname and remove_eventname methods.

6. When you mix callbacks and postbacks in your Ajax-enabled ASP.NET applications, you might encounter this dreaded error. This error occurs when the response object is modified due to calls to Response.Write() and Response.Redirect() and usage of response filters and HttpModules. This error is a result of mixing postbacks and callbacks in your code.

7. The PageRequestManagerServerErrorException occurs PageRequestManagerServerErrorException for any unhandled errors at the server side. The PageRequestManagerTimeoutException can occur if the response is not sent by the server within a specific period of time.

PART III

Advanced Concepts

HOUR 14

Working with Web Services Using Ajax

What You'll Learn in This Hour:

▶ The features of the asynchronous communication layer
▶ Components in the client and server asynchronous communication layer
▶ Using the Microsoft Ajax Library to make HTTP requests and invoking web services from the client

In this hour, we will explore the asynchronous communication layer in the Microsoft Ajax Library, which can also be thought of as a network layer responsible for the communication between the server and client.

The Asynchronous Communication Layer

The asynchronous communication layer is a set of classes exposed as an API that enables the communication between server and client. The Microsoft Ajax Library is browser independent, and JavaScript or ECMAScript can use this API to perform an asynchronous request from any browser to the server. This API is nothing but abstracting the asynchronous behavior provided by the XMLHttp object. This forms the foundation for presenting a quick and very responsive web application. This hour focuses on how the web request is generated and managed using this Library. Also we'll explore how web services are invoked from the client using this Library.

What Does the Asynchronous Communication Layer Support?

The asynchronous communication layer provides the following features:

▶ Asynchronous postbacks using JavaScript to make asynchronous calls to the server.

▶ Ability to call ASP.NET web services on the server from the client script.

▶ Support for various serialization formats for passing data between the server and client browser. These formats include JSON, XML, text, and so on.

▶ Ability to call specific ASP.NET static page methods.

▶ Ability to enhance web service interactions by generating web service proxies to communicate with the web services on the server.

In essence, this layer abstracts the underlying complexity in the browser and the server to facilitate easier communication between the server and client in an asynchronous fashion.

By the Way

Calling a web service from the client in ASP.NET Ajax application is a configurable option—that is, it can be enabled or disabled.

To gain insight into the architecture of the asynchronous communication layer, let's explore Figure 14.1.

FIGURE 14.1
The asynchronous communication layer

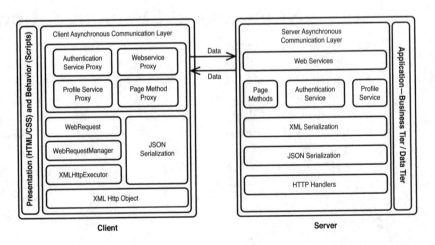

Figure 14.1 illustrates the components in the asynchronous communication layer of both the client and server.

The client asynchronous communication layer has the components necessary to initiate requests to the server. The web requests are based on the XMLHttp object of the browser and on the executor objects that dispatches the request to the server. The WebRequest, WebRequestManager, and XMLHttpExecutor classes are responsible for sending the HTTP request. These classes abstract the execution of the XMLHttp object of the browser. Here is a brief description of these classes:

▶ **Sys.Net.WebRequest**—This is the client HTTP request object.

▶ **WebRequestManager**—This is the object responsible for managing requests by invoking the executor object.

▶ **XmlHttpExecutor**—This object calls the instance of the XMLHttp object of the corresponding browser and provides the status of the request.

With the help of the preceding three objects, making an HTTP request is simple. Let's explore this with the help of that familiar example of accessing the Items.xml file on the server.

Sending an HTTP Request from the Client

To send an HTTP request from the client, follow these steps:

1. Create an instance of the Sys.Net.WebRequest object.

2. Set its url property to the file on the server.

3. Next, attach an event handler to the add_completed function, which is called when the response is received at the client. Finally, call the invoke method to initiate the asynchronous request.

4. Create a new aspx page in the existing solution and write the code shown here:

```
<%@ Page Language="C#" AutoEventWireup="true"
CodeFile="HttpRequest.aspx.cs"
➥Inherits="HttpRequest" %>
<!DOCTYPE html PUBLIC "-//W3C//DTD XHTML 1.0 Transitional//EN"
➥"http://www.w3.org/TR/xhtml1/DTD/xhtml1-transitional.dtd">
<html xmlns="http://www.w3.org/1999/xhtml">
<head runat="server">
    <title>Example for making HTTP Request</title>
    <script language="javascript" type="text/javascript">
    var outputElement;
```

```
// This function performs a GET Web request.
function WebRequest()
{
    alert("Making web request...");
    // Instantiate a WebRequest.
    var request = new Sys.Net.WebRequest();
    // Set the request URL.
    request.set_url("Items.xml");
    // Set the request callback function.
    request.add_completed(OnWebRequestCompleted);
    outputElement = document.getElementById("divOutput");
    // Clear the output area.
    outputElement.innerHTML = "";
    // Execute the request.
    request.invoke();
}
// This callback function processes the
// request return values. It is called asynchronously
// by the current executor.
function OnWebRequestCompleted(executor, eventArgs)
{
alert("Fetching Response...");
    if(executor.get_responseAvailable())
    {
        // Clear the previous results.
        outputElement.innerHTML = "";
        // Display Web request status.
        outputElement.innerHTML +=
          "Status: [" + executor.get_statusCode() + " " +
                    executor.get_statusText() + "]" + "<br/>";
        // Display Web request headers.
        outputElement.innerHTML +=
            "Headers: ";
        outputElement.innerHTML +=
            executor.getAllResponseHeaders() + "<br/>";
        // Display Web request body.
        outputElement.innerHTML +=
            "Body:";
      if(document.all)
        outputElement.innerText +=
            executor.get_responseData();
      else
        outputElement.textContent +=
            executor.get_responseData();
    }
}
    </script>
</head>
<body>
    <form id="form1" runat="server">
        <asp:ScriptManager runat="server" ID="ScriptManagerId">
        </asp:ScriptManager>
        <table>
        <tr align="left">
            <td>
                Make HTTP Request:</td>
            <td>
                <button id="Button1" onclick="WebRequest()" type="button">
```

```
                       Request</button>
                  </td>
              </tr>
          </table>
          <hr />
          <div id="divOutput"/>
          </form>
      </body>
      </html>
```

After the preceding code is executed in the browser, the output is as shown in Figure 14.2.

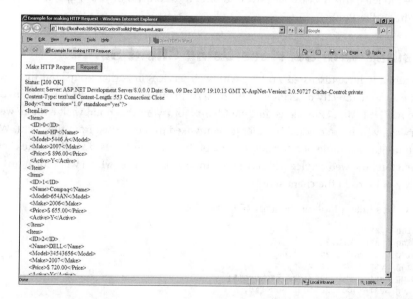

FIGURE 14.2
Sending Http
requests to the
server from the
client side

Let's now briefly discuss the code example shown earlier. The HTML source contains a button called Request that calls the method WebRequest; this instantiates the Sys.Net.WebRequest object and calls the xml file requested on the server with its invoke method. This object is associated with the callback method when the response is fetched. In our example, this callback method is OnWebRequestCompleted. This method has two parameters: executor and eventArgs. The first parameter, executor, is of type Sys.Net.WebRequestExecutor and contains information about the status of the asynchronous request. The second parameter, EventArgs, is by default set to Sys.EventArgs.Empty, which indicates the absence of Event Arguments.

The executor object is an instance of the Sys.Net.XMLHttpExecutor class, which is inherited from the Sys.Net.WebRequestExecutor class. The XMLHttpExecutor class overrides the implementation of the executeRequest method for specifying how an HTTP request is sent from the client script. The XMLHttpExecutor sends a request using the XMLHttpRequest object. In the preceding example, the OnWebRequestCompleted method checks if the response is available through the executor's get_ResponseAvailable() method, and if the response is available, displays the status codes, header information, and the content of the xml file onto the divOutput tag in HTML. Here, the XML data is rendered as text. You can use XML-DOM to fetch this as XmlDocument and bind it to controls in your page, as described in the earlier hours.

Calling Web Services Using Client Script

We already have discussed working with web services in earlier hours, but those web services were directly associated with the server controls in the Toolkit, which used the ASP.NET Ajax extensions and the Client Library. In this hour, we'll explore web services, which are created in order to be invoked and executed from the client. We will use the example of returning the list of items in the Items.xml file to the client. Therefore, the web service will have a method FetchItems, which will return an array of items to the client script.

First, let's take a look at the asmx file, as follows:

```
using System;
using System.Web;
using System.Collections;
using System.Web.Services;
using System.Web.Services.Protocols;
using System.Collections.Generic;
using System.Data;
using System.Web.Script.Services;
```

The namespace System.Web.Script.Services is required for script services and has to be used if web service from the client has to be called. The next thing is to add the declarative attribute [ScriptService] for Ajax-enabled services. This attribute is added for the web service class, as shown next:

```
[WebService(Namespace = "http://tempuri.org/")]
[WebServiceBinding(ConformsTo = WsiProfiles.BasicProfile1_1)]
[ScriptService]
public class ItemService : System.Web.Services.WebService {
```

We'll have a web method `FetchItems` that will read the xml file `Items.xml` and create and return a list of item names to the client script. The code snippet for the web
method is as follows:

```
[WebMethod]
public List<string> FetchItems() {
        DataSet dsItems = new DataSet();
        dsItems.ReadXml(HttpContext.Current.Request.PhysicalApplicationPath
➥+ @"Items.xml");
        List<string> items = new List<string>();
        foreach (DataRow dr in dsItems.Tables["Item"].Rows)
        {
            string name = dr["Name"].ToString();
            items.Add(name);
        }
        return items;
    }
```

The web method `FetchItems` reads the xml file `Items.xml` into a DataSet and then
loops through each item and adds the item name to a list and returns the list to the
client. Paste the preceding code in a web service file called `ItemService.asmx`.

Now, create an aspx page called `WebServiceRequest.aspx` to call this web service
from JavaScript. Paste the following code in this aspx page:

```
<%@ Page Language="C#" AutoEventWireup="true"
CodeFile="WebServiceRequest.aspx.cs"
    Inherits="WebServiceRequest" %>
<!DOCTYPE html PUBLIC "-//W3C//DTD XHTML 1.0 Transitional//EN"
➥"http://www.w3.org/TR/xhtml1/DTD/xhtml1-transitional.dtd">
<html xmlns="http://www.w3.org/1999/xhtml">
<head runat="server">
    <title>Web service request</title>
    <script type="text/javascript">
            // This function calls the Web Service method.
            function GetItems()
            {
                ItemService.FetchItems(OnProcessed);
            }
            // This is the callback function that
            // processes the Web Service return value.
            function OnProcessed(output)
            {
                var outputElement = document.getElementById("divOutput");
                outputElement.innerHTML = output;
            }
    </script>
</head>
<body>
    <form id="Form1" runat="server">
        <asp:ScriptManager runat="server" ID="scriptManager">
            <Services>
                <asp:ServiceReference Path="ItemService.asmx" />
            </Services>
        </asp:ScriptManager>
```

```
        <div>
            <h2>
                Item List</h2>
            <p>
                Calling a service that returns the list of items.</p>
            <input id="btnFetchItems" type="button" value="Fetch Item(s)"
➥onclick="GetItems()" />
        </div>
    </form>
    <hr />
    <div>
        <span id="divOutput"></span>
    </div>
</body>
</html>
```

In the preceding code, the ScriptManager control contains the reference to the web service to be invoked in its path attribute of the ServiceReference tag. Button btnFetchItems, when clicked, calls JavaScript function GetItems, and this method in turn calls the web service method FetchItems of the ItemService class. This method has an argument that is a callback method, fired when the web service is processed and the result is returned. The callback method in this example is OnProcessed. This method displays the output in the div tag divOutput. After executing this example, the browser shows the output in Figure 14.3.

FIGURE 14.3
Calling a web service from the client

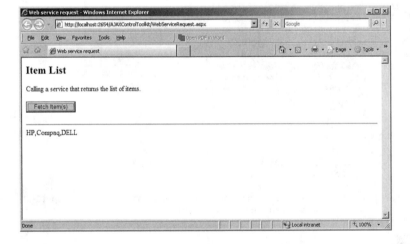

The output is retrieved as string and assigned to the divOutput tag.

Working with the Web Service Proxy Classes

The asynchronous communication layer automatically generates client-script proxy classes, which can be used to make asynchronous requests to the server from the client script.

There are two ways to make a web service request. Let's examine both.

Calling Web Services by Using the HTTP POST Verb

A POST request sends the body that contains data to the server. This request does not have any size limitation, as opposed to a GET request. The serialization and de-serialization in ASP.NET Ajax is, by default, done in JSON. So any data sent by the browser is first serialized into JSON and then sent. The server de-serializes JSON into .NET data types and processes the web service.

Calling Web Services by Using the HTTP GET Verb

A GET request has a data size that is limited to the URL length allowed by the browser.

Using this verb, the browser uses a query string to send the parameters to the server.

The web service has to be configured with the attribute [ScriptMethod(UseHttpGet = true)] in order to be called by the GET request.

Working with the Page Method Proxy Classes

This proxy class provides infrastructure to call the static methods in an asp.net page quite similar to the web service methods. This can be in any aspx or ascx page. To use a page method using Ajax, your page should have the namespace System.Web.Services, included. The page methods should be static and should have the attribute [WebMethod]. And in the aspx page, the ScriptManager control should have its EnablePageMethods property set to true.

> **By the Way**
>
> All page methods should be static. The reason for this is that a page method call does not instantiate your page class and does not contain the view state for the page when the request is made. So it cannot even have access to any controls or the nonstatic members of your page class.

Let's take a small example of returning a server date and time in a static method in an aspx page:

```
[WebMethod]
    public static string GetServerDateTime()
    {
        return DateTime.Now.ToString();
    }
```

The preceding static method is in the code-behind of an aspx page. The aspx page has the ScriptManager, Button, and Div, as follows:

```
<form id="form1" runat="server">
        <div>
            <asp:ScriptManager ID="ScriptManager1" runat="server"
➥EnablePageMethods="True">
            <Scripts>
                    <asp:ScriptReference Path="PageMethod.js"/>
            </Scripts>
            </asp:ScriptManager>
        </div>
        <div>
            <h2>
                Testing Page Methods</h2>
            <input id="button1" type="button" value="Click Me"
➥onclick="GetValue()" />
        </div>
        <div id="divOutput"></div>
    </form>
```

When the button is clicked, the GetValue function is called. The source for this function is the JS file PageMethod.js, which is shown next:

```
function GetValue()
        {
            PageMethods.GetServerDateTime(OnSucceeded, OnFailed);
        }

        // Callback function invoked on successful
        // completion of the page method.
        function OnSucceeded(result, userContext, methodName)
        {
            if (methodName == "GetServerDateTime")
            {
                var outputElement = document.getElementById("divOutput");
                outputElement.innerHTML = result;
            }
        }
        // Callback function invoked on failure
        // of the page method.
        function OnFailed(error, userContext, methodName)
        {
            if(error !== null)
            {
                outputElement.innerHTML = "An error occurred: " +
                    error.get_message();
            }
        }
```

The GetValue() method invokes the GetServerDateTime() method on the server and returns the server date and time to the client in its callback method. If you observe, there are two callback methods for page methods—one for success and the other one for failure. The output of the successful execution is shown in Figure 14.4.

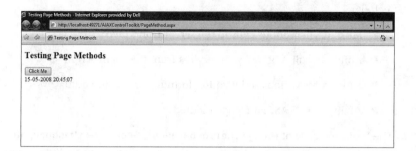

FIGURE 14.4
Calling page methods using Ajax

Summary

This hour focused on the asynchronous communication layer, an API in the Microsoft Ajax Library to make asynchronous web requests and network calls to the server from JavaScript. This layer abstracts the underlying complexity in the browser and the server to facilitate easier communication between the server and client in an asynchronous fashion. We explored this concept with a working example on accessing web services and making HTTP requests from JavaScript. Other application services like authentication and profile services will be discussed in the next hour.

Workshop

Quiz

1. What is asynchronous communication layer? What are its basic features?

2. What is the basic objective of the Sys.Net.WebRequest, WebRequestManager, and XmlHttpExecutor classes?

3. In how many ways can web services be called from the client side using Ajax?

4. What is the purpose of the GetValue() method?

5. What are the benefits of the asynchronous communication layer?

6. What is the purpose of the WebRequestManager object?

Answers

1. The asynchronous communication layer is an API in the Microsoft Ajax Library to make asynchronous web requests and network calls to the server from JavaScript. The basic features of the asynchronous communication layer include

   ▶ Make asynchronous calls to the server using JavaScript

   ▶ Ability to call ASP.NET web services from the client script

   ▶ Support for various serialization formats for passing data

   ▶ Ability to call ASP.NET page methods

2. The basic objective of the `Sys.Net.WebRequest`, `WebRequestManager`, and `XmlHttpExecutor` classes is to abstract the execution of the `XMLHttp` object.

3. There are two ways, that is, using the HTTP POST verb and using the HTTP GET verb.

4. The `GetValue()` method invokes the `GetServerDateTime()` method on the server and returns the server date and time to the client in its callback method.

5. The asynchronous communication layer supports the following:

   ▶ Asynchronous postbacks by enabling JavaScript to make asynchronous calls to the server.

   ▶ Ability to call ASP.NET web services on the server from the client script.

   ▶ Support for various serialization formats for passing data between the server and client browser. These formats include JSON, XML, text, and so on.

   ▶ Ability to call specific ASP.NET static page methods.

   ▶ Enhancing web service interactions by generating web service proxies to communicate with the web services on the server.

6. The `WebRequestManager` object is responsible for managing requests by invoking the executor object.

HOUR 15

Working with Authentication Service Using ASP.NET Ajax

What You'll Learn in This Hour:

▶ An overview of authentication in ASP.NET

▶ Types of authentication in ASP.NET

▶ Using authentication with ASP.NET Ajax

The built-in server-side services of ASP.NET 2.0, such as authentication, profiles, member-ship, roles, and so on, are awesome. They enable you to use these services in your ASP.NET applications without having to write much code. However, because these are server-side services, consuming them from your client-side scripts can be a nightmare.

Fortunately, ASP.NET Ajax provides support for calling such services from your client-side scripts. In this hour and the next, we explore how we can invoke these services using Ajax in your applications seamlessly. In this hour in particular, we learn about the role of Ajax in ASP.NET authentication and discuss how you can call the ASP.NET authentication service using client-side scripts with Ajax.

Before we delve deep into this topic, let's have a quick look at what exactly authentication is, its types, and how you can use it in a typical ASP.NET application. When we're done, we will do the same with Ajax and discuss how we can use authentication through Ajax, access the ASP.NET authentication service using Ajax, and more.

What Is Authentication? What Are Its Types?

Authentication is the process of identifying and validating the user's credentials—it is a process that verifies the authenticity of a user. Once a user is authenticated, a process called *authorization* is responsible for checking to see what resources this authenticated user can have access to.

By the Way

> Authorization works only for a user who has already been authenticated.

In ASP.NET, you can use one of the following types of authentication:

- ▶ Forms authentication

- ▶ Windows authentication

- ▶ Passport authentication

Using authentication in applications is also simple; just specify the type of authentication that you need in your application's `web.config` file. Here is the syntax for specifying authentication in the application's `web.config` file:

```
<configuration>
  <system.web>
    <authentication mode="[Windows/Forms/Passport/None]">
    </authentication>
  </system.web>
</configuration>
```

By the Way

> You can also use custom authentication in ASP.NET. To do so, you should turn off the default authentication in your `web.config` file and write your own authentication provider. Here is how you can turn off authentication in your application's web.config file:
>
> ```
> <authentication mode="none">
> ```

The following three code snippets illustrate how you can specify the three forms of authentication in your application's `web.config` file.

Forms Authentication:

```
<configuration>
  <system.web>
    <authentication mode="Forms">
    <forms name="loginForm" loginUrl="loginForm.aspx" />
    <authorization>
        <deny users="?"/>
```

```
      </authorization>
    </system.web>
</configuration>
```

Windows Authentication:

```
<authentication mode="Windows"/>
<authorization>
<allow users ="*" />
</authorization>
```

Passport Authentication:

```
    <authentication mode = "Passport">
      <passportredirectUrl = "loginForm.aspx" />
    </authentication>
    <authorization>
      <deny users="?"/>
    </authorization>
```

Refer to the following code snippet:

```
    <configuration>
      <system.web>
        <authorization>
          <deny users="?"/>
          <allow users="*"/>
        </authorization>
      </system.web>
    </configuration>
```

The symbol "*" in the statement <allow user = "*"> in the preceding code snippet implies all users, inclusive of authenticated and anonymous users. On the other hand, the symbol "?" in the <deny users = "?"> statement implies only authenticated users. Thus, although the former statement implies "allow all users inclusive of authenticated and anonymous users," the latter implies "deny only the authenticated users."

By the Way

Working with Authentication Service Using Client-Side Scripts

Let's discuss how we can use forms authentication using ASP.NET Ajax. We will learn how to access the ASP.NET authentication service from client-side JavaScript using Ajax.

First, you have the AuthenticationService class that allows you to access the ASP.NET authentication service using client-side scripts. In this class, you have two methods: `login` and `logout`. Whereas the `login` method allows you to validate the user's credentials, the `logout` method clears the forms authentication cookie in order to log out the user.

> If you add the `ScriptManager` control in your web page, the `AuthenticationService` object is available to any client-side scripts for that web page by default.

Now, you need to enable the authentication service so that you can use it from client-side scripts. Here is how you can do this:

```
<system.web.extensions>
  <scripting>
    <webServices>
      <authenticationService enabled="true" />
    </webServices>
  </scripting>
</system.web.extensions>
```

> When using the `AuthenticationService` object in your application, you should either have cookies enabled in your web browser (the `AuthenticationService` class makes use of cookies for creating the authentication ticket to preserve the identity of the logged-in user for subsequent requests) or alternatively, you can set the cookieless attribute to `true` in the `<SessionState>` tag in your `web.config` file.
>
> To use the authentication service, forms authentication should be enabled in your application using the `<authentication mode>` tag in the application's `web.config` file.

Implementing a Sample Application

We'll explore using the authentication service with ASP.NET Ajax in a sample example. This example demonstrates logging into the system using the authentication service. Follow these steps to code and test the example:

1. Open Visual Studio 2005, and create a new Ajax-enabled web site named AJAXAuthentication with code-behind as c#.

2. We will be using ASP.NET membership to test the login. So let's create a user first. Go to ASP.NET configuration from the solution explorer. This would open up the Website Administration Tool of this web site.

3. Go to the Security tab of this tool. In the Users sections, click the link Select Authentication Type. The user will be prompted to select either the option From the Internet or From a Local Network. Select the option From the Internet because we will be using a database, and click the Done button.

4. Click the link Create User in the Users section, create a user named joydip with the password joydip@24h. This information is stored in the SQL Server Express database on the local server. After you create the user, you can find this database ASPNETDB.MDF in the App_data folder of the solution, as shown in Figure 15.1.

FIGURE 15.1
The ASPNETDB.MDF file when viewed in the Solution Explorer

Figure 15.2 shows the tables list used to store the users and roles of this application.

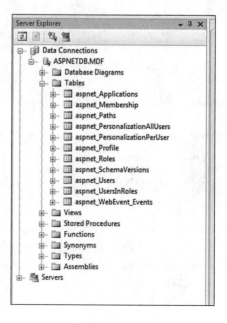

FIGURE 15.2
List of tables viewed in the Server Explorer

5. The ASP.NET membership provider model uses this database. You can have this created in your SQL Server database and use it by adding RoleManager and Membership tags to the web.config file and pointing the connection to your database. In this example, we are concentrating on using the default connection of the SQL Server Express database on the local server. The default provider configuration can be found in the Machine.Config file, which is as follows:

```
<roleManager>
  <providers>
    <add name="AspNetSqlRoleProvider"
        connectionStringName="LocalSqlServer"
        applicationName="/"
        type="System.Web.Security.SqlRoleProvider, ..." />
    <add name="AspNetWindowsTokenRoleProvider"
        applicationName="/"
        type="System.Web.Security.WindowsTokenRoleProvider, ..." />
  </providers>
</roleManager>
```

Because we are using the default provider pointing to the SQL Server Express database, you need not do anything in this step.

6. Now that we have a user ready for logging into the system, we'll go ahead and create an authentication service overriding the default one of ASP.NET Ajax. The first step toward creating this service is to enable the authentication service by adding the following to the web.config file just after the <configSections> tag:

```
<system.web.extensions>
  <scripting>
    <webServices>
      <authenticationService enabled="true" />
    </webServices>
  </scripting>
</system.web.extensions>
```

7. Next, add the following to the web.config file to enable forms authentication:

```
<system.web>
  <authentication mode="Forms">
    <forms cookieless="UseCookies"
          loginUrl="~/login.aspx"/>
  </authentication>
<system.web>
```

8. Add the web service name to the ScriptManager control to perform the authentication asynchronously from the client script. The ScriptManager control has a property called AuthenticationService. Set the value of its Path

attribute to the name of the web service. In this case, the web service name is
Authenticate.asmx. The following is the markup code for this in the
Default.aspx file:

```
<asp:ScriptManager ID="ScriptManager1" runat="server" >
        <AuthenticationService Path="Authenticate.asmx" />
    </asp:ScriptManager>
```

9. Create the web service Authenticate.asmx and implement the methods Login
and Logout to perform the authentication. The authenticate web service class
should use the ScriptService attribute to implement authentication. The following is the code for this web service:

```
using System;
using System.Web;
using System.Collections;
using System.Web.Services;
using System.Web.Services.Protocols;
using System.Web.Script.Services;
using System.Web.Security;
/// <summary>
/// Summary description for Authenticate
/// </summary>
[WebService(Namespace = "http://tempuri.org/")]
[WebServiceBinding(ConformsTo = WsiProfiles.BasicProfile1_1)]
[ScriptService]
public class Authenticate : System.Web.Services.WebService {
    public Authenticate () {
        //Uncomment the following line if using designed components
            //InitializeComponent();
    }
    [WebMethod]
    public bool Login(string userName, string password, bool
➥createPersistentCookie)
    {
        if (Membership.Provider.ValidateUser(userName, password))
        {
            FormsAuthentication.SetAuthCookie(userName,
➥createPersistentCookie);
            return true;
        }
        return false;
    }
    [WebMethod]
    public void Logout()
    {
        FormsAuthentication.SignOut();
    }
}
```

10. The login method has three arguments in `username`, `password`, and `createPersistentCookie`. This method validates the user using the ASP.NET Membership API and creates a cookie using forms authentication upon successful validation and sends this cookie back to the browser. This cookie would be used for subsequent requests from the browser.

The logout method signs out the user from the system and clears the cookie from the client browser.

11. The infrastructure for authentication is ready except for the user interface and client script accessing this service. So let's create the script calls from the aspx page to perform authentication. The script interacts with the authentication service and registers for callbacks and notifies the user about the status of Login and Logout. We'll have a login form, login.aspx, to perform this action. This form contains Username and Password textboxes and a Login button. The body of the login HTML is as follows:

```
<body onload="javascript:document.getElementById('txtUsername').focus();">
    <form id="form1" runat="server">
        <asp:ScriptManager ID="ScriptManager1" runat="server" >
            <AuthenticationService Path="Authenticate.asmx" />
        </asp:ScriptManager>
        <div>
            <p>Authentication Service using ASP.NET AJAX</p>
        </div>
        <div id="divLogin">
            Username :
            <input type="text" id="txtUsername"/><br />
            Password :
            <input type="password" id="txtPassword" /><br />
            <button id="btnLogin" onclick="Login_OnClick(); return
➥false;">Login</button>
        </div>
        <div id="divHome" style="display: none">
            You have successfully logged in to the system !!<br /><br />
            <button id="btnLogout" onclick="Logout_OnClick(); return
➥false;">Logout</button>
        </div>
    </form>
</body>
```

The Login and Logout buttons have `onclick` events in `Login_OnClick` and `Logout_OnClick`.

12. After the user clicks Login, the `Sys.Services.AuthenticationService` class sets the default callback events for the `OnLoginCompleted`, `OnFailed`, and `OnLogoutCompleted` methods. It then calls the login service by passing the user credentials. The `ScriptManager` control generates the `AuthenticationService` and emits it to the browser and then manages the

entire authentication process. In this example, the `OnLoginCompleted` method
verifies the credentials, hides the `Login` controls contained in a `<div>` tag
called `divLogin`, and displays a `divHome` block containing the message, "You
have successfully logged in to the system !!" Upon clicking the Logout button,
the `Sys.Services.AuthenticationService.logout` method is called, which
logs out the user from the application. In addition, the callback event
`OnLogoutCompleted` is called, which displays the block `divLogin`. In case of
failure of the Login or Logout operations, the `OnFailed` method is called,
which alerts the user with the error message. The script code for this process is
as follows:

```javascript
<script language="javascript" type="text/javascript">
        function Login_OnClick()
        {
            if (document.getElementById("txtUsername").value == "")
            {
                alert("Please enter Username.");
                document.getElementById("txtUsername").focus();
                return;
            }
            if (document.getElementById("txtPassword").value == "")
            {
                alert("Please enter Password.");
                document.getElementById("txtPassword").focus();
                return;
            }
Sys.Services.AuthenticationService.set_defaultLoginCompletedCallback
➥(OnLoginCompleted);
Sys.Services.AuthenticationService.set_defaultFailedCallback(OnFailed);
Sys.Services.AuthenticationService.set_defaultLogoutCompletedCallback
➥ (OnLogoutCompleted);
Sys.Services.AuthenticationService.login(document.getElementById
➥("txtUsername").value, document.getElementById("txtPassword").value,
➥false,null,null,null,null,"User Context");
return;
}
        function Logout_OnClick()
        {
            Sys.Services.AuthenticationService.logout(null, null, null,
➥null);
        }
        function OnLoginCompleted(validCredentials, userContext,
methodName)
        {
            if (validCredentials == true)
            {
                document.getElementById("divLogin").style.display = 'none';
                document.getElementById("divHome").style.display = 'block';
            }
            else
            {
                alert("Invalid Login credentials !");
                document.getElementById("txtUsername").focus();
```

```
        }
        return;
    }
    function OnFailed(error, userContext, methodName)
    {
        alert("Unable to log in to the site. Details : " + error.get_
➥message() + ". " + error.get_statusCode());
        return;
    }
    function OnLogoutCompleted(result)
    {
        document.getElementById("divLogin").style.display = 'block';
        document.getElementById("divHome").style.display = 'none';
        return;
    }
</script>
```

13. Set the login.aspx as the Startup page and execute the application by pressing F5. Figure 15.3 displays the page before logging into the application.

FIGURE 15.3
The application
at work!

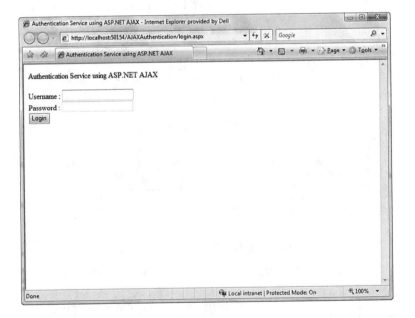

If you remember, we have configured a user, joydip, with the password joydip@24h
for this web site. Initially, let's try to validate the system with a different user to find
out the response of the site. Let's start with a username/password called test/test,
which does not exist in the system. Figure 15.4 displays the validation when tested
against the test user.

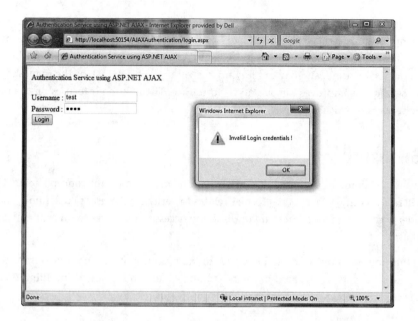

FIGURE 15.4
Invalid login

Now, let's try this with the correct username and password—joydip and joy-dip@24h. Figure 15.5 displays the page after a successful login.

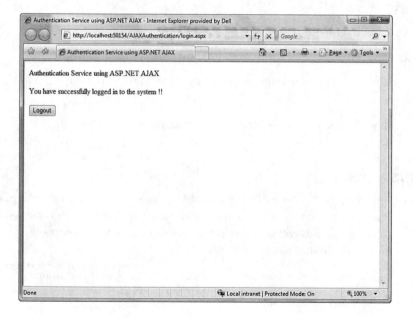

FIGURE 15.5
Login succeeded

When you click the Logout button, the currently logged-in user will be logged out of the application, and you would be back to the Login form again. This hour examined how to use authentication service using ASP.NET Ajax, so as to perform the actions asynchronously to avoid having to send the entire HTML as the request to the server; this improves the overall performance. The next hour focuses on the profile services of ASP.NET Ajax.

Summary

Authentication and authorization are two of the most important concepts related to ASP.NET security. Whereas the former relates to verifying the user's credentials, the latter is concerned with enabling or disabling access to resources to an authenticated user.

In this hour, we have discussed how we can access authentication services from client-side scripts using Ajax. In the next hour, we take a look at the profiling service and how we can use it with ASP.NET Ajax.

Workshop

Quiz

1. What is authentication? What are its types?

2. How can you enable forms authentication in your application?

3. What is the purpose of the `AuthenticationService` class? What are its methods?

4. How can you enable authentication service for your application?

Answers

1. Authentication is the process of identifying and validating a user's credentials. It is a process that verifies the authenticity of a user. After a user is authenticated, the process called authorization checks to see what resources this authenticated user can have access to.

    In ASP.NET, you can use one of the following types of authentication:

    ▶ Forms authentication

    ▶ Windows authentication

    ▶ Passport authentication

2. You can enable forms authentication in your application's web.config file by specifying the authentication mode attribute, as shown in the following code snippet:

```
<configuration>
  <system.web>
    <authentication mode="Forms"/>
    <forms name="loginForm" loginUrl="loginForm.aspx" />
    <authorization>
        <deny users="?"/>
    </authorization>
  </system.web>
</configuration>
```

3. The AuthenticationService class allows you to access the ASP.NET authentication service using a client-side script. This class is comprised of two methods: login and logout. Whereas the login method allows you to validate the user's credentials, the logout method clears the forms authentication cookie in order to log the user out.

4. You can enable authentication service as shown in the following code snippet:

```
<system.web.extensions>
  <scripting>
    <webServices>
      <authenticationService enabled="true" />
    </webServices>
  </scripting>
</system.web.extensions>
```

Note that you should enable forms authentication for your application before using authentication service.

Working with Profile Service Using ASP.NET Ajax

What You'll Learn in This Hour:

▶ An overview of the ASP.NET profile service

▶ Defining a Profile Section

▶ Working with the profile service in ASP.NET Ajax

The ASP.NET profile object can be used to store profile information for both authenticated and anonymous users. You can use it to store a user's profile information for subsequent visits to the web application. Both authentication and profile services are part of the ASP.NET Ajax Extensions Library. These are available as classes named Sys.Services.AuthenticationService and Sys.Services.ProfileService in the ASP.NET Ajax Extensions Library. We discussed how we can use the authentication service in the previous hour.

Working with the Profile Service

In this section, we will explore the profile service and learn how to use it in our application.

Enabling the Profile Service

To enable the profile service for your Ajax-enabled ASP.NET application, specify the following in the application's web.config file:

```
<system.web.extensions>
  <scripting>
    <webServices>
      <profileService enabled="true" />
```

```
      </webServices>
    </scripting>
  </system.web.extensions>
```

In the preceding code snippet, notice how the profile service has been set on using the `profileService` attribute.

Defining the Profile Section

You can use the `<profile>` section inside the `<system.web.extensions>` section of the application's `web.config` file to define your profile properties. Here is the simplest example of how you can use the `<profile>` section:

```
<profile enabled="true">
          <properties>
              <add name="FirstAuthor" defaultValue="Joydip Kanjilal"
➥type="string"
                    allowAnonymous="true" />
              <add name="SecondAuthor" defaultValue="Sriram Putrevu"
➥type="string"
                    allowAnonymous="true" />
          </properties>
      </profile>
```

You can also use groups to group your profile information. The code snippet that follows illustrates how this can be achieved:

```
<profile enabled="true">
<add name=" Backgroundcolor" type="System.String"
     defaultValue="white" />
  <add name=" Foregroundcolor" type="System.String"
     defaultValue="blue" />
        <properties>
        <group name="Address">
          <add name="Address1" type="string"/>
          <add name="Address2" type="string"/>
          <add name="City" type="string"/>
          <add name="State" type="string"/>
          <add name="PinCode" type="string"/>
          <add name="Country" type="string"/>
        </group>
        <group name="Contact">
          <add name="Name" type="string"/>
          <add name="Address" type="string"/>
          <add name="Phone" type="string"/>
          <add name="Mobile" type="string"/>
        </group>
        </properties>
      </profile>
```

Implementing a Sample Application

In this section, we implement a sample application that will make use of the profiling service using Ajax. The application also will make use of the authentication service to authenticate users. After a user is authenticated, then the profile information of the user is stored in a database and retrieved later when it is needed.

To implement this application, follow these steps:

1. Open Visual Studio 2005 and create a new Ajax-enabled web site named AJAXProfileService.

2. Similar to what we did in the previous hour, switch to the ASP.NET configuration from the solution explorer. This opens up the Website Administration Tool of this web site.

3. Go to the Security tab of this tool. In the Users sections, click the link Select Authentication Type. The user is prompted to select either the option From the Internet or From a Local Network. Select the option From the Internet because we will be using a database and click the Done button.

4. Click the link Create User in the Users section and create a user named joydip with the password joydip@24h. Create another user called sriram and set the password for this user as sriram@24h. This information is stored in the SQL Server Express database on the local server. After you create the user, you can find this database ASPNETDB.MDF in the App_data folder of the solution, as shown in Figure 16.1.

FIGURE 16.1
ASPNETDB.MDF database in the App_Date folder

5. Now, we go ahead and create an authentication service that overrides the default one of ASP.NET Ajax. The first step toward creating this service is to enable the authentication service by adding the following to the web.config file:

```
<system.web.extensions>
  <scripting>
```

```
    <webServices>
      <authenticationService enabled="true" />
    </webServices>
  </scripting>
</system.web.extensions>
```

6. Next, add the following section to the application's web.config file to enable
   forms authentication:

```
<system.web>
  <authentication mode="Forms">
    <forms cookieless="UseCookies"
          loginUrl="~/login.aspx"/>
  </authentication>
<system.web>
```

7. Add the web service name to the ScriptManager control to perform the
   authentication asynchronously from the client script. The ScriptManager control has a property called AuthenticationService. Set the value of its Path
   attribute to the name of the web service. In this case, the web service name is
   Authenticate.asmx. The following is the markup code for this:

```
<asp:ScriptManager ID="ScriptManager1" runat="server" >
        <AuthenticationService Path="Authenticate.asmx" />
      </asp:ScriptManager>
```

8. Create the web service Authenticate.asmx and implement the methods
   Login and Logout to perform the authentication. The authenticate web service class should use the ScriptService attribute to implement authentication. The following is the code for this web service:

```
using System;
using System.Web;
using System.Collections;
using System.Web.Services;
using System.Web.Services.Protocols;
using System.Web.Script.Services;
using System.Web.Security;
/// <summary>
/// Summary description for Authenticate
/// </summary>
[WebService(Namespace = "http://tempuri.org/")]
[WebServiceBinding(ConformsTo = WsiProfiles.BasicProfile1_1)]
[ScriptService]
public class Authenticate : System.Web.Services.WebService {
    public Authenticate () {
        //Uncomment the following line if using designed components
            //InitializeComponent();
    }
    [WebMethod]
    public bool Login(string userName, string password, bool
➥createPersistentCookie)
    {
```

```
            if (Membership.Provider.ValidateUser(userName, password))
            {
                FormsAuthentication.SetAuthCookie(userName,
    ➥createPersistentCookie);
                return true;
            }
            return false;
        }
        [WebMethod]
        public void Logout()
        {
            FormsAuthentication.SignOut();
        }
    }
```

9. The Login method has three arguments: username, password, and createPersistentCookie. This method validates the user using the ASP.NET Membership API, creates a cookie using forms authentication upon successful validation, and sends this cookie back to the browser. This cookie will be used for subsequent requests from the browser.

   The Logout method signs out the user from the system and clears the cookie from the client browser.

10. Let's first define the profile section we will use. We define this in the application's web.config file. Here is the profile section that we will use:

```
<profile enabled="true">
                        <properties>
                            <add name="Backgroundcolor" type="string"
    ➥defaultValue="white" />
                            <group name="Contact">
                                <add name="FirstName" type="string" />
                                <add name="LastName" type="string" />
                                <add name="Age" type="int"/>
                                <add name="Email" type="string"/>
                            </group>
                            <group name="Address">
                                <add name="Street" type="string" />
                                <add name="City" type="string"/>
                                <add name="PostalCode" type="string"
    />
                            </group>
                        </properties>
                </profile>
```

11. By default, the <ProfileService> section would be commented under the <webServices> section in web.config file. Uncomment this section and overwrite the section with the following:

```
<profileService enabled="true"
```

```
readAccessProperties="Backgroundcolor,Contact.FirstName,
➥Contact.Lastname,Contact.Age,Contact.Email,Address.Street,
➥Address.City,Address.PostalCode"
                        writeAccessProperties="Backgroundcolor,
➥Contact.FirstName,Contact.Lastname,Contact.Age,Contact.Email,
➥Address.Street,Address.City,Address.PostalCode" />
```

The `ProfileService` section has two attributes—`readAccessProperties` and `writeAccessProperties`. These attributes hold the values defined in the `<property>` tab as discussed in step 10. In essence, we are setting the properties that have read or write access.

12. The following is the markup code in the `Default.aspx` file that we will use to display and save the profiling information:

```
<body onload="javascript:document.getElementById('txtUsername').focus();">
    <form id="form1" runat="server">
        <asp:ScriptManager ID="ScriptManager1" runat="server" >
            <AuthenticationService Path="Authenticate.asmx" />
        </asp:ScriptManager>
        <div>
            <p>
                Profile Service using ASP.NET AJAX</p>
        </div>
        <div id="divLogin">
            Username :
            <input type="text" id="txtUsername"/><br />
            Password :
            <input type="password" id="txtPassword" /><br />
            <button id="btnLogin" onclick="Login_OnClick(); return
➥false;">Login</button>
        </div>
        <div id="divHome" style="display: none">
            You have successfully logged in to the system !!<br /><br />
            <button id="btnLogout" onclick="Logout_OnClick(); return
➥false;">Logout</button>
        </div><br />
        <div id="divProfile" style="display: none">
        <table>
        <tr>
            <td align="center" colspan="2" style="font-size:large;font-
weight:
➥bold">Your Profile</td>
        </tr>
        <tr>
            <td align="center" colspan="2">Contact Information</td>
        </tr>
        <tr>
            <td>First Name: </td>
            <td><input type="text" id="txtFirstName" /></td>
        </tr>
        <tr>
            <td>Last Name: </td>
            <td><input type="text" id="txtLastName" /></td>
        </tr>
        <tr>
```

```
        <td>Age: </td>
        <td><input type="text" id="txtAge" /></td>
    </tr>
    <tr>
        <td>Email: </td>
        <td><input type="text" id="txtEmail" /></td>
    </tr>
    <tr>
        <td align="center" colspan="2">Address Information</td>
    </tr>
    <tr>
        <td>Street: </td>
        <td><input type="text" id="txtStreet" /></td>
    </tr>
    <tr>
        <td>City: </td>
        <td><input type="text" id="txtCity" /></td>
    </tr>
    <tr>
        <td>Postal Code: </td>
        <td><input type="text" id="txtPostalCode" /></td>
    </tr>
    <tr>
        <td colspan="2"> </td>
    </tr>
    <tr>
        <td>Backgroundcolor: </td>
        <td><input type="text" id="txtBackgroundcolor" /></td>
    </tr>
    <tr>
        <td align="center" colspan="2"><input type="button"
➥id="btnSaveProfile" value="Save Profile" onclick="SaveProfile();" /></td>
    </tr>
    </table>
    </div>
    </form>
</body>
```

13. Next, we use the necessary scripts to call the authentication and the profile services. Here are the scripts:

```
<script language="javascript" type="text/javascript">
        function Login_OnClick()
        {
            if (document.getElementById("txtUsername").value == "")
            {
                alert("Please enter Username.");
                document.getElementById("txtUsername").focus();
                return;
            }
            if (document.getElementById("txtPassword").value == "")
            {
                alert("Please enter Password.");
                document.getElementById("txtPassword").focus();
                return;
            }
```

```
                    Sys.Services.AuthenticationService.set_
➥defaultLoginCompletedCallback(OnLoginCompleted);
                    Sys.Services.AuthenticationService.set_
➥defaultFailedCallback(OnFailed);
                    Sys.Services.AuthenticationService.set_
➥defaultLogoutCompletedCallback(OnLogoutCompleted);
                    Sys.Services.AuthenticationService.login
➥ (document.getElementById("txtUsername").value,
➥document.getElementById("txtPassword").value,
➥false,null,null,null,null,"User Context");
                return;
        }
        function Logout_OnClick()
        {
                Sys.Services.AuthenticationService.logout(null, null, null,
null);
        }
        function OnLoginCompleted(validCredentials, userContext,
methodName)
        {
            if (validCredentials == true)
            {
                document.getElementById("divLogin").style.display = 'none';
                document.getElementById("divHome").style.display = 'block';
                document.getElementById("divProfile").style.display =
'block';
                LoadProfile();
            }
            else
            {
                alert("Invalid Login credentials !");
                document.getElementById("txtUsername").focus();
            }
            return;
        }

        function OnFailed(error, userContext, methodName)
        {
            alert("Unable to log in to the site. Details : " +
➥error.get_message() + ". " + error.get_statusCode());
            return;
        }
        function OnLogoutCompleted(result)
        {
            document.getElementById("divLogin").style.display = 'block';
            document.getElementById("divHome").style.display = 'none';
            document.getElementById("divProfile").style.display = 'none';
            return;
        }
        //Profiling in AJAX
        function LoadProfile()
        {
                Sys.Services.ProfileService.load(null,
➥OnLoadCompletedCallback, OnProfileFailedCallback, null);
        }
        // Reads the profile information and displays it.
        function OnLoadCompletedCallback(numProperties, userContext,
➥methodName)
```

```
        {
                // Get Contact Information.
                document.getElementById("txtFirstName").value =
➥Sys.Services.ProfileService.properties.Contact.FirstName;
                document.getElementById("txtLastName").value =
➥Sys.Services.ProfileService.properties.Contact.LastName;
                document.getElementById("txtAge").value =
➥Sys.Services.ProfileService.properties.Contact.Age;
                document.getElementById("txtEmail").value=
➥Sys.Services.ProfileService.properties.Contact.Email;
                // Get Address Information.
                document.getElementById("txtStreet").value =
➥Sys.Services.ProfileService.properties.Address.Street;
                document.getElementById("txtCity").value =
➥Sys.Services.ProfileService.properties.Address.City;
                document.getElementById("txtPostalCode").value =
➥ Sys.Services.ProfileService.properties.Address.PostalCode;
                // Get Backgroundcolor.
                document.getElementById("txtBackgroundcolor").value =
➥Sys.Services.ProfileService.properties.Backgroundcolor;
                document.body.bgColor =
➥Sys.Services.ProfileService.properties.Backgroundcolor;
        }
        function OnProfileFailedCallback(error_object, userContext,
➥methodName)
        {
                alert("Profile service failed. Details : " + error_
➥object.get_message());
        }
        function SaveProfile()
        {
                // Set Contact Information.
                Sys.Services.ProfileService.properties.Contact.FirstName =
➥document.getElementById("txtFirstName").value;
                Sys.Services.ProfileService.properties.Contact.LastName =
➥document.getElementById("txtLastName").value;
                Sys.Services.ProfileService.properties.Contact.Age =
➥document.getElementById("txtAge").value;
                Sys.Services.ProfileService.properties.Contact.Email =
➥document.getElementById("txtEmail").value;
                // Set Address Information.
                Sys.Services.ProfileService.properties.Address.Street =
➥document.getElementById("txtStreet").value;
                Sys.Services.ProfileService.properties.Address.City =
➥document.getElementById("txtCity").value;
                Sys.Services.ProfileService.properties.Address.PostalCode =
➥document.getElementById("txtPostalCode").value;
                // Set Backgroundcolor.
                Sys.Services.ProfileService.properties.Backgroundcolor =
➥document.getElementById("txtBackgroundcolor").value;

                // Save profile information.
                Sys.Services.ProfileService.save(null, OnSaveCompletedCallback,
➥OnProfileFailedCallback, null);
        }

        // This is the callback function called
        // if the profile was saved successfully.
```

```
function OnSaveCompletedCallback(numProperties, userContext,
➥methodName)
    {
        alert("User Profile saved successfully !");
        LoadProfile();
    }
</script>
```

After the user clicks Login, the `Sys.Services.AuthenticationService` class
sets the default callback events for the `OnLoginCompleted`, `OnFailed`, and
`OnLogoutCompleted` methods. It then calls the login service by passing the
user credentials. The `ScriptManager` control generates the authentication
service and emits it to the browser and then manages the entire authentication process. In this example, the `OnLoginCompleted` method verifies the credentials, hides the Login controls contained in a <div> tag called `divLogin`,
and displays a `divHome` block containing the message, "You have successfully
logged in to the system!!" Upon clicking the Logout button, the
`Sys.Services.AuthenticationService.logout` method is called, which logs
out the user from the application. In addition, the callback event
`OnLogoutCompleted` is called, which displays the block `divLogin`. In case of
failure of the Login or Logout operations, the `OnFailed` method is called,
which alerts the user with the error message.

After the user has been successfully logged in, the `LoadProfile()` method is
called. Here is the source code of this method:

```
function LoadProfile()
    {
        Sys.Services.ProfileService.load(null, OnLoadCompletedCallback,
➥OnProfileFailedCallback, null);
    }
```

14. The `OnLoadCompletedCallback` handler, which is invoked from within the
`LoadProfile()` method, loads the default profile information, as follows:

```
// Reads the profile information and displays it.
    function OnLoadCompletedCallback(numProperties, userContext,
➥methodName)
        {
            // Get Contact Information.
            document.getElementById("txtFirstName").value =
➥Sys.Services.ProfileService.properties.Contact.FirstName;
            document.getElementById("txtLastName").value =
➥Sys.Services.ProfileService.properties.Contact.LastName;
            document.getElementById("txtAge").value =
➥Sys.Services.ProfileService.properties.Contact.Age;
            document.getElementById("txtEmail").value=
➥Sys.Services.ProfileService.properties.Contact.Email;
            // Get Address Information.
```

```
        document.getElementById("txtStreet").value =
➥Sys.Services.ProfileService.properties.Address.Street;
        document.getElementById("txtCity").value =
➥Sys.Services.ProfileService.properties.Address.City;
        document.getElementById("txtPostalCode").value =
➥Sys.Services.ProfileService.properties.Address.PostalCode;
        // Get Backgroundcolor.
        document.getElementById("txtBackgroundcolor").value =
➥Sys.Services.ProfileService.properties.Backgroundcolor;
        document.body.bgColor =
➥Sys.Services.ProfileService.properties.Backgroundcolor;
    }
```

15. When you execute the application, the default profile information is used. The
output is shown in Figure 16.2.

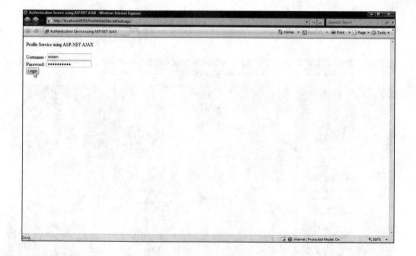

FIGURE 16.2
The application
at work!

Now, log in to the system using the username and password for the user sriram. After logging in, the default profile is used, as shown in Figure 16.3.

Change the profile information and click Save. After you change the profile
information and save it, the SaveProfile() method gets called, which saves
the profile information in the database. Figure 16.4 shows what the output
looks like now. Note that the background color for the user sriram has been
changed from the default white to blue.

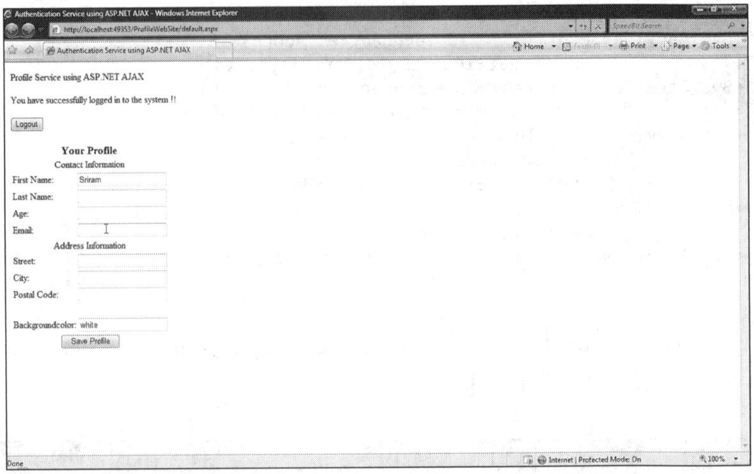

FIGURE 16.3
Successful login

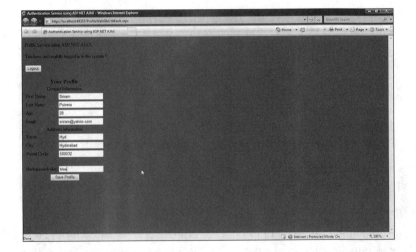

FIGURE 16.4
Profile saved

Here is the source code of the SaveProfile() method:

```
function SaveProfile()
        {
            // Set Contact Information.
            Sys.Services.ProfileService.properties.Contact.FirstName =
➥document.getElementById("txtFirstName").value;
            Sys.Services.ProfileService.properties.Contact.LastName =
➥ document.getElementById("txtLastName").value;
            Sys.Services.ProfileService.properties.Contact.Age =
➥document.getElementById("txtAge").value;
            Sys.Services.ProfileService.properties.Contact.Email =
➥document.getElementById("txtEmail").value;
            // Set Address Information.
```

```
            Sys.Services.ProfileService.properties.Address.Street =
➥ document.getElementById("txtStreet").value;
            Sys.Services.ProfileService.properties.Address.City =
➥document.getElementById("txtCity").value;
            Sys.Services.ProfileService.properties.Address.PostalCode =
➥document.getElementById("txtPostalCode").value;
            // Set Backgroundcolor.
            Sys.Services.ProfileService.properties.Backgroundcolor =
➥document.getElementById("txtBackgroundcolor").value;
            // Save profile information.
            Sys.Services.ProfileService.save(null, OnSaveCompletedCallback,
➥OnProfileFailedCallback, null);
        }
```

Summary

This hour has examined how we can use the profile service in our Ajax-enabled
ASP.NET web applications. It started with an overview of the ASP.NET Ajax profile
service available as a class named `Sys.Services.ProfileService` in the ASP.NET
Ajax Extensions Library. In the next hour we will examine the ASP.NET Ajax
authentication service.

Workshop

Quiz

1. Where are the authentication and the profile service in the Ajax Library available?

2. What is the purpose of the ASP.NET profile object?

3. How do you enable the profile service?

4. How can you define profile information using groups to group the profile data?

Answers

1. Both authentication and profile services are part of the ASP.NET Ajax
   Extensions Library. These are available as classes named
   `Sys.Services.AuthenticationService` and `Sys.Services.ProfileService`
   in the ASP.NET Ajax Extensions Library.

2. The ASP.NET profile object can be used to store profile information for both authenticated and anonymous users. You can use it to store a user's profile information for subsequent visits to the web application.

3. To enable the profile service for your Ajax-enabled ASP.NET application, specify the following in the application's `web.config` file:

```
<system.web.extensions>
  <scripting>
    <webServices>
      <profileService enabled="true" />
    </webServices>
  </scripting>
</system.web.extensions>
```

4. You can also use groups to group your profile information. The code snippet that follows illustrates how this can be achieved:

```
<profile enabled="true">
<add name=" Backgroundcolor" type="System.String"
     defaultValue="white" />
  <add name=" Foregroundcolor" type="System.String"
     defaultValue="blue" />
        <properties>
        <group name="Address">
          <add name="Address1" type="string"/>
          <add name="Address2" type="string"/>
          <add name="City" type="string"/>
          <add name="State" type="string"/>
          <add name="PinCode" type="string"/>
          <add name="Country" type="string"/>
        </group>
        <group name="Contact">
          <add name="Name" type="string"/>
          <add name="Address" type="string"/>
          <add name="Phone" type="string"/>
          <add name="Mobile" type="string"/>
        </group>
      </properties>
    </profile>
```

Extending the Microsoft Ajax Library

What You'll Learn in This Hour:

▶ Creating a custom client control by extending the Microsoft Ajax Library

▶ Using the custom client control in our application

▶ Extending the Microsoft Ajax Library

In the last two hours, we discussed how we can work with authentication and profiling services using Ajax. In this hour, we will learn how we can extend the Microsoft Ajax Library to add new functionalities to it.

How Do You Extend the Microsoft Ajax Library?

So what are the ways to extend the Microsoft Ajax Library? The Microsoft Ajax Library provides you with three ways in which you can extend the Library:

▶ Nonvisual controls that extend the Sys.Component class

▶ Visual controls that extend the Sys.UI.Control class

▶ Behaviors that extend the Sys.UI.Behavior class

Both Sys.UI.Behavior and Sys.UI.Control classes extend the Sys.Component base class.

By the Way

Components are nonvisual—that is, they have no UI representation and extend the Sys.Component base class. A typical example is the Timer control. You know that it is working at regular intervals of time, but it is not visible on your web page—it doesn't have any UI representation. Other examples are the Application and the Validator controls.

Controls are visual and represent a DOM element; they are derived from the Control class, which in turn is derived from the Component base class.

Behaviors extend the Behavior class, which also extends the Component base class, and are used to extend the behavior of DOM elements by adding functionalities to them.

Figure 17.1 shows how these classes are related to each other.

FIGURE 17.1
Relationship between Component, Control, and the Behavior classes

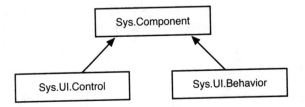

Extending the Ajax Library Using Components

In this section, we discuss how we can create a nonvisual client component by extending the Sys.Component base class. Essentially, any nonvisual client component in Ajax contains JavaScript. When you derive from the Sys.Component base class to create your custom component, you inherit some features by default, such as the features covered next.

Creating the Custom Client Component

Here is how you register the namespace. In our example, the namespace used is AjaxSTYSeries:

```
Type.registerNamespace("AjaxSTYSeries");
```

Let's now define our sample component:

```
AjaxSTYSeries.MyComponent = function()
{
    AjaxSTYSeries.MyComponent.initializeBase(this);
    this._myProp = 0;
}
```

> Note that the `initializeBase` method is called on the custom component and the current instance of the custom component—that is, this is passed to it as a parameter. This is done for default initialization purposes.

By the
Way

We now create a prototype and a get and set accessor for a property that can be used to get or set values for our property. We also write our custom method called MyMethod that displays an alert box:

```
AjaxSTYSeries.MyComponent.prototype =
{
    SetMyprop: function(myNumber)
    {
        this._myProp = myNumber;
    },

    GetMyprop: function()
    {
        return this._myProp;
    },
    MyMethod: function()
    {
        alert('This is a component method.');
    }
}
```

Now, you need to declare the base class from which our custom client component will derive. The base class for all components is Sys.Component, so we will invoke the `inheritsFrom` method to declare the name of the class from which our custom client component inherits. Here is how you do this:

```
AjaxSTYSeries.MyComponent.inheritsFrom(Sys.Component);
```

The next step is registering the client component class. This can be done by making a call to the `registerClass` method on the component instance, as shown here:

```
AjaxSTYSeries.MyComponent.registerClass('AjaxSTYSeries.MyComponent',
➥Sys.Component);
```

The next step is initializing the base class from within the constructor. Here is how the constructor of our custom client component initializes its base—that is, the Sys.Component class:

```
STYAjaxSeries.MyComponent = function()
{
    STYAjaxSeries.MyComponent.initializeBase(this);
}
```

The following is the complete source code of our custom client component class:

```
Type.registerNamespace("AjaxSTYSeries");

AjaxSTYSeries.MyComponent = function()
{
    AjaxSTYSeries.MyComponent.initializeBase(this);
    this._var = 0;
}
AjaxSTYSeries.MyComponent.prototype =
{
    SetValue: function(_value)
    {
        this._var = _value;
    },

    GetValue: function()
    {
        return this._var;
    }
}
AjaxSTYSeries.MyComponent.inheritsFrom(Sys.Component);
AjaxSTYSeries.MyComponent.registerClass('AjaxSTYSeries.MyComponent',
➥Sys.Component);
```

Create a file called MyControl.js and place the preceding code in that file.

Using the Custom Client Component

Now that we are done creating our custom client control, let's discuss how we can use it in our application.

To use the control, you need to do the following:

▶ Register the script library for the control.

▶ Create an instance of the component and use the control.

You can register the script for our custom client control using the ScriptReference element of the ScriptManager control, as shown here:

```
<form id="form1" runat="server">
  <asp:ScriptManager runat="server" ID="ScriptManager1">
    <scripts>
      <asp:ScriptReference path="MyControl.js" />
    </scripts>
  </asp:ScriptManager>
</form>
```

By the Way

If your script is embedded in an assembly, you should specify the name of the assembly when referencing the script using the `ScriptManager` control's `ScriptReference` attribute, as shown in the following code:

```
<asp:ScriptManager ID="ScriptManager1" runat="server">
  <Scripts>
    <asp:ScriptReference
        Name="MyControls.js" Assembly="STYAjaxSeries"/>
  </Scripts>
</asp:ScriptManager>
```

Here is how you can instantiate and use the control in your application:

```
<script type="text/javascript">
var myControlObject;
function pageLoad(sender, args){
    myControlObject = new STYAjaxSeries.MyControl();
    myControlObject.SetValue(100);
}
</script>
```

Next, we take a `Button` control in our web form and click event handler. We call a method that retrieves the value we passed earlier using the set accessor.

The following is the markup code for the button control:

```
<input id="btnClick" type="button" value="Click Here" onclick="return
btnClick_Onclick()" />
```

Here is how we invoke the `GetMyprop` method on the custom control instance to retrieve the value we passed earlier:

```
function btnClick_Onclick()
{
    var valueReturned = myControlObject.GetValue();
    alert("The value returned is: "+valueReturned);
}
```

The following is the complete markup code to use the control we just created:

```
<script type="text/javascript">
var myControlObject;
function pageLoad(sender, args)
{
    myControlObject = new AjaxSTYSeries.MyComponent();
    myControlObject.SetValue(100);
}

function btnClick_Onclick()
{
    var valueReturned = myControlObject.GetValue();
    alert("The value returned is: "+valueReturned);
}
```

```
</script>

    <title>Implementing a Custom Client Control</title>
</head>
<body>
    <form id="form1" runat="server">
    <asp:ScriptManager runat="server" ID="ScriptManager1">
      <scripts>
        <asp:ScriptReference path="MyControl.js" />
      </scripts>
    </asp:ScriptManager>
    <input id="btnClick" type="button" value="Click Here"
➥onclick="return btnClick_Onclick()" />
    </form>
</body>
```

When you execute the application, the output is similar to what is shown in Figure 17.2.

FIGURE 17.2
Implementing the Custom Control

Now when you click on the Button control, the alert box is displayed with the message "The value returned is: 100" (see Figure 17.3).

FIGURE 17.3
The Custom Control at Work!

You can include the following statement at the end of each script file so that the script files can be processed correctly by the ScriptManager control:

```
if (typeof(Sys) !== 'undefined') Sys.Application.notifyScriptLoaded();
```

Extending the Ajax Library Using Controls

The Ajax Library enables you to create your own custom control by extending the Control base class. The following is the sequence of steps that you need to follow to do this:

1. Register the control's namespace.

   Registering a namespace is simple; just call the registerNamespace method, as shown here:

   ```
   Type.registerNamespace("STYAjax");
   ```

2. Inherit from the Control base class.

   You can specify the base class from which your custom control inherits, as shown here:

   ```
   AjaxSTYSeries.MyControl.inheritsFrom(Sys.UI.Control);
   ```

3. Initialize the base class in the control's constructor.

4. Implement the prototype pattern to override Initialize, Dispose, and the other methods and properties.

5. Register the control. Here is how you can register your control:

   ```
   STYAjax.MyControl.registerClass("STYAjax.MyControl", Sys.UI.Control);
   if (typeof(Sys) !== 'undefined') Sys.Application.notifyScriptLoaded();
   ```

After the custom control is registered, it is ready for use in your application. Here is the complete code structure for the custom control. Note that the methods and the properties sections have been kept blank:

```
Type.registerNamespace('STYAjax');
STYAjax.MyControl = function()
{
    // Specify the properties of the class here.
}
STYAjax.MyControl.prototype =
{
    // Specify the methods of the class here.
}
STYAjax.MyControl.registerClass('STYAjax.MyControl');
```

Here is how you can instantiate and use the custom control in your application.

You can create an instance of your control in the web page by calling the `Sys.Application.create` (or the `$create` statement as a shortcut) method in the init event of the web page. Here is how you can add a handler called `OnInit` for the init event of your web page:

```
Sys.Application.add_init(onInit);
```

Be sure that your ScriptManager control references the script file where you have placed the control's code, as follows:

```
<asp:ScriptManager id="ScriptManager1" runat="Server">
    <Scripts>
        <asp:ScriptReference Path="MyControl.js" />
    </Scripts>
</asp:ScriptManager>
```

Extending the Ajax Library Using Behaviors

You can also add new functionalities to an existing control by attaching behaviors. Behaviors can be used to provide more elegant user interfaces with added functionalities. Behaviors generally respond to user interaction or events. You can now implement cross browser-compliant behaviors and attach them to a control seamlessly.

Summary

In this hour, we explored the ways to extend the Microsoft Ajax Library to add new functionalities to it. We discussed how we can extend the Microsoft Ajax Library in all three possible ways: using components, controls, and behaviors using sample programs wherever applicable. The next hour discusses how we can implement localization and globalization using ASP.NET Ajax.

Workshop

Quiz

1. What are the possible ways in which you can extend the Microsoft Ajax Library?

2. List the sequence of steps that should be followed for creating a custom control by extending the Ajax Library.

3. How do you reference an external script file in the `ScriptManager` control?

4. How do you specify that your custom control inherits from `Sys.UI.Control` class?

5. What are behaviors?

Answers

1. The Microsoft Ajax Library can be extended in three ways, as follows:

   ▶ Nonvisual controls that extend the `Sys.Component` class

   ▶ Visual controls that extend the `Sys.UI.Control` class

   ▶ Behaviors that extend the `Sys.UI.Behavior` class

2. The sequence of steps is as follows:

   1. Register the control's namespace.

   2. Inherit from the `Control` base class.

   3. Initialize the base class in the control's constructor.

   4. Implement the prototype pattern to override Initialize, Dispose, and the other methods and properties.

   5. Register the control.

3. To refer to an external script file using the ScriptManager control, use the `ScriptReference` attribute of the control, as shown in the following code snippet:

```
<asp:ScriptManager id="ScriptManager1" runat="Server">
    <Scripts>
        <asp:ScriptReference Path="MyControl.js" />
    </Scripts>
</asp:ScriptManager>
```

4. You can specify the base class from which your custom control inherits, as follows:

```
AjaxSTYSeries.MyControl.inheritsFrom(Sys.UI.Control);
```

   In this statement, `AjaxSTYSeries` is the namespace and `MyControl` is the name of a custom control class that inherits the `Sys.UI.Control` class.

5. Behaviors are used to add new functionalities to an existing control and provide a more elegant user interface with added functionalities in it.

Implementing Localization and Globalization Using ASP.NET Ajax

---

What You'll Learn in This Hour:

▶ An overview of localization and globalization

▶ The System.Globalization namespace

▶ The role of the ScriptManager control in localization and globalization

▶ Embedding JavaScript resources in an assembly

In this hour, we discuss localization and globalization and how we can implement them in ASP.NET Ajax applications. There are times when you need to internationalize your application so that it can support different locales. Microsoft .NET provides excellent support for implementing multilingual applications—that is, applications that support different locales. In this context, we need to discuss resource files, satellite assemblies, localization, globalization, and so on. Don't be confused by these concepts; we explore each of them as we move ahead in this hour. In this hour, we discuss these and related concepts and then implement an application that supports different locales using ASP.NET Ajax.

Understanding Localization and Globalization

Localization and globalization are often misunderstood terms; it is easy to get confused and relate one to the other. More often than not, we assume that both mean the same thing. They are distinct concepts, however, and there are subtle differences between them. Let's now discuss what each of these terms implies. *Localization* is defined as the process of adapting an application for a specific locale. You use *localization* to create and configure your application to support a specific language or locale. *Globalization*, on the other hand, is defined as the process of identifying the specific portion or portions of the application that should be different based on the language it is meant for, and identifying how those portions can be isolated from the application's core. In essence, globalization is the process of identifying the resources that need to be localized in application to suit it for the locale it is meant for.

The Microsoft .NET Library provides support for globalization and localization using the System.Globalization and System.Resources namespaces.

The System.Globalization namespace provides support for developing multilingual applications in Microsoft .NET by allowing the developers to define culture-specific information. The sections that follow discuss cultures and how to work with them in .NET. The System.Resources namespace provides support for creating, storing, and managing various culture-specific resources used in an application. It contains a class called ResourceManager that allows access to resources either from the main assembly or those that are present in satellite assemblies.

> You can store text specific to a particular culture in resource files. When you compile the resource files (files having .resx extensions), compiled resources files are generated. These files have .resources extensions. So a resource file named Test.resx generates a compiled resource file called Test.resources when it is compiled.

The default language setting in your browser is English. You can change this to French (or another language) by changing the language settings of the browser. This is discussed later in this chapter. Now, ASP.NET Ajax supports localization and globalization through one of the properties of the ScriptManager control, called EnableScriptGlobalization. This property is set to false by default. Here is how you can set it to true and implement script globalization in your Ajax-enabled ASP.NET applications:

```
<asp:ScriptManager ID="ScriptManager1" runat="server"
➡EnableScriptLocalization="true" EnableScriptGlobalization="true">
```

We now make use of this property to display localized strings in the client side.

If you set the EnableScriptGlobalization to true, the localeFormat() method will send strings to the client side based on the locale you have selected. Let's now implement a simple application that will demonstrate how the localeFormat() method can be used to display a currency and the current date in different locales. To create this application, follow these steps:

1. Create a new ASP.NET Ajax web site.

2. Open the `Default.aspx` file that is created by default.

3. Switch to the design view of the `Default.aspx` file.

4. Drag and drop a ScriptManager control and two Button controls from the tool-box.

   The following is the markup code of the `Default.aspx` file after you insert the controls discussed earlier:

```
<body>
    <form id="form1" runat="server">
    <div>
        <asp:ScriptManager ID="ScriptManager1" runat="server"
➥EnableScriptLocalization="true" EnableScriptGlobalization="true">
        </asp:ScriptManager>
        <asp:Button ID="Button1" runat="server"/>
        <asp:Button ID="Button2" runat="server"/>
    </div>
    </form>
</body>
```

5. Now, add events corresponding to each of the buttons in the `OnClientClick` event:

```
<asp:ScriptManager ID="ScriptManager1" runat="server"
➥EnableScriptLocalization="true" EnableScriptGlobalization="true">
</asp:ScriptManager>
<asp:Button ID="Button1" runat="server"
➥OnClientClick="return DisplayCurrency();"  Text="Click Me"/>
<asp:Button ID="Button2" runat="server" OnClientClick="return
DisplayDate();"
➥Text="Get Today's Date"/>
```

   Here are the two JavaScript methods, `DisplayCurrency()` and `DisplayDate()`:

```
function DisplayCurrency()
{
alert(String.localeFormat("{0:c}", 12345678.90));
return false;
}
function DisplayDate()
{
alert(String.localeFormat("{0:dddd, dd MMMM yyyy hh:mm:ss tt}", new
Date()));
return false;
}
```

Place these JavaScript methods in the same `.aspx` file where you have your
ScriptManager control. When you do this, the complete markup code in the `.aspx`
file looks like this:

```
<head runat="server">
    <title>Implementing Internationalization Using ASP.NET Ajax</title>
    <script language ="javascript" type="text/javascript">
    function DisplayCurrency()
    {
        alert(String.localeFormat("{0:c}", 12345678.90));
        return false;
    }
    function DisplayDate()
    {
        alert(String.localeFormat("{0:dddd, dd MMMM yyyy hh:mm:ss tt}",
    ➥new Date()));
        return false;
    }

    </script>
</head>
<body>
    <form id="form1" runat="server">
    <div>
        <asp:ScriptManager ID="ScriptManager1" runat="server"
    ➥EnableScriptLocalization="true" EnableScriptGlobalization="true">
        </asp:ScriptManager>
        <asp:Button ID="Button1" runat="server" OnClientClick="return
    ➥DisplayCurrency();"  Text="Click Me"/>
        <asp:Button ID="Button2" runat="server" OnClientClick="return
    ➥DisplayDate();"  Text="Get Today's Date"/>
    </div>
    </form>
</body>
```

You are done! After you execute the application, the output is similar to what is
shown in Figure 18.1.

FIGURE 18.1
Implementing
internationaliza-
tion using
ASP.NET Ajax

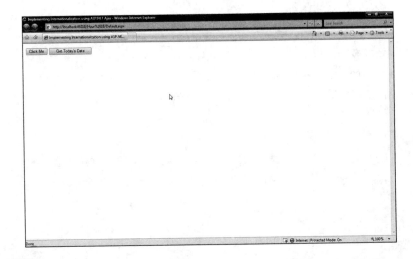

Now, when you click on the button to the right, the current date is displayed in a message box. The output is shown in Figure 18.2.

FIGURE 18.2
The Current Date displayed in the Default Locale

To change the language that is displayed, click Tools, Internet Options, Languages from the toolbar and select French (see Figure 18.3).

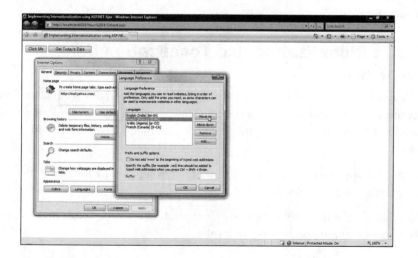

FIGURE 18.3
Changing the locale

Refresh the screen and click the same button control once again to see that the date is now displayed in French. The output is shown in Figure 18.4.

FIGURE 18.4
The current
date displayed
in French locale

Note that only the format of the date was changed, not the text. This is because we used String.localeFormat to display the date to the user in the alert message box. The texts used as captions of the Button controls have been set directly.

This was the easiest way of implementing localization in your applications. Note that the statement return false was used in each of the JavaScript methods to eliminate postbacks.

Script Globalization and Localization Using JavaScript

Let's take a look at how we can use JavaScript files to support different cultures and use them in our applications. This is a static model, where you need to create one JavaScript file per locale and use the files to display messages as per the locale selected.

Figure 18.5 displays the folder structure where we will place the JavaScript files that correspond to a specific locale.

Note that each of these JavaScript files corresponds to a specific locale and follows the standard naming convention for locales.

You need to set the `EnableScriptLocalization` and `EnableScriptGlobalization` properties of the `ScriptManager` control to true and specify the script reference path, as shown next:

```
<asp:ScriptReference Path="Scripts/Display.en-GB.js"
➥ResourceUICultures="en-GB" />
```

The `ScriptManager` control should be present on every web page that needs to leverage the benefits of Ajax. You can also use the `ScriptManager` control to define the UI or custom UI cultures that you would use. We will learn more about the role of the `ScriptManager` control later as we progress through this hour.

We will also add a `Button` control that will invoke the `DisplayText()` method when clicked. Here is the corresponding markup code:

```
<asp:Button ID="Button3" runat="server" OnClientClick="return DisplayText();"
➥Text="Click here"/>
```

The `DisplayText()` method in the `Display.en-GB.js` file is as follows:

```
function DisplayText()
{
  window.alert("This is in English - Great Britain");
  return false;
}
```

We will use the same method in the other `.js` files stored in the Scripts directory, but the text displayed will differ. Here is the `DisplayText()` method of the `Display.fr.js` file:

```
function DisplayText()
{
  window.alert("This is in French");
  return false;
}
```

Notice that the script reference path in the `ScriptManager` control's `ScriptReference` property has been set to the `Display.en-GB.js` file. This eventually implies that when the `Button` control is clicked, the `DisplayText()` method of the same file is called. The following is the complete markup code of the `ScriptManager` control:

```
<asp:ScriptManager ID="ScriptManager1" runat="server"
➥EnableScriptLocalization="true" EnableScriptGlobalization="true">
<Scripts>
<asp:ScriptReference Path="Scripts/Display.en-GB.js" ResourceUICultures="en-GB"
/>
</Scripts>
</asp:ScriptManager>
<asp:Button ID="Button3" runat="server" OnClientClick="return DisplayText();"
➥Text="Click here"/>
```

When you execute the application and click on the `Button` control, the output is similar to Figure 18.6.

FIGURE 18.6
Displaying
Message in
English

Now, change the script reference to point to the `Display.fr.js` as follows:

```
<asp:ScriptManager ID="ScriptManager1" runat="server"
➥EnableScriptLocalization="true" EnableScriptGlobalization="true">
<Scripts>
<asp:ScriptReference Path="Scripts/Display.fr.js" ResourceUICultures="fr-FR" />
</Scripts>
</asp:ScriptManager>
<asp:Button ID="Button3" runat="server" OnClientClick="return DisplayText();"
➥Text="Click here"/>
```

When you execute the application and click the Button control again, a different text is shown. Here is how the output looks this time (see Figure 18.7).

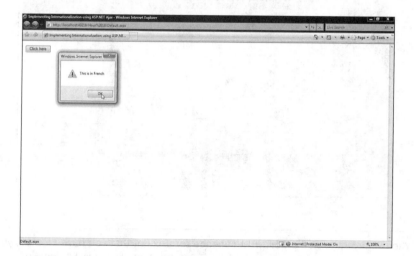

FIGURE 18.7
Displaying message in French

Embedding Script Resources in an Assembly

Script localization is a feature that enables you to specify texts in your JavaScript files based on a particular locale. Script globalization is used to format and parse your script text based on a specific culture. ASP.NET Ajax provides excellent support for script localization and globalization. In this section, we take a look at how these can be used in your applications.

Let's examine how we can create an assembly that contains an embedded JavaScript file. Here is the list of the steps that you need to follow to do this:

1. Create a class library project and name it LocalizationTest. You can do this by either adding a new project to your existing solution or creating a new web site and then adding the project to it (see Figure 18.8).

2. Next, add references to the System.Web and System.Web.Extensions assemblies.

FIGURE 18.8
Creating the
class library

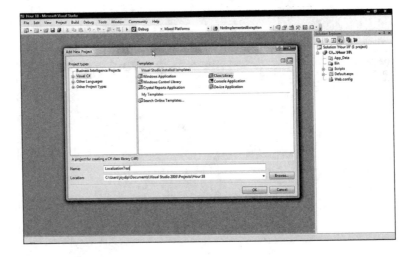

When you want to add a `ScriptReference` for a script that you have created, you should define the `WebResource` for this script. Incidentally, the `WebResource` attribute is present in the `System.Web.UI` namespace.

3. Now, create a new JScript file called `Message.js` and add the following code to it:

```
function DisplayMessage(var message)
{
   alert(message);
}
```

4. Set the build action to this JScript file to Embedded Resource by right-clicking it and setting the build action in its Properties window (see Figure 18.9).

5. Right-click the project that you have just created and add a resource file to it. Name this resource file `TestResource.resx`. Refer to Figure 18.10.

6. Set the build action of this resource to Embedded Resource, as shown in Figure 18.9.

FIGURE 18.9
Setting the build action to Embedded Resource

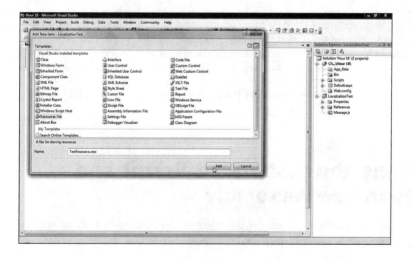

FIGURE 18.10
Adding the resource file to the project

7. Add text to this resource file, as shown in Figure 18.11.

FIGURE 18.11
Adding text to
the resource file

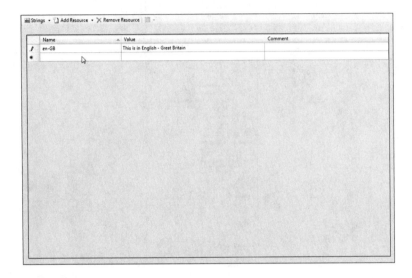

> Localized resources specific to a culture are defined using name/value pairs in
> the resource files. These files have `.resx` extensions. When compiled, these
> `.resx` files generate their `.resources` counterparts.

By the Way

8. Now save all files and build the project. The assembly named
`LocalizationTest.dll` is created.

Using the Embedded Script and Resource Assembly

Let's now discuss how we can use the assembly we just created in our applications.
To reference the assembly and use it in your applications, here are the steps that
you need to follow:

1. Add a new ASP.NET Ajax web site or use the existing one (if you have created
it already).

2. Create a bin folder to the root of the web site and add a reference to the
assembly you have created.

3. Create a new web page and add a `ScriptManager` control to it.

4. Add a script reference to the JScript file called `Message.js` using the `ScriptReference` attribute of the `ScriptManager` control. Refer to the following code snippet, which shows the markup code of the `ScriptManager` once you have set the script reference:

```
<asp:ScriptManager runat="server" ID="ScriptManager1" >
    <Scripts>
        <asp:ScriptReference Name="LocalizationTest.Message.js"
Assembly="LocalizationTest" />
    </Scripts>
    </asp:ScriptManager>
```

> **By the Way**
>
> You can add script references to a web page using the `<script>` tag and then setting the `src` attribute of it to `text/javascript`, as shown in the following code snippet:
>
> ```
> <script type="text/javascript" src="Message.js"></script>
> ```
>
> This is an example of adding scripts using the `<script>` tag. However, we are using the `<Scripts>` tag of the `ScriptManager` control in this example to add scripts to the `Scripts` collection and implement script globalization and localization. This collection can contain one of more script references. You can mention a script reference using the `ScriptReference` property.

5. Now add a drop-down list control and a text box control to the web page.

6. Attach a client-side script method that in turn calls the `DisplayMessage()` method based on the locale typed by the user in a text box control.

You are done!

Summary

This hour was focused on how we can implement localization and globalization using ASP.NET Ajax. Although these terms seem synonymous, there are distinct differences between the two. While the former relates to designing your application to suit different cultures, the latter is concerned with identifying the portions of your application that need to be localized.

Workshop

Quiz

1. What is the difference between localization and globalization?

2. What is the role of the `ScriptManager` control in implementing multilingual applications?

3. What is the purpose of the `EnableScriptGlobalization` property?

4. Name the namespaces in the .NET library that provide support for globalization and localization.

5. Define the terms script localization and script globalization.

Answers

1. Although the terms localization and globalization seem synonymous, there are distinct differences between the two. Whereas the former relates to designing your application to suit different cultures, the latter is concerned with identifying the portions of your application that need to be localized. In other words, localization is the process of adapting a software application for a specific locale. It is defined as the process of creating and configuring an application for supporting a specific language or locale. Globalization is defined as the process of identifying the specific portion of the application that needs to be different for different languages and identifying how to isolate them from the application's core.

2. The `ScriptManager` control can be used to define the UI or custom UI cultures that you would use in your applications. You can set the `EnableScriptLocalization` and `EnableScriptGlobalization` properties of the `ScriptManager` control to true and specify the script reference path as per your requirements.

3. ASP.NET Ajax supports localization and globalization through one of its properties called `EnableScriptGlobalization`. This property is set to `false` by default.

4. The Microsoft .NET Library provides support for globalization and localization using the `System.Globalization` and `System.Resources` namespaces.

5. Script localization is a feature that enables you to specify texts in your JavaScript files based on a particular locale. Script globalization is used to format and parse your script text based on a specific culture.

HOUR 19

Debugging and Tracing in ASP.NET Ajax

What You'll Learn in This Hour:

▶ An overview of debugging and tracing
▶ The Sys.Debug namespace
▶ Debugging and tracing Ajax-enabled applications

Debugging and tracing are two of the most important techniques for enhancing productivity and tracking potential errors that might occur post-deployment of any application. When you debug an application, you essentially set a breakpoint and step into the code to search for potential errors. The ASP.NET Ajax applications are comprised of both server-side and client-side code. The applications can work both on synchronous and asynchronous requests. This becomes a major constraint in debugging the applications built using ASP.NET Ajax. This hour is an attempt to provide the reader with an overview of debugging and tracing Ajax-enabled ASP.NET applications. We will take a look at why debugging and tracing is important and how efficiently we can debug our Ajax-enabled ASP.NET applications.

You can use one or more of the following approaches to debug your Ajax-enabled ASP.NET applications:

▶ Enable debugging support in the web browser

▶ Enable debugging support in the application's `web.config` file

▶ Attach the Visual Studio debugger to the web browser

▶ Use the `Sys.Debug` class

We examine each of these techniques as we progress through this hour.

Debugging and Tracing—A Quick Look

Microsoft's ASP.NET Ajax framework provides a platform for designing and developing high-performance web applications with rich user experiences and fast responses—and eventually, an awesome user experience. However, regardless of how good a platform is, bugs can always creep in; it is rare for an application to be free of bugs at its development cycle. *Debugging* may be defined as the practice of detecting potential bugs in your source code.

Earlier, debugging your JavaScript code was quite tedious; you only had the option of using alert messages to trace the potential bugs in your JavaScript code.

Debugging and tracing enable you to efficiently track bugs that would otherwise become a nightmare post-deployment of the application.

Working with the Sys.Debug Class

The Debug class pertaining to the Sys namespace can be used for providing tracing and debugging functionality in your applications. The Debug class contains a list of methods that can be used to define breakpoints in your scripts and handle trace output. Table 19.1 lists the members of this class.

TABLE 19.1   Members of the Debug Class

Member	Purpose
Sys.Debug.trace(message)	Displays the message as text in the debugger console or to the TraceConsole text area.
Sys.Debug.clearTrace()	Used to clear all trace information from the TraceConsole text area.
Sys.Debug.fail(message)	Breaks the debugger and displays a message in the TraceConsole text area.
Sys.Debug.assert(condition, message, displayCaller)	Checks whether the condition specified is false; if so, it displays a message and prompts the user to break into the debugger.
Sys.Debug.traceDump(object, name)	Dumps an object to the debugger console or to the TraceConsole text area.

Before you deploy your Ajax-enabled web application, you should set the release version of the Ajax-enabled web application to release mode and set the debug attribute to `false` in the application's `web.config` file. Further, the `ScriptMode` property of the ScriptManager control in all Ajax-enabled web pages in your application should also be set to release.

The Debug class enables you to display trace messages, use assertions, break into the debugger, and even display objects in human-readable format.

There are two possible ways to view the trace messages. First, you can attach the Visual Studio debugger to your web browser and then execute the application. When you do so, you can easily see the trace messages in the output window. Second, you can use a TextArea object and set its ID to TraceConsole, as shown in the following code snippet:

```
<textarea id='TraceConsole' rows="25" cols="50" title="TraceConsole"></textarea>
```

> To use Sys.Debug, the debug attribute of the compilation section in the web. config file should be set to true and the ScriptMode attribute of the ScriptManager control set to debug. Here is how you can set the ScriptMode attribute of the ScriptManager control:
>
> ```
> <asp:ScriptManager ID="ScriptManager1" runat="server" ScriptMode="Debug">
> ```

By the Way

We now take a look at how we can use the Debug class to programmatically demonstrate tracing.

To get started, create a new Ajax-enabled ASP.NET web application. Next, open the Default.aspx file in its source view and paste the following markup code inside it:

```
<form id="Form1" runat="server">
    <asp:ScriptManager ID="ScriptManager1" runat="server" />
        <asp:Label ID="Label1" runat="server" Text="Enter first name:">
➥</asp:Label>
            <input id="Text1" maxlength="50" type="text" />
            <asp:Label ID="Label2" runat="server" Text="Enter last name:">
➥</asp:Label>
            <input id="Text2" maxlength="50" type="text" />
            <br /><br />
            <table>
            <tr>
            <td>
            <input id="btnShowTrace" type="button" value="Show Trace"
➥style="width: 80px" onclick="ShowTrace();" /><br />
            </td>
            <td>
            <input id="btnClearTrace" type="button" value="Clear Trace"
➥style="width: 80px" onclick="ClearTrace();" /><br />
            </td>
            </tr>
            </table>
            <br />
        <textarea id='TraceConsole' rows="5" cols="50" title="TraceConsole">
➥</textarea>
    </form>
```

Refer to the preceding code snippet. We have taken a `TextArea` control that has its ID property set to `TraceConsole` and two buttons that correspond to the `ShowTrace()` and `ClearTrace()` methods. The `TraceConsole TextArea` control will be used to display the trace output. We also have two label controls and text box controls to accept first name and last name from the user and display appropriate static messages.

Although the `ShowTrace()` method displays the trace output in a `TextArea`, the `ClearTrace()` method will clear the trace console in its entirety. Here is the source code of the `ShowTrace()` and the `ClearTrace()` methods:

```javascript
<script language="javascript" type="text/javascript">
function ShowTrace()
{
    v = Form1.Text1.value + ' ' + Form1.Text2.value;
    Sys.Debug.trace(v);
    if(Form1.Text1.value.length > 0)
    alert("The name entered is: "+v);
}
function ClearTrace()
{
    Sys.Debug.clearTrace();
    alert("The Trace Console has been cleared.");
}
</script>
```

Here is the complete code:

```javascript
<script language="javascript" type="text/javascript">
function ShowTrace()
{
    v = Form1.Text1.value + ' ' + Form1.Text2.value;
    Sys.Debug.trace(v);
}
function ClearTrace()
{
    Sys.Debug.clearTrace();
}
</script>
</head>
<body>
    <form id="Form1" runat="server">
        <asp:ScriptManager ID="ScriptManager1" runat="server" />
            <asp:Label ID="Label1" runat="server" Text="Enter first name:">
➥</asp:Label>
            <input id="Text1" maxlength="50" type="text" />
            <asp:Label ID="Label2" runat="server" Text="Enter last name:">
➥</asp:Label>
            <input id="Text2" maxlength="50" type="text" />
            <br /><br />
            <table>
            <tr>
            <td>
```

```
            <input id="btnShowTrace" type="button" value="Show Trace"
►style="width: 80px" onclick="ShowTrace();" /><br />
            </td>
            <td>
            <input id="btnClearTrace" type="button" value="Clear Trace"
►style="width: 80px" onclick="ClearTrace();" /><br />
            </td>
            </tr>
            </table>
            <br />
        <textarea id='TraceConsole' rows="5" cols="50" title="TraceConsole">
►</textarea>
    </form>
```

When you execute the application, the output is similar to what is shown in Figure 19.1.

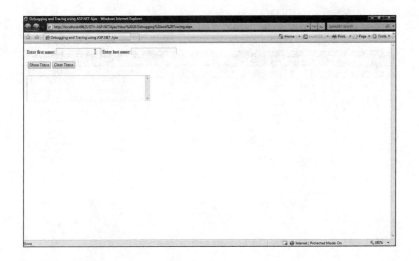

FIGURE 19.1
Debugging and tracing using ASP.NET Ajax

Now, enter first and last name in the respective text box controls and click the Show Trace button to see the trace output displayed in the text area beneath (see Figure 19.2).

You can also click the Clear Trace button to clear the trace console. Once you do that, the content of the text area beneath is cleared; Figure 19.3 shows the output.

FIGURE 19.2
The trace out-
put

FIGURE 19.3
The trace out-
put is now
cleared

How Do I Debug My Code?

You can use debugging in both your server- and client-side code. Using debugging
for server-side code is simple; just set a break point in your code for the debugger to
step in when the application has been executed. However, debugging should be
enabled in your application's web.config file.

By the Way

To start an application in Visual Studio in debug mode, simply press the F5 key or click the Start Debugging option from the Debug menu.

Now, debugging your JavaScript code is not so simple—the browser's environment is not contained within your Visual Studio environment. Your Visual Studio IDE has absolutely no control over how your browser will react to the JavaScript code.

The simplest way to debug your JavaScript code is using alert statements. The following is an example that illustrates how you can use alert statements to debug your JavaScript code:

```
<script language="javascript" type="text/javascript">
function Display()
{
 if(Validate())
  alert('The name entered is: '+Form1.Text1.value + '  '+ Form1.Text2.value);
  else
 alert('Please re-enter');
}
function Validate()
{
  if((Form1.Text1.value.length > 0) && (Form1.Text2.value.length > 0))
   return true;
   return false;
}
</script>
<body>
    <form id="Form1" runat="server">
        <div>
            <asp:Label ID="Label1" runat="server" Text="Enter first name:">
➥</asp:Label>
            <input id="Text1" maxlength="50" type="text" />
            <asp:Label ID="Label2" runat="server" Text="Enter last name:">
➥</asp:Label>
            <input id="Text2" maxlength="50" type="text" />
            <br /><br />
            <input id="btnCheckName" type="button" value="Display"
➥style="width: 100px" onclick="Display();" />
        </div>
    </form>
</body>
```

Although this is the simplest approach, this may not be the most suitable one because you need to use alert statements to debug your code.

By the Way

The debug attribute of the @Page directive of a web page has no effect in particular if you need to debug your scripts. Rather, you should set the debug attribute of the compilation section of the application's `web.config` file, `IsDebuggingEnabled` attribute, and the `ScriptMode` property of the ScriptManager control to debug your scripts.

Enabling Debugging Support in the `web.config` File

You can enable debugging by setting the debug attribute of the compilation tag in the application's `web.config` file to true, as shown in the following code snippet:

```
<configuration>
  <system.web>
    <compilation debug="true">
    </compilation>
  </system.web>
<configuration>
```

If you execute an application in debug mode for which the debug attribute is not set in the application's `web.config` file, you are prompted for "set debugging on." When you click OK, your application's `web.config` file is updated with the debugging support.

Enabling Debugging Support in Internet Explorer

To enable debugging in Internet Explorer, follow these simple steps:

1. Go to the Tools menu of the browser.

2. Click Internet Options (see Figure 19.4).

FIGURE 19.4
Enabling debugging support
in IE

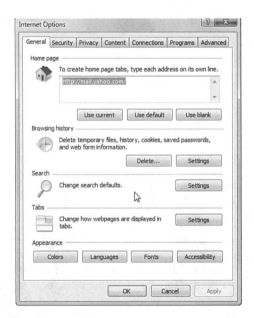

3. Switch to the Advanced tab and uncheck the Disable Script Debugging and Disable Script Debugging (Other) checkboxes (see Figure 19.5).

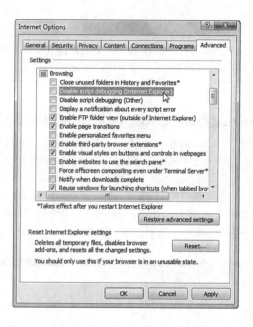

FIGURE 19.5
Enabling script debugging

4. Optionally, you can also uncheck the Display a Notification About Every Script Error and Show Friendly HTTP Error Messages checkboxes (see Figure 19.6).

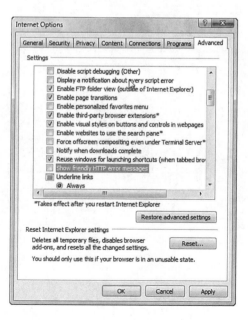

FIGURE 19.6
Enabling display notifications and HTTP messages

5. Now, click OK.

You are done!

> Every Ajax-enabled web page should have one and only one ScriptManager control and, optionally, one or more UpdatePanel controls.

Enabling Debugging Support in Visual Studio

You can debug your application in Visual Studio by pressing the F5 key or clicking the Start Debugging option in the Debug menu. You can also attach the Visual Studio debugger when the application is already running. For this, you need to click the Attach to Process option in the Debug menu of Visual Studio and then select the instance of the Internet Explorer to which you would like to attach the debugger. The steps are depicted diagrammatically in Figures 19.7 and 19.8.

FIGURE 19.7
The Attach to Process option

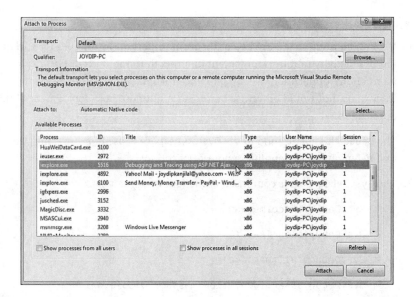

FIGURE 19.8
Attaching the process from the list of available processes

Summary

This hour examined how we can debug our Ajax-enabled ASP.NET applications using two of the most important techniques for enhancing application performance and tracking potential errors—debugging and tracing. We also looked at how we can enable debugging support in Visual Studio and the application's configuration file. In the next hour, we look at the future of Ajax.

Workshop

Quiz

1. Why are debugging and tracing required?

2. What is the purpose of the `Debug` class?

3. Name the members of the `Sys.Debug` class.

4. How can you enable or disable debugging support in the `web.config` file?

5. How do you enable debugging support in Visual Studio?

Answers

1. Debugging and tracing are two of the most important techniques for enhancing productivity and tracking potential errors that might occur post-deployment of any application. Debugging and tracing enable you to efficiently track bugs that would otherwise become a nightmare post-deployment of the application.

2. The Debug class pertaining to the Sys namespace is used for providing tracing and debugging functionality in your applications.

3. The Sys.Debug class is comprised of the following members:

   - ▶ Sys.Debug.trace(message)

   - ▶ Sys.Debug.clearTrace()

   - ▶ Sys.Debug.fail(message)

   - ▶ Sys.Debug.assert(condition,message,displaycaller)

   - ▶ Sys.Debug.traceDump(object,name)

4. You can enable debugging by setting the debug attribute of the compilation tag in the application's web.config file to true, as shown in the following code snippet:

```
<configuration>
  <system.web>
    <compilation debug="true">
    </compilation>
  </system.web>
<configuration>
```

5. You can debug your application in Visual Studio by pressing the F5 key or clicking the Start Debugging option in the Debug menu. You can also attach the Visual Studio debugger when the application is already running. For this, you need to click the Attach to Process option in the Debug menu of Visual Studio and then select the instance of the explorer to which you would like to attach the debugger.

HOUR 20

The ASP.NET Ajax Futures CTP

What You'll Learn in This Hour:

▶ An overview of the ASP.NET Ajax Futures CTP

▶ Dynamic data controls and dynamic web sites

▶ Ajax and beyond

We are now close to the end of our journey! We have already explored a lot about Ajax and how we can leverage its awesome power in our applications. In this hour, we examine the ASP.NET Ajax Futures CTP and also explore what the future has in store for Ajax— one of the most popular technologies in recent times.

The ASP.NET Ajax Futures CTP Release

The three major components that comprise the Microsoft Ajax framework are the following:

▶ ASP.NET Ajax extensions

▶ ASP.NET Ajax Control Toolkit

▶ ASP.NET Ajax Futures CTP

We have already discussed the first two components in detail earlier in this book. In this section, we examine the ASP.NET Ajax Futures CTP and its contents.

ASP.NET Ajax Futures is a package that contains the updates and enhancements to Ajax. The ASP.NET Ajax Pure Client-Side Library, introduced as part of the CTP release, contains a handful of controls that can be used to provide drag and drop, fading, and animation effects. The AutoCompleteExtender control provides you with an auto-suggest functionality much the same as Google. In the sections that follow, we look at the new additions to

Ajax with its Futures CTP release. We also discuss what the future has in store for Ajax—a technology that has taken the web programming world by storm over the past few years.

Pure Client-Side Controls in the `Sys.Preview.UI` Namespace

Were the controls that we discussed earlier in this book pure client-side? No! If we take a look back, ASP.NET Ajax 1.0 contains a lot of controls, but none of them were pure client-side controls in the strict sense. Now, with the ASP.NET Ajax Futures release, you have a number of pure and rich client-side controls. The `Sys.Preview.UI` namespace bundles a collection of such controls in it. Here is the list of the controls contained in this namespace:

▶ `Sys.Preview.UI.Window`

▶ `Sys.Preview.UI.Label`

▶ `Sys.Preview.UI.Image`

▶ `Sys.Preview.UI.HyperLink`

▶ `Sys.Preview.UI.Button`

▶ `Sys.Preview.UI.CheckBox`

▶ `Sys.Preview.UI.Selector`

▶ `Sys.Preview.UI.TextBox`

By the Way

One noticeable change from the beta versions of ASP.NET Ajax Futures and the CTP versions that have been released later is in the ease of declaring the ScriptManager control—one of the most important controls in ASP.NET Ajax.

Here is how you had to declare the ScriptManager control in your web page in the beta versions:

```
<asp:ScriptManager ID="myScriptManagerControl" runat="server">
    <Scripts>
        <asp:ScriptReference Assembly="Microsoft.Web.Preview"
➥Name="Microsoft.Web.Resources.ScriptLibrary.PreviewScript.js" />
        <asp:ScriptReference Assembly="Microsoft.Web.Preview"
➥Name="Microsoft.Web.Resources.ScriptLibrary.PreviewDragDrop.js" />
    </Scripts>
</asp:ScriptManager>
```

And now you have an easier way of writing the same. Here is how you can declare the ScriptManager control using the ASP.NET Ajax Futures CTP releases:

```
<asp:ScriptManager ID="myScriptManagerControl" runat="server">
    <Scripts>
        <asp:ScriptReference Assembly="Microsoft.Web.Preview"
➡Name="PreviewScript.js" />
        <asp:ScriptReference Assembly="Microsoft.Web.Preview"
Name="PreviewDragDrop.js" />
    </Scripts>
</asp:ScriptManager>
```

What Are Dynamic Data Web Sites?

To work with dynamic data web sites, ensure that ASP.NET Futures CTP is already installed in your system. You should also configure your connection string properly to connect to the database you will use.

To create a dynamic data web site, follow these steps:

1. Open Visual Studio 2005 or 2008.

2. Select File, New Web Site.

3. Select Dynamic Data Web Site from the list of templates displayed.

4. Map the connection string using the dynamicData settings in your application's web.config file.

5. Create a dynamic data web form. To do this, right-click the project and select Add, New Item, Dynamic Data Web Form.

6. After your dynamic data web form has been created, you can simply play with the dynamic data controls—drag and drop them from the toolbox onto your web form and write code to do what you need to.

> **By the Way**
>
> In a dynamic data web site, when you create a web form—also known as dynamic data form—by default, the name of the web form coincides with that of your database table. In essence, it is mapped with your database table. You can, however, change this setting in the application's configuration file.

Now that we know how to create dynamic web sites, we will now learn what dynamic data controls are and how we can work with them in our data-driven web applications.

Dynamic Data Controls—Manipulate Data with Even Less Code

The dynamic data controls are an addition to ASP.NET Futures that enable you to perform CRUD (Create, Read, Update, and Delete) operations with the least amount of code. They provide you with a simple, intuitive user interface for data-driven dynamic web sites and can retrieve the database schema information at runtime.

Actually, dynamic data support is a feature that has been introduced as a part of the ASP.NET 3.5 extensions release. The dynamic data controls can retrieve database schema information at runtime and can be used to display data in user-defined or custom formats.

As Scott Guthrie says in his esteemed blog, "The ASP.NET 3.5 extensions release delivers new features that enable faster creation of data-driven web sites. It provides a rich scaffolding framework, and will enable rapid data-driven site development using both ASP.NET web forms and ASP.NET MVC."

The ASP.NET Futures CTP includes the following dynamic data controls:

- The DynamicList control
- The DynamicInsert control
- The DynamicDetails control
- The DynamicFilter control
- The DynamicAutoData control
- The DynamicRssLink control
- The DynamicNavigator control

You also have two more controls in the ASP.NET Futures CTP—namely, the SearchDataSource and History controls.

To use these Ajax–enabled controls of the ASP.NET Futures CTP release, you should use an ASP.NET Futures Ajax web site. To do this, follow these simple steps:

1. In the Visual Studio click File, New—Web Site.

2. Select ASP.NET Futures Ajax Web Site from the list of the templates displayed, as shown in figure 20.1.

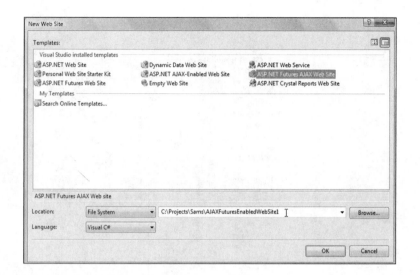

FIGURE 20.1
Selecting
ASPNET Futures
Ajax Web Site

3. Lastly, save the web site with a name.

You are done! You can now use any of the controls of the ASP.NET Futures CTP release.

Note that all these controls are Ajax-enabled. Let's have a quick look at what these controls are used for. Figure 20.2 shows a diagrammatic view of these controls in the toolbox.

You can use the DynamicList control to display the table data as a GridView control. The DynamicInsert control can be used to insert rows in a database table. The DynamicDetails control can be used to display the columns of a particular row of the database table. The DynamicFilter control can be used to select a particular row based on the column selected. The DynamicAutoData control displays data from the database table as a GridView control. The DynamicRssLink control can be used to implement an Rss feed for your web page. The DynamicNavigator control can be used to display all the tables and views.

FIGURE 20.2
The Ajax-
enabled con-
trols of the
ASP.NET Futures
CTP Release

To work with the DynamicFilter control, you need to set its ColumnName property, as shown in the following code snippet:

```
<asp:DynamicFilter ID="DynamicFilter1" runat="server" ColumnName="City"
➥ FilterStyle="Radio" />
```

**Did you
Know?**

> To customize the display of a dynamic data control, you can use the following code:
>
> ```
> <asp:DropDownList runat="server" ID="drpEmployee" BackColor="Cyan"
> ➥Font-Italic="true" Font-Bold="true" />
> <cc1:DynamicFilter ID="DynamicFilter1" runat="server"
> ➥ColumnName="EmployeeName" ControlID="drpEmployee"
> ➥FilterStyle="DropDown" />
> ```

Here is the markup code generated when you drag and drop these controls one by one from the toolbox onto your dynamic data web form:

```
<asp:DynamicNavigator ID="DynamicNavigator1" runat="server" />
<asp:DynamicAutoData id="AutoData1" runat="server" />
<asp:DynamicRssLink ID="DynamicRssLink1" runat="server" />
<asp:DynamicFilter ID="DynamicFilter1" runat="server" />
<asp:DynamicInsert ID="DynamicInsert1" runat="server" />
<asp:DynamicDetails ID="DynamicDetails1" runat="server" />
<asp:DynamicList ID="DynamicList1" runat="server" />
```

> To specify the connection string to a Dynamic Data Control, you can use the following.
>
> ```
> <dynamicDataControls showAllTables="true"
>    dataLayerType="Microsoft.Web.DynamicDataControls.SqlDataLayer"
>         connectionString="MyConnectionString" >
>     <nameMap>
>     </nameMap>
> </dynamicDataControls>
> ```
>
> If you don't specify the connection string when defining a dynamic data control, the connection string specified in the application's web.config file is used by default.

Did you Know?

The following is a markup code that illustrates how you can use the
DynamicAutoData and DynamicDetailsView controls to display records from a
table:

```
<div>
            <asp:DynamicAutoData ID="AutoData1" runat="server" />
            <asp:DynamicDetails ID="DynamicDetails1" runat="server"
➥ControlID="MyDetails" />
            <asp:DetailsView ID="MyDetails" runat="server"
AutoGenerateRows="False"
➥DataKeyNames="DepartmentID" DataSourceID="SqlDataSource1">
                <Fields>
                    <asp:BoundField DataField="CustomerID"
➥HeaderText="Customer ID" InsertVisible="False"
                        ReadOnly="True" SortExpression="CustomerID" />
                    <asp:BoundField DataField="CustomerName"
➥HeaderText="Customer Name" SortExpression="CustomerName" />
                </Fields>
            </asp:DetailsView>
            <asp:SqlDataSource ID="SqlDataSource1" runat="server"
➥ConnectionString="<%$ ConnectionStrings:TestConnectionString %>"
                SelectCommand="SELECT [CustomerID], [CustomerName]
➥FROM [CustomerMaster]">
            </asp:SqlDataSource>
        </div>
```

You can use a GridView control as a template for the DynamicList control to display its data. Let's say you have a GridView control with the following markup:

```
<asp:GridView ID="GridView1" runat="server" BackColor="White"
BorderColor="Blue" BorderStyle="None"
GridLines="Horizontal">
<RowStyle BackColor="Cyan" ForeColor="#4A3C8C" />
<PagerStyle BackColor="Black" ForeColor="White" />
<SelectedRowStyle BackColor="Yellow" ForeColor="Black" />
<HeaderStyle BackColor="Red" Font-Bold="True"/>
<AlternatingRowStyle BackColor="Blue" />
</asp:GridView>
```

You can now map the `ControlID` property of your `DynamicList` control to the `GridView` control, as shown in the following code snippet:

```
<asp:DynamicList ID="DynamicList1" runat="server" ControlID="GridView1" />
```

> To map a dynamic data control to a table or a view, you can create a folder that contains one or more pages that display data from the table in varying ways. For example, suppose you have a folder called EmployeeDDControls in which you have the following .aspx pages: `EmployeeList.aspx` and `EmployeeDetails.aspx`.
>
> You can now map your dynamic data control using the `<nameMap>` tag, as shown in the following code snippet:
>
> ```
> <dynamicDataControls listView="EmployeeList" detailsView="EmployeeDetails">
>     <nameMap>
>         <add table="Employee" pathPrefix="~/EmployeeDDControls" />
>     </nameMap>
> </dynamicDataControls>
> ```

You can use the `DynamicInsert` control to insert new rows into a database table. Note that the `DynamicInsert` control uses the `DetailsView` control to generate the layout. The `DynamicNavigator` control is a dynamic data control that can be used to retrieve schema information of all tables and views at execution time. Note that it displays a list of all the table and views whose names coincides with the page file name. However, you can configure it to display all tables and views. To do this, set its `showAllTables` attribute to `true` in the `<dynamicDataControls>` section in the application's configuration file.

Support for Returning DataSet, DataTable, or DataRow Instances

Prior to this release, ASP.NET Ajax has had no support for DataSets, DataTables, and so on. The ASP.NET Ajax Futures release now incorporates this awesome feature. The ability to return ADO.NET objects, such as DataSet, DataTable, or DataRow, is one of the most striking features in the ASP.NET Ajax Futures release. You can now return DataSet, DataTable, or DataRow instances from a web service or even a page method! You couldn't do this earlier. Fantastic, isn't it? Here is what you need to specify in your application's `web.config` to make this work:

```
<system.web.extensions>
    <scripting>
      <webServices>
        <jsonSerialization>
          <converters>
            <add name="DataSetConverter"
➥type="Microsoft.Web.Preview.Script.Serialization.Converters.
➥DataSetConverter, Microsoft.Web.Preview"/>
```

```
            <add name="DataRowConverter"
➦type="Microsoft.Web.Preview.Script.Serialization.Converters.
➦DataRowConverter, Microsoft.Web.Preview"/>
            <add name="DataTableConverter"
➦type="Microsoft.Web.Preview.Script.Serialization.Converters.
➦DataTableConverter, Microsoft.Web.Preview"/>
          </converters>
        </jsonSerialization>
      </webServices>
    </scripting>
  </system.web.extensions>
```

Ajax—What About Tomorrow?

In this section, we discuss what the future has in store for one of Microsoft's most popular technologies ever: Ajax. Ajax, an acronym for Asynchronous JavaScript and XML, is a technology that can reduce web page postbacks significantly and yield better response times for your web applications. It is a technology with cross-platform, cross-architecture, and even cross-browser support. In fact, Ajax has already become recognized by the development communities world-wide as the technology of choice for building lightning-fast web applications with improved response times, which results in awesome user experiences.

So, is Ajax our future? Yes! Let's discuss why. The advent of Ajax has put an end to the arduous struggle of web application development communities worldwide to find a technology that can not only can save you bandwidth and give you improved response times, but also allow for asynchronous processing—this is a dramatic departure from the traditional model, where you had to rely on postbacks to bring in your data. In essence, Ajax-enabled web applications are a paradigm shift from the way the traditional web applications were designed. Keeping aside the downsides in using Ajax in application development and its implementation difficulties, Ajax is still making its presence felt in enterprise-level Web applications, SOA, mobile applications, and so on.

And, with Microsoft taking Ajax to new heights and quickly coming up with newer releases, Ajax is all set to become the next-generation technology of choice for building fast and responsive web applications. Fine, but what has the future in store for one of the most popular collection of technologies in recent times? Let's take a look.

Most web applications these days are Ajax-enabled. With Ajax, there has been a sudden departure from the traditional way of designing web applications. Gmail, Google Maps, and Google Suggest are some of the best examples where Ajax has been put to the best use. Moreover, most of the modern day's web browsers come with Ajax support. The greatest benefit in using Ajax is that it can dramatically reduce the bandwidth consumption of your application—which is a decrease in the cost, too! A lot of companies around the globe have invested huge amounts of money in designing their future applications—and they have already designed and architected their future applications with Ajax in mind.

Summary

This hour has examined the ASP.NET Ajax Futures CTP release. We have also discussed the future of Ajax. This concludes our discussion on ASP.NET Ajax. We are now nearing the end of our journey!

In the forthcoming hours, we discuss the implementation of a sample application, where we make use of the concepts and controls we have covered so far in this book. We design a simple shopping cart application that covers almost all the concepts we have discussed. So, stay tuned!

Workshop

Quiz

1. What are the client-side controls that are available as part of the `Sys.Preview.UI` namespace in the ASP.NET Ajax Futures release?

2. Name some of the most popular Ajax implementations of today.

3. Name the Ajax-enabled dynamic data controls of the ASP.NET Futures release. Briefly explain what each of them is used for.

4. How can you use a `DynamicList` control that is mapped to a `GridView` control to use as its template?

5. I have a `DynamicList` control with its ID as "DynamicList1" and a `GridView` control with its ID as "GridView1". How do I map the `ControlID` property of the `DynamicList` control to the `GridView` control?

6. What should you specify in your application's `web.config` file to provide the support for returning DataSet, DataTable, or DataRow instances from a web service or even a page method?

Answers

1. The controls available as part of the `Sys.Preview.UI` namespace are as follows:

   ▶ `Sys.Preview.UI.Window`

   ▶ `Sys.Preview.UI.Label`

   ▶ `Sys.Preview.UI.Image`

   ▶ `Sys.Preview.UI.HyperLink`

   ▶ `Sys.Preview.UI.Button`

   ▶ `Sys.Preview.UI.CheckBox`

   ▶ `Sys.Preview.UI.Selector`

   ▶ `Sys.Preview.UI.TextBox`

2. With Ajax, there has been a sudden departure from the traditional way of designing web applications. Gmail, Google Maps, and Google Suggest are some of the best examples where Ajax has been put to good use.

3. The ASP.NET Futures CTP includes the following dynamic data controls:

   ▶ The `DynamicList` control

   ▶ The `DynamicInsert` control

   ▶ The `DynamicDetails` control

   ▶ The `DynamicFilter` control

   ▶ The `DynamicAutoData` control

   ▶ The `DynamicRssLink` control

   ▶ The `DynamicNavigator` control

   The `DynamicList` control can be used to display the table data as a `GridView` control. The `DynamicInsert` control can be used to insert rows in a database table. The `DynamicDetails` control can be used to display the columns of a particular row of the database table. The `DynamicFilter` control can be used to select a particular row based on the column selected. The `DynamicAutoData` control displays data from the database table as a `GridView` control. The

`DynamicRssLink` control can be used to implement an Rss feed for your web page. The `DynamicNavigator` control can be used to display all the tables and views.

4. You can use a `GridView` control as a template for the `DynamicList` control to display its data. Let's say you have a `GridView` control with the following markup:

```
<asp:GridView ID="GridView1" runat="server" BackColor="White"
BorderColor="Blue" BorderStyle="None"
GridLines="Horizontal">
<RowStyle BackColor="Cyan" ForeColor="#4A3C8C" />
<PagerStyle BackColor="Black" ForeColor="White" />
<SelectedRowStyle BackColor="Yellow" ForeColor="Black" />
<HeaderStyle BackColor="Red" Font-Bold="True"/>
<AlternatingRowStyle BackColor="Blue" />
</asp:GridView>
```

You can now map the `ControlID` property of your `DynamicList` control to the `GridView` control, as shown in the following code snippet:

```
<asp:DynamicList ID="DynamicList1" runat="server" ControlID="GridView1" />
```

5. To map the `ControlID` property of the `DynamicList` control to the `GridView` control, use the following code:

```
<asp:DynamicList ID="DynamicList1" runat="server" ControlID="GridView1" />
```

6. To do this, here is what you should specify in your application's `web.config` file:

```
<system.web.extensions>
<scripting>
<webServices>
<jsonSerialization>
<converters>
<add name="DataSetConverter"
 type="Microsoft.Web.Preview.Script.Serialization.Converters.
 DataSetConverter, Microsoft.Web.Preview"/>

<add name="DataRowConverter"
 type="Microsoft.Web.Preview.Script.Serialization.Converters.
 DataRowConverter, Microsoft.Web.Preview"/>
<add name="DataTableConverter"
 type="Microsoft.Web.Preview.Script.Serialization.Converters.
 DataTableConverter, Microsoft.Web.Preview"/>
</converters>
</jsonSerialization>
</webServices>
</scripting>
</system.web.extensions>
```

PART IV

Using ASP.NET Ajax to Build a Sample e-Commerce Application

HOUR 21

Introducing e-Commerce and Designing an Application

What You'll Learn in This Hour:

▶ An introduction to e-commerce
▶ A general system design and modules in an e-commerce application
▶ The operational flow in the application
▶ The database design of the application

This hour starts a series of four hours that demonstrate building a sample e-commerce application using ASP.NET Ajax. We maintain calling it a sample, as building a complete and full-fledged e-commerce application would require an entire book altogether. The entire source code of the application is provided on this book's web site (www.informit.com/title/9780672329678). This hour focuses on kick-starting a sample e-commerce application and discussing its underlying system design, the different modules, and its functionality and overall operational flow. The next three hours focus on the development of different modules of this sample application with code snippets. The code snippets will be related to the source code provided on this book's web site. Let's start by getting an overview of the e-commerce application.

Introducing e-Commerce

To start with, e-commerce is an online store for buying and selling goods—a concept that has grown in leaps and bounds over the last eight years or so and has taken shopping for goods to a completely new level of automation. Needless to say, the process of order delivery is manual. There are two kinds of business that happen on the Internet: B2B (Business to Business) and B2C (Business to Consumer). B2B represents an electronic commerce between enterprises, and B2C represents an electronic commerce between the merchants and consumers directly. E-commerce applications help businesses automate their order fulfillment apart from globalizing their sales rather than sticking to a geographical location. This helps them to reach out to more customers and enhance their business. Today, almost every business that exists is either online or on the way to being online. All that the consumer needs is to have an Internet connection, and they are ready to buy their products online. The following section focuses on the different modules that make up the application.

Modules in the Application

The e-commerce application we will be discussing is a B2C system, which is an online shopping web site that accommodates viewing and searching products, buying products, making orders, giving feedback, and managing the users. In general, this can be broadly classified into the following modules:

- ▶ Home page, registration, and login
- ▶ Product display/search and shopping cart management
- ▶ Order generation and online payment
- ▶ User and role management
- ▶ Order and product management

These are the basic modules that make up a simple e-commerce application. However, there can be many more interesting modules that can be added to the preceding list based on your innovation. You can add modules like news, a feedback section, a wish-list section, and so on, to make the user more attached to the web site and encourage him/her to visit the site more often and recommend it to others. The first three modules listed previously are used by the consumer visiting the site: buying products, adding them to the cart, creating orders, and making payments online. The last two modules listed are administrative activities in the sense that the Manager and the executives of the site take care of the order status of different orders, communicating with the consumers who have made orders, managing the product categories, products, and its stock, and managing different users of the site and their roles. Let's have a brief look at each of these modules and their activities.

Home Page, Registration, and Login

This module showcases the most important part of the web site: the home page. The home page consists of all the important information a web site needs to display. The most important part of the home page is content display and navigation. In this case, the content display is organized into product categories display, product category search, product search, a login section, and providing navigation to the user by providing hyperlinks, images, and other UI elements. If users are visiting the site and shopping for the first time, they will need to register at the site by submitting personal details such as their name, email, phone, billing address, shipping address, and so on. After the user registers to the site, he/she can log in and shop for the products to buy online. In our application, we would be covering these pages in `Login.aspx`, `Registration.aspx`, and `Default.aspx`.

Product Display/Search and Shopping Cart Management

This is an integral part and the core of a shopping web site. This module contains searching of products, viewing them in a detail page, and adding them to the cart. The user has the flexibility of adding and deleting items in the cart and can also save the items in the cart for a specific period. A cart in a shopping web site generally holds items and their quantity, individual price, and the total price of all the items together. It is represented in a tabular form for easy reading and manipulation. Each record in the cart table holds an item, the quantity, the price of the item, and the total (which is the price of the item multiplied by quantity). A cart can hold any number of such records, and the total price of all the items is calculated. This is the order amount excluding the taxes and shipping charges. After the cart is ready, the user can check out to generate the order. The pages that are covered in this module are `Products.aspx`, `ProductDetails.aspx`, and `Cart.aspx`.

Order Generation and Online Payment

This module takes care of generating orders once the cart is ready with items. An order consists of the cart information—that is, the product name, quantity, individual price, and total price. Apart from these, it also includes taxes, discounts, and shipping charges. All these make up the total order amount the customer has to pay. The customer has to provide the billing and shipping address and then confirm the order. Upon confirmation, the customer is redirected to a payment gateway site for paying the amount using a credit card.

Most web sites today implement an API provided by the credit card gateways to keep the user on the web site without redirecting them to a payment site.

By the Way

Upon successful transaction, the customer is redirected back to the site. However, in our application, we will not redirect the customer to any payment gateway site. After you make the application real, you can go to any popular payment gateway site, such as PayPal, Verisign, and so on. The different pages in this module include `Order.aspx` and `TrackOrder.aspx`.

User and Role Management

This module is an admin-related activity. First, roles need to be defined, and each user being created is associated with a role. The different roles defined in our application are Administrator, Manager, and Customer:

▶ **Administrator**—The super user of the site. The Administrator has complete access to all the information in the site, including order management and product management, receives alerts on key events and activities being performed in the site, has access to all the sales reports and dashboard, and is the one who creates the users with the Manager role.

All these features mentioned are not a part of the application we are building, however. We will be concentrating more on the front end—that is, the shopping cart and order generation—and less on the administration activity, as it is not possible to cover all of them practically in four hours.

▶ **Manager**—The user responsible for managing products and orders, tracking shipments and delivery of products purchased from the site, and communicating with the customer.

▶ **Customer**—The end user. The customer is the person who shops for the products and buys them online.

This module allows the user to perform add/edit/delete/select operations on users and roles.

Order and Product Management

This module is about managing products and orders. The Manager takes care of maintaining this information, although the Administrator also has the privilege of doing this. The operations include adding/editing/deleting/selecting categories and products, keeping track of the stock of the products, keeping track of the orders and their status, and taking care of the delivery of orders. The following section briefly describes the architecture of the application.

Architecture and Operational Flow

The application is a web site; therefore, it generally follows a three-tier architecture that includes the presentation layer, business layer, and data access layer. Because this application is based on ASP.NET with Ajax, there might be a tendency to write more of the logic on the client side, making it more client-centric. But it is always a safe bet to write your logic on the server side. We will build the application to be more server-centric and apply Ajax techniques to leverage its power with ASP.NET. We will be using the built-in ASP.NET Ajax controls and extenders, which make the application more user-interactive and provide faster performance. These controls perform the logic on the server side and emit lots of JavaScript onto the client to get the client-side behavior. The business logic in the application can be found in custom classes and web services. The database used is SQL Server 2005. Figure 21.1 illustrates the architecture and model of the application.

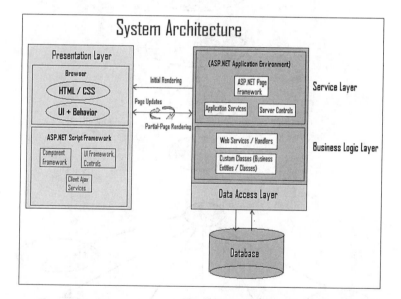

FIGURE 21.1
System architecture and model of the application.

Figures 21.2 and 21.3 display the operational flow of the application with respect to the user/customer and Manager/Administrator of the application.

FIGURE 21.2
User's or customer's operational flow

FIGURE 21.3
Manager's or Administrator's operational flow

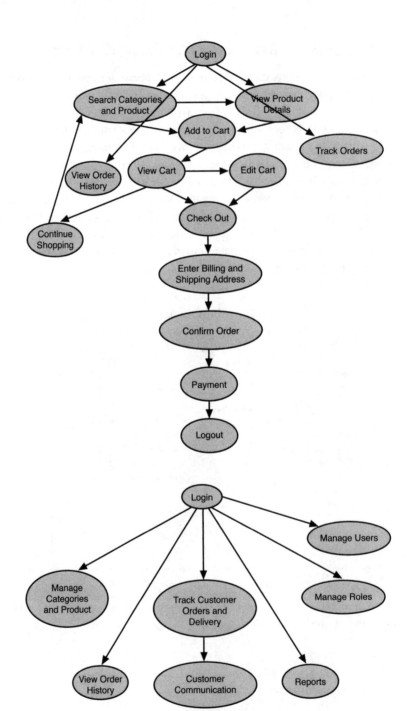

Database Design

This section discusses a very important topic: the database. It is assumed that the reader has installed a SQL Server 2005 edition before designing the database. The sample application we are developing uses a SQL login sa/sa. This login can be created as a default login during the SQL Server 2005 installation process. If it has not been done during installation, proceed to create a SQL login with the username as "sa" and password as "sa." Following are the steps to create a SQL login:

1. Open SQL Server Management Studio.

2. In the Object Explorer window, under the root, open the Security folder. You'll find a folder called Logins. Right-click this folder and click New Login. Figure 21.4 displays the New Login window.

3. Enter the username **sa**. Select the option SQL Server Authentication, enter and confirm the password as sa, and click OK. We now have aSQL login ready!

FIGURE 21.4
Creating a SQL login

Now let's design a database named "shoppingcart." Under the root of the Object Explorer, right-click the Databases folder and click New Database. Enter the database name as shoppingcart and click OK. Figure 21.5 displays the New Database window. We will be using SQL Server authentication for this application, as this is targeted for use on the Internet.

FIGURE 21.5
Creating the
database
shoppingcart

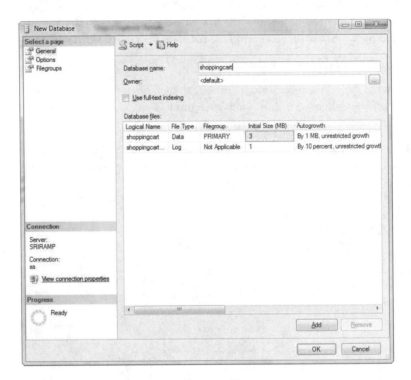

After creating the database, we have to map the user sa to the database shopping-cart. Go to the user sa in the Object Explorer (root, Security, Logins), right-click the Logins folder, and click Properties. Select the option User Mapping under the left tab, Select a Page. Check the option for the database shoppingcart under the section Users Mapped to This Login. Also check the option db_owner under the section Database Role Membership For. Figure 22.6 displays the Login properties for the user sa. This ensures that the user sa is the owner of the database shoppingcart and has the permissions to perform any operation on this database.

FIGURE 21.6
Mapping user sa to the database shopping-cart.

If the user sa is created as a default login during the SQL Server 2005 installation process, this user is automatically given the permissions of db_owner for any database that is either already created or will be created on the server. In that case, we would not need to manually do the mapping process as we've done in the previous steps.

By the Way

Now let's proceed further by creating tables for maintaining the shopping cart. Before we begin creating the tables, however, it needs to be stressed that we will be using a custom ASP.NET membership and role provider for managing roles, users, and logins in our application. The process of creating this custom provider and using it in the application will be detailed in the next hour. The schema generated by the Membership and Role Provider tool has around 11 tables and several stored procedures. However, three tables are of utmost importance to us: aspnet_Roles, aspnet_Users, and aspnet_UsersInRole. The rest of the tables generated by this tool revolve around these three base tables. Let's discuss the schema and relationships of these three tables and the other application-specific tables we are about to create.

Tables and Relationships

All the tables defined in this section are described by their structure and relationship(s) with other tables.

aspnet_Roles **Table**

This is a master table holding the different roles used in the system. The different roles in this application are Customer, Manager, and Administrator. The role of the Customer is to browse through the products, add them to the cart, and buy them. The role of the Manager is to maintain the web site, manage the orders, track their status, communicate with customers, keep track of stock of the products, and have the ability to add/edit/delete/select product categories and products. The role of the Administrator is to create and manage users—that is, managers. The Administrator is the super user of the system. He or she also has all the privileges of the Manager. Table 21.1 shows the structure of the Role table.

TABLE 21.1 aspnet_Roles

Column Name	Datatype	Key	Description
ApplicationId	UniqueIdentifier	Foreign Key	This maps to the ApplicationId in the aspnet_Applications table. This holds a unique ID for each application.
RoleId	UniqueIdentifier	Not Null	The unique ID for the role.
RoleName	nvarchar(256)	Not Null	The name of the role, such as Administrator, Manager, or customer.
LoweredRoleName	nvarchar(256)	Not Null	Creates the lowered case role name of the RoleName field.
Description	nvarchar(256)	Allow Null	An optional field describing the role.

aspnet_Users **Table**

This table holds the users of the system—that is, the Administrator, Manager, and customer. The RoleId is attached to every user, which defines his/her privileges in the application (see Table 21.2).

TABLE 21.2 aspnet_Users

Column Name	Datatype	Key	Description
ApplicationId	UniqueIdentifier	Foreign Key	This maps to the ApplicationId in the asp-net_Applications table. This holds a unique ID for each application.
UserId	UniqueIdentifier	Not Null	The unique ID of the user.
UserName	nvarchar(256)	Not Null	The login name of the user.
LoweredUserName	nvarchar(256)	Not Null	The lowered case of the user name.
MobileAlias	nvarchar(16)	Allow Null	The mobile number of the user.
IsAnonymous	bit	Not Null	Bit field indicating whether the user is anonymous or not.
LastActivityDate	datetime	Not Null	Created date or last-modified date.

aspnet_UsersInRoles **Table**

This table holds the mapping information of the users and roles in the system (see Table 21.3).

TABLE 21.3 aspnet_UsersInRoles

Column Name	Datatype	Key	Description
UserId	UniqueIdentifier	Foreign Key	This column maps to the UserId of the aspnet_Users table.
RoleId	UniqueIdentifier	Foreign Key	This column maps to the RoleId of the aspnet_Roles table.

Categories **Table**

This table holds the information of all the categories to be displayed in the site. This application showcases products in computer peripherals in different categories. Each category will have a set of products for display and purchase. Table 21.4 displays the structure of the Categories table.

TABLE 21.4   Categories

Column Name	Datatype	Key	Description
CategoryId	Int	Primary Key	Identity field (auto-generated number to identify the uniqueness of the record).
CategoryName	Varchar(50)	Not Null	The name of the product category.
Description	Varchar(250)	Not Null	The product category description.
CreatedDate	Datetime	Not Null [Default—Getdate()]	Date of creation of the category.
CreatedBy	Int	Not Null	Logged-in user. Either the Manager's UserId or the Administrator's UserId.

Product **Table**

This table holds all the products on display in the site. Each product is tied to a category, has a price, and also has its stock maintained. Whenever the product has reached its reorder level, an alert is raised to the Manager and Administrator of the site to procure it. The Product table structure is shown in Table 21.5.

TABLE 21.5   Product

Column Name	Datatype	Key	Description
ProductId	Int	Primary Key	Identity field (auto-generated number to identify the uniqueness of the record).
ProductName	Varchar(50)	Not Null	The name of the product.
Description	Varchar(250)	Not Null	The description of the product.
CategoryId	Int	Foreign Key	The product associated with a category.
QuantityInStock	Int	Not Null	The current quantity of products.
ReorderLevel	Int	Not Null	The minimum quantity of a product before it has to be procured.
CostPrice	money	Not Null	The purchase price from the supplier.

TABLE 21.5   continued

Column Name	Datatype	Key	Description
SellingPrice	money	Not Null	The sale price to the customer.
ImageId table	Int	Foreign Key	Fetched from the images.
Notes	Varchar(250)	Allow Null	Any notes/remarks on the product.
CreatedDate	Datetime	Not Null [Default—Getdate()]	The date of creation of the product in the system.
CreatedBy	Int	Not Null [Logged-in user. Either the Manager's UserId or the Administrator's UserId.]	The UserId of the user who created this record.

Images **Table**

The Images table is used to store the images that are used in the application. Earlier, images were stored on the file system in the web server. The advantage of storing images in database is the ease of portability; whereas in file system, the administrator would have the extra task of moving the images. Each product is associated with an image (see Table 21.6).

TABLE 21.6   Images

Column Name	Datatype	Key	Description
ImageId	Int	Primary Key	Identity field (auto-generated number to identiy the uniqueness of the record).
ImageName	Varchar(50)	Not Null	The name or description of the image.
ImageData	image	Not Null	Image data.

Cart **and** CartDetails **Tables**

The Cart table holds the CartId and UserId whose products have been added to the cart. The CartDetails table holds the products, their quantity, the price, and the total price of all the products added to the cart. The customer can add the items to the cart and can purchase them at a later point in time. In general, this data would be maintained only for a certain period of time. The customer can modify the cart, but this cart is active for a customer only for one month in this application. If the customer does not order the items before this period, his/her cart would be emptied by a batch process. Table 21.7 shows the structure of the Cart table, and Table 21.8 displays the CartDetails table.

TABLE 21.7 Cart

Column Name	Datatype	Key	Description
CartId	Int	Primary Key	Identity field (auto-generated number to identify the uniqueness of the record).
UserId	UniqueIdentifier	Foreign Key	The UserId of the customer who has added the products to the cart.

TABLE 21.8 CartDetails

Column Name	Datatype	Key	Description
CartDetailsId	Int	Primary Key	
CartId	Int	Foreign Key	The details are associated with the CartId in the Cart table.
ProductId	Int	Foreign Key	The product held by the cart.
QuantityOrdered	Int	Not Null	The quantity ordered per each product.
Price	money	Not Null	The price of this item. It holds the price of the product multiplied by the quantity ordered.
ShopDate	Datetime	Not Null	The date of shopping the product in the cart.

Order **Table**

After the customer finalizes the cart and proceeds to order the items, he/she has to provide the billing and shipping address. Taxes and shipping charges are applicable accordingly and the total amount to be paid is calculated. Once the customer confirms the order, he/she pays with a credit card through a payment gateway service and then is returned back to the site. The order table holds the order information of the customer and its status. Table 21.9 displays the structure of the Order table.

TABLE 21.9 Order

Column Name	Datatype	Key	Description
OrderId	Int	Primary Key	Identity field (auto-generated number to identify the uniqueness of the record).
CartId	Int	Foreign Key	The order mapped to the customer's cart.
OrderDate	Datetime	Not Null	Date of purchase/order.
Tax	Money	Allow Null	Amount of taxes to be paid.
Discount	Money	Allow Null	Discount, if applicable.
ShippingCharges	Money	AllowNull	Shipping charges, if applicable.
TotalAmount	Money		Not Null The total amount after applying taxes, discounts, and shipping charges.
OrderStatus	Varchar(20)		Not Null The status of the order: Confirmed, Dispatched, Shipped.
DispatchDate	datetime	Allow Null	The date when the order has been dispatched to the customer.
ShippedDate	datetime	Allow Null	The date of shipping the order to the customer.

Address **Table**

This table holds the address information of the customer. The customer is prompted to enter a shipping address when placing an order. This happens when the customer is shopping in this site for the first time. The address details are automatically populated in the order page for subsequent visits to the site. However, the customer can update the shipping address details, which are saved back to the Address table. Table 21.10 displays the structure of the Address table.

TABLE 21.10 Address

Column Name	Datatype	Key	Description
AddressId	Int	Primary Key	Identity field (auto-generated number to identify the uniqueness of the record).
UserId	uniqueidentifier	Foreign Key	The UserId of the customer.
Address	Varchar(250)	Allow Null	Door number, street number of the customer.
City	Varchar(250)	Allow Null	City of the customer.

TABLE 21.10   Continued

Column Name	Datatype	Key	Description
State	Varchar(250)	Allow Null	State of the customer.
Country	Varchar(250)	Allow Null	Country of the customer.
Zipcode	Varchar(20)	Allow Null	Zip code of the customer.
ContactNo	Varchar(20)	Allow Null	Contact number of the customer.

The preceding tables define the database design of the sample e-commerce application. The database diagram representing the tables and its relationships is provided in Figure 21.7.

FIGURE 21.7
Database design of the sample e-commerce application

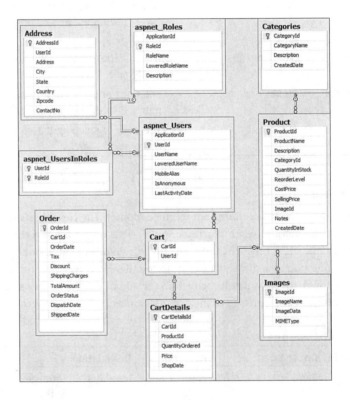

We come to the end of this hour by finalizing the data model of the application. The next hour starts the development of the site.

Summary

This hour gave us an overview of an e-commerce application and covered the basic functionality and design of the application we will develop in the next three hours. This hour explained the different modules of the application in login, product search, and cart management; user and role management; and administering by managing products and orders. It also discussed the architecture and the database design, giving us a glimpse of the shopping cart model in its entirety. The next hour focuses on building the application and begins with the development of the home page, registration, and product search.

Workshop

Quiz

1. What are the different features provided in a shopping web site?

2. What is e-commerce?

3. Is a shopping web site a B2C type of a business or B2B?

4. Name three important tables from the list of the tables generated by the ASP.NET Membership and Role Provider tool.

5. What does the term "role" refer to when related to an application's user?

6. Name the modules in this shopping cart application.

Answers

1. A shopping web site basically provides product and category search, product display, adding products to cart, managing the cart, processing orders, tracking orders, and status updates of order shipments.

2. E-commerce, or electronic commerce, refers to an online store that is used for buying and selling goods—a concept that has grown in leaps and bounds over the last few years.

3. B2C type of business. B2C (Business to Consumer) is a commerce between merchants and consumers.

4. The three most important tables generated by the ASP.NET Membership and Role Provider tool include

- ▶ `aspnet_Roles`

- ▶ `aspnet_Users`

- ▶ `aspnet_UsersInRole`

5. A user's role here implies the privileges that he/she has when accessing the application, that is, the modules that the user can access, the operations that can be performed, and so on. A typical role can be administrator or admin user, guest user, and so on. Note that the administrator is the super user of the application; he/she can create users, define roles, drop users, provide or revoke privileges, and so on.

6. This application is comprised of the following modules:

- ▶ Home page, registration, and login

- ▶ Product display/search and shopping cart management

- ▶ Order generation and online payment

- ▶ User and role management

- ▶ Order and product management

HOUR 22

Setting Up the Application

What You'll Learn in This Hour:

▶ Developing a master page for the site

▶ Managing users and roles

▶ Developing the registration page

▶ Logging in and navigating the site

This hour focuses on setting up the application by starting the development of ASP.NET Ajax pages for the sample e-commerce application. We begin the development by creating a master page, which will be used across the application, and then creating pages to manage roles and users. After the users are set up, we will come up with the registration page to register the customer in the system and give you a glimpse of what will appear on the home page.

Getting Started with the Master Page

Create a new ASP.NET Ajax-enabled site named STY-ASP.NETAjaxApp. This is the site that we'll use to create the sample e-commerce application that we were discussing earlier. We will use this hour and the next two hours to build up this application, and as we go along, we will provide code listings and snippets. The entire application is provided on this book's web site.

After creating the web site, add a master page, `MasterPage.master`, and make sure the option Place Code in Separate File is checked. The master page in an ASP.NET application is used to hold the repeating elements in every page of the application. This will generally be the header of the site, the search interface, and any navigation menu(s) or sitemap. Let's proceed to create these elements in our master page. In our application, this master page will also hold the Login and Search interfaces. Open the source view of MasterPage.master and add the following lines of code:

```
<html xmlns="http://www.w3.org/1999/xhtml" >
<head runat="server">
    <title>STY ASP.NET AJAX in 24 Hours - Sample e-commerce application</title>
    <link rel="stylesheet" href="StyleSheet.css" type="text/css" />
</head>
<body>
    <form id="form1" runat="server">
    <div>
        <table border="0" style="height:100%">
        <tr style="height: 20%">
            <td colspan="2">
                <table border="0" class="Title">
                <tr>
                    <td style="width: 25%; height: 20%;" align="left">
➥Sams Teach Yourself ASP.NET AJAX</td>
                    <td style="width: 75%; height: 20%;" align="right">A Sample
➥e-commerce site !</td>
                </tr>
                </table>
            </td>
        </tr>
        <tr style="height: 5%">
            <td style="width: 30%"> <asp:Label ID="lblTime"
➥runat="server" CssClass="LabelText"></asp:Label></td>
            <td style="width: 70%" align="left"><asp:Label
ID="lblPageSubHeading"
➥ runat="server" CssClass="PageSubHeading" Text=">> You are at Home
➥Page"></asp:Label></td>
        </tr>
        <tr style="height: 75%">
            <td valign="top">
                <table border="0">
                <tr>
                    <td>
                        <asp:LoginStatus ID="LoginStatus1" runat="server"
➥CssClass="Hyperlink" />
                        <br />
                        <asp:LoginView ID="LoginView1" runat="server" >
                        <LoggedInTemplate>
                        <span class="WarningText">Welcome</span>
                        <asp:LoginName ID="LoginName1" runat="server"
                        CssClass="WarningText"/>
                        </LoggedInTemplate>
                        </asp:LoginView>
                    </td>
                </tr>
                <tr>
                    <td>
                        <asp:Login ID="Login1" runat="server"
➥BackColor="#E3EAEB" BorderColor="#E6E2D8" BorderPadding="4"
➥BorderStyle="Solid" BorderWidth="1px" Font-Names="Verdana"
➥Font-Size="0.8em" ForeColor="#333333" TextLayout="TextOnTop">
```

```
                                    <TitleTextStyle BackColor="#1C5E55" Font-Bold="True"
➥Font-Size="0.9em" ForeColor="White" />
                                    <InstructionTextStyle Font-Italic="True"
➥ForeColor="Black" />
                                    <TextBoxStyle Font-Size="0.8em" />
                                    <LoginButtonStyle BackColor="White"
➥BorderColor="#C5BBAF" BorderStyle="Solid" BorderWidth="1px"
                                        Font-Names="Verdana" Font-Size="0.8em"
➥ForeColor="#1C5E55" />
                                </asp:Login>
                            </td>
                        </tr>
                        <tr>
                            <td>
                                <table border="0" class="Table">
                                <tr>
                                    <td class="LabelText">Search Categories</td>
                                </tr>
                                <tr>
                                    <td><asp:TextBox ID="txtSearchCategory"
➥runat="server"></asp:TextBox> 
                                        <asp:Button ID="btnSearchCategory"
➥CssClass="ButtonText" runat="server" Text="Go" />
                                    </td>
                                </tr>
                                <tr>
                                    <td class="LabelText">Search Products</td>
                                </tr>
                                <tr>
                                    <td><asp:TextBox ID="txtSearchProduct"
➥runat="server"></asp:TextBox> 
                                        <asp:Button ID="btnSearchProduct"
➥CssClass="ButtonText" runat="server" Text="Go" />
                                    </td>
                                </tr>
                                </table>
                            </td>
                        </tr>
                        </table>
                    </td>
                    <td valign="top">
                        <asp:Label ID="lblErrorMessage" runat="server"
➥CssClass="ErrorText"></asp:Label><br />
                        <asp:contentplaceholder id="ContentPlaceHolder1"
➥runat="server">
                        </asp:contentplaceholder>
                    </td>
                </tr>
                </table>
        </div>
        </form>
</body>
</html>
```

The preceding code listing of the `MasterPage.master` holds the header information at the top, and a `Login` and a `Search` interface at the left side of the page. The rest of the page holds a `ContentPlaceHolder`, which holds all the other pages in the site that use this master page. The `Login` interface has three ASP.NET controls: `LoginStatus`, `LoginView`, and `Login`. The `LoginStatus` control displays the status of Login on a user. The `LoginView` control has a `LoggedInTemplate`, which displays information after a successful login. In this case, it displays a welcome message of the logged-in username. Finally, the `Login` control is a new ASP.NET control in version 2.0, which is associated with the ASP.NET role and membership provider. We will have a brief discussion about this in the next section when setting up the roles and users for this system. All you need to keep in mind is that the `Login` control uses a membership provider to login to the system, and the entire user context across the application can be accessed through this provider. The design view of this master page is shown in Figure 22.1.

FIGURE 22.1
Design view
of the
MasterPage.
master page

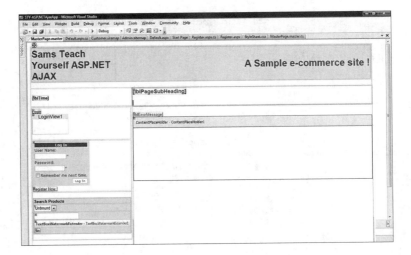

In Figure 22.1, you can see that there are three labels. One label, named `lblTime`, displays the current time, which is placed just above the `Login` interface. The second label, named `lblPageHeading`, is used to display the heading of the page that it is navigated to. By default, the home page is displayed. To change its text from other pages, we expose a public property called `PageSubHeading` from the code-behind of the master page. The third label, named `lblErrorMessage`, is used to display an error or warning message if any during the course of a transaction. To assign text to this label, we expose this as a public property called `ErrorMessage` from the code behind of the master page. The code snippet is as follows:

```
public Label PageSubHeading
{
get { return lblPageSubHeading; }
      set { lblPageSubHeading = value; }
```

```
}
public Label ErrorMessage
    {
        get { return lblErrorMessage; }
        set { lblErrorMessage = value; }
    }
protected void Page_Load(object sender, EventArgs e)
{
this.lblTime.Text = DateTime.Now.ToString();
    if (Page.User.Identity.IsAuthenticated == false)
            this.LoginStatus1.Visible = false;
    else
            this.LoginStatus1.Visible = true;
}
```

In the page load event, we are setting the current time to the Label `lblTime` and also checking if a user is logged on. If logged on, the `LoginStatus` control will be made visible, and this will show the welcome message of the logged-in user and a link for logging out. If no user is logged in, this control will be made invisible. If you have observed the HTML of the `MasterPage.master`, we have applied a stylesheet for all the display elements in the site. The styles have been stored in `Stylesheet.css` in the application. The following are the styles used in this site from this file:

```
body
{
        font-family: Arial;
}
.Title
{
        font-weight: bold;
        font-size: xx-large;
        color: blue;
        background-color: #E3EAEB;
}
.Table
{
        background-color: #E3EAEB;
}
.PageSubHeading
{
        font-weight: bold;
        font-size: large;
        color: #284E98;
}
.Hyperlink
{
        font-weight: normal;
        font-size: small;
        color: Blue;
        text-decoration: underline;
}
.ButtonText
{
```

```
            font-weight: bold;
            font-size: x-small;
            color: Black;
}
.LabelText
{
            font-weight: bold;
            font-size: small;
            color: Black;
}
.ContentMedium
{
            font-weight: normal;
            font-size: small;
            color: Black;
}
.ContentSmall
{
            font-weight: normal;
            font-size: x-small;
            color: Black;
}
.ErrorText
{
            font-weight: normal;
            font-size: small;
            color: Red;
}
.WarningText
{
            font-weight: bold;
            font-size: Small;
            color: Red;
}
.Transparent
{
            font-weight: normal;
            font-size: xx-small;
            color: Gray;
}
.ProductList
{
            display:inline;
            float:left;
            margin-left:20px;
            margin-bottom:20px;
}
```

User and Role Management

Now that the master page is ready, we need to set up the roles and users in the system for performing operations in the site. As discussed in the previous hour, we will have three roles in the system: Administrator, Manager, and Customer. This section guides us through creating the roles in the application using the ASP.NET 2.0 mem-

bership and role providers. The default membership and role providers used by
ASP.NET are SqlMembershipProvider and SqlRoleProvider, which serialize the
information to a SQL Server database. This information is stored in a pre-defined set
of tables and accessed through a number of pre-defined stored procedures. If you
create roles and users through the default providers, ASP.NET will create SQL Server
2005 Express Edition database ASPNET.MDF in your application's App_data folder
with a pre-defined schema and a set of stored procedures.

For our sample application, we have defined our own database in SQL Server 2005.
To map the users and roles with our existing database, we need to create a custom
membership and role provider. To do this, ASP.NET 2.0 has provided a tool called
ASP.NET SQL Server Registration Tool (aspnet_regsql.exe). This can be found in
the following folder: %Windows%\Microsoft.NET\Framework\v2.0.5.727. Running
this tool opens up the ASP.NET SQL Server Setup Wizard, which allows you to configure a SQL Server database for application services. Select this option in the wizard;
then select the database named shoppingcart, provide SQL Server authentication
details sa/sa, and click Finish. This will set up the schema in our existing database
shoppingcart. Figure 22.2 displays the database schema consisting of the tables
generated from this tool. You can also find the application-specific tables that we
created in the previous hour.

Even though we have the membership and role schema merged into our existing
database, the default providers SqlMembershipProvider and SqlRoleProvider will
still make use of the ASPNET.MDF and will send the requests there. To make the
providers use our existing database, we need to add our own provider instances in
the web.config file. To customize the providers, we need to add the following in the
web.config file:

```
<configuration>
  <connectionStrings>
<add name="MyConn" connectionString="Data Source=localhost; Initial Catalog=
➥shoppingcart; User Id=sa; password= sa" providerName="System.Data.SqlClient"/>
</connectionStrings>
<system.web>
<!—Other configurations —>
  <roleManager enabled="true" defaultProvider="CustomizedRoleProvider">
      <providers>
<add connectionStringName="MyConn" name="CustomizedRoleProvider"
➥type="System.Web.Security.SqlRoleProvider" />
      </providers>
 </roleManager>
  <membership defaultProvider="CustomizedMembershipProvider">
      <providers>
<add name="CustomizedMembershipProvider" type="System.Web.
➥Security.SqlMembershipProvider" connectionStringName="MyConn" />
      </providers>
  </membership>
 </system.web>
</configuration>
```

FIGURE 22.2
List of database
tables to be
used in develop-
ing the sample
application

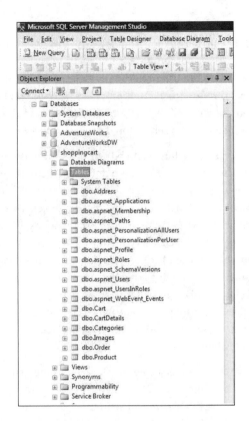

FIGURE 22.2
List of database
tables to be
used in develop-
ing the sample
application

The infrastructure for custom membership and roles is set up. Now, to add the roles and users, click the Web Site Administration Tool in the solution explorer of your project. This opens up an IE browser to administer the site. Click the Security tab. If this tab fails to open up or is in error, then there is a configuration error in the web.config file. The problem will be more specifically on the connection between application and the database server. So verify the connection string to fix this issue. The security tab will be as displayed in Figure 22.3.

In Figure 22.3, you find three sections: Users, Roles, and Access Rules. Users and Roles are important for us in the context of our application. First, create the roles Administrator, Manager, and Customer. Figure 22.4 illustrates the creation of the three roles.

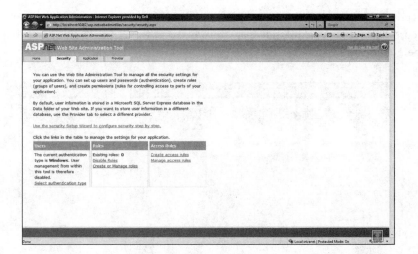

FIGURE 22.3
Security tab in the Web Site Administration tool

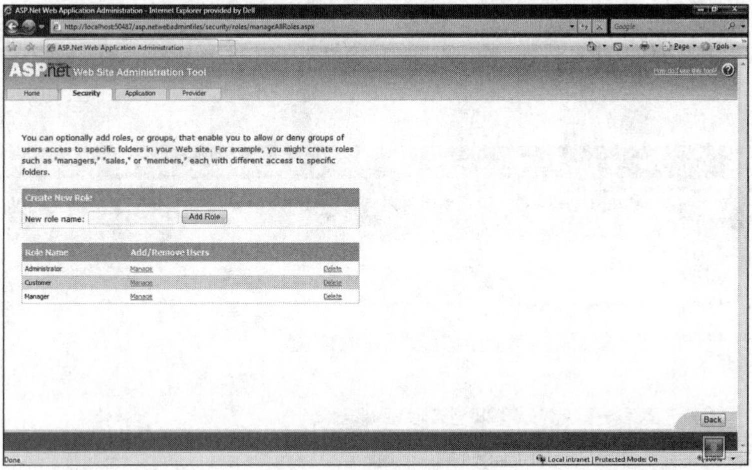

FIGURE 22.4
The roles used in the sample application

In the Users section, click the link Select Authentication Type, select the option From the Internet, and click Done because this application is developed for users of the Internet and not the local network. Let's add two users: one Administrator and one Manager. The first user sriram with password sriram@24h is the Administrator of the site. The second user joydip with the password joydip@24h is the Manager of the site. We will not add customers from here as it does not make sense. This tool is only for Administrators and Managers of the site. The customer will register from the front end of the site. The customer registration is covered in the next section.

Figures 22.5 and 22.6 show the Create User screen and User List screen, respectively. Figure 22.6 displays the users `sriram` and `joydip` added to the site using the Web Site Administration Tool.

FIGURE 22.5
Creating user
"sriram"

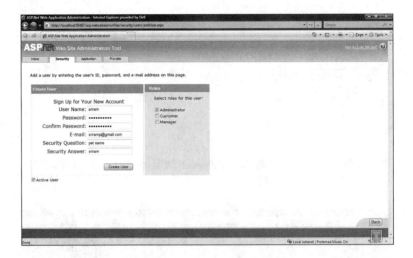

FIGURE 22.6
Displaying
users "joydip"
and "sriram"

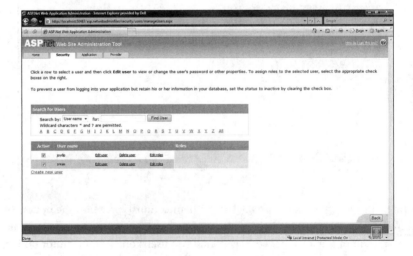

The next section demonstrates registering a customer from the site.

Registering a Customer

Before we proceed to develop the customer registration page, let's add a page called
Default.aspx that acts as a home page for the application. As of now, this page
will hold only static content and will use the master page MasterPage.master. This
page will be the starting point of the application. Later in the book, we will add the
products list to this page. The current HTML source of the Default.aspx page is as
follows:

```
<%@ Page Language="C#" MasterPageFile="~/MasterPage.master"
AutoEventWireup="true"
➥CodeFile="Default.aspx.cs" Inherits="_Default" Title="Home Page" %>
<%@ MasterType TypeName="MasterPage" %>
<asp:Content ID="Content1" ContentPlaceHolderID="ContentPlaceHolder1"
➥runat="server">
    <div class="ContentMedium">
        Welcome to this shopping site. You can search / view all the products
➥available <br />
        in this site and can order them. Below are the list of few products.
        <br />
    </div>
    <br />
</asp:Content>
```

We will assign the text "You are at Home Page!" to the PageSubHeading property of
the master page in the page_load event of the Default.aspx page. As discussed
earlier in the hour, we have to set this property in each page accordingly to display
the user to which page he/she is currently in.

```
protected void Page_Load(object sender, EventArgs e)
    {
        this.Master.PageSubHeading.Text = ">> You are at Home Page !";
    }
```

Registering a customer is done from the front end of the site. We've added a link
called "Register Now" just below the Login control. Clicking this link will open a
customer registration page. We will be using the same database schema for storing
the customers as we did for the Managers and Administrators. Doing this will
enable us to use the custom membership and role provider to access the context of
the Customer login throughout the application. Also the registration form we are
using is an in-built CreateUserWizard of ASP.NET 2.0. Therefore, we will use the
Membership API to insert the new customer into our database. Now, these users can
be seen from the Web Site Administrator tool. Instead of using the basic wizard,
we'll make the CreateUserWizard a little more interesting by customizing it using
the ContentTemplate and adding Ajax extenders to validate the user input and
enrich the user experience.

Create a new ASPX page called `Register.aspx` and make sure to select the master page `MasterPage.master`.

> When creating a new web form in our application, select the option Select Master Page. This should be done because every page in the application uses the master page.

Add the `MasterType` attribute to make use of the properties of the master page:

```
<%@ MasterType TypeName="MasterPage" %>
```

Because we will be using Ajax extenders in this page, we have to add two dlls—`AjaxControlToolkit.dll` and `Microsoft.Web.Preview.dll`—to our solution. Create a physical folder called Ajax Extensions and place these two dlls from the installed location of ASP.NET Ajax 1.0 into the folder. After copying these two dlls, go to the solution explorer and add a reference to these two dlls. Next, create a new tab "AJAX Control Toolkit" in the toolbox and choose items from the `AjaxControlToolkit.dll`. Refer to Hour 10 to see the steps in creating this tab. Figure 22.7 displays the selected extenders in the new tab, AJAX Control Toolkit.

FIGURE 22.7
The Ajax Control Toolkit

Because Ajax controls are being used, the page needs to have the ScriptManager control to process these controls.

> Because every page might use some Ajax-related feature, it is better to have the ScriptManager control placed in the master page MasterPage.master rather than having it in every page.

By the Way

> It is better to add Ajax-related features after adding all the required content in the page, as IDE support for ASP.NET controls will not be there when an Ajax control like UpdatePanel is placed. Therefore, get all the ASP.NET activity done first, and add Ajax last.

Did you Know?

Place the ScriptManager control in the MasterPage.master:

```
<asp:ScriptManager ID="ScriptManager1" runat="server" EnablePageMethods="true">
        </asp:ScriptManager>
```

Now place the Content tag in the Register.aspx page as this uses the master page MasterPage.master:

```
<asp:Content ID="Content1" ContentPlaceHolderID="ContentPlaceHolder1"
➥runat="server">
    <div>
    </div>
</asp:Content>
```

Drag the CreateUserWizard control from the Login tab of the toolbox and set the AutoFormat to Professional. The following is the source of the default CreateUserWizard:

```
<asp:CreateUserWizard ID="CreateUserWizard1" runat="server" BackColor="#E3EAEB"
➥BorderColor="#E6E2D8"
            BorderStyle="Solid" BorderWidth="1px" Font-Names="Verdana"
➥Font-Size="0.8em"
            OnCreatedUser="CreateUserWizard1_CreatedUser"
            EmailRegularExpression="\w+([-+.']\w+)*@\w+([-.]\w+)*\.\w+([-
.]\w+)*"
➥ContinueDestinationPageUrl="~/Default.aspx">
            <WizardSteps>
                <asp:CreateUserWizardStep runat="server">
                </asp:CreateUserWizardStep>
                <asp:CompleteWizardStep runat="server">
                </asp:CompleteWizardStep>
            </WizardSteps>
            <SideBarStyle BackColor="#1C5E55" Font-Size="0.9em"
➥VerticalAlign="Top" />
            <TitleTextStyle BackColor="#1C5E55" Font-Bold="True"
➥ForeColor="White" />
```

```
            <SideBarButtonStyle ForeColor="White" />
            <NavigationButtonStyle BackColor="White" BorderColor="#C5BBAF"
➥BorderStyle="Solid"
                BorderWidth="1px" Font-Names="Verdana" ForeColor="#1C5E55" />
            <HeaderStyle BackColor="#666666" BorderColor="#E6E2D8"
➥BorderStyle="Solid" BorderWidth="2px"
                Font-Bold="True" Font-Size="0.9em" ForeColor="White"
➥HorizontalAlign="Center" />
            <CreateUserButtonStyle BackColor="White" BorderColor="#C5BBAF"
➥BorderStyle="Solid"
                BorderWidth="1px" Font-Names="Verdana" ForeColor="#1C5E55" />
            <ContinueButtonStyle BackColor="White" BorderColor="#C5BBAF"
➥BorderStyle="Solid"
                BorderWidth="1px" Font-Names="Verdana" ForeColor="#1C5E55" />
            <StepStyle BorderWidth="0px" />
        </asp:CreateUserWizard>
```

In the preceding code snippet, we have included three important attributes:
`OnCreatedUser`, `EmailRegularExpression`, and `ContinueDestinationPageUrl`.

The `OnCreatedUser` is an attribute that holds an event to be fired when a user is
added. We require this event in order to add the role for this user. The code-behind
of this event is as follows:

```
protected void CreateUserWizard1_CreatedUser(object sender, System.EventArgs e)
    {
        Roles.AddUserToRole(CreateUserWizard1.UserName, "Customer");
    }
```

This event is raised immediately after a user is added. We are adding the Customer
role to this user, as every user who registers from the front end is a customer in our
application.

The `EmailRegularExpression` attribute is used to validate the EmailId field in the
control, and the third attribute we mentioned, the `ContinueDestinationPageUrl`, is
used to redirect to the set page in this attribute after completing the registration and
clicking the Continue button.

Next, the `WizardSteps` tag in the CreateUser Wizard has two key elements:
CreateUserWizardStep and CompleteWizardStep. To customize these two elements, we
need to create `ContentTemplate` tags in each of these elements and place our HTML
in it. The only restriction is that the IDs of the fields—such as UserName, Password,
ConfirmPassword, Email, and so on—should not be changed. In our example, we are
customizing it to introduce Ajax to these elements. Following is the code listing that
holds a table containing these fields: UserName, Password, ConfirmPassword,
EmailId, Security Question, Answer, and Required Validators. Apart from these,

we have also added Ajax extenders, such as TextBoxWaterMarkExtender, PasswordStrengthExtender, and ValidatorCalloutExtender:

```
        <WizardSteps>
        <asp:CreateUserWizardStep ID="CreateUserWizardStep1" runat="server">
        <ContentTemplate>
          <table border="0">
            <tr>
              <td align="center" colspan="2">
                Sign Up for Your New Account</td>
            </tr>
            <tr>
              <td align="right">
                <label class="ContentSmall" for="UserName">
                  User Name:</label></td>
              <td>
                <asp:TextBox ID="UserName" runat="server"></asp:TextBox>
                <cc1:TextBoxWatermarkExtender ID="TextBoxWatermarkExtender1"
➥runat="server" Enabled="True"
                        TargetControlID="UserName" WatermarkText=
➥"Enter User Name" WatermarkCssClass="Transparent">
                    </cc1:TextBoxWatermarkExtender>
                <asp:RequiredFieldValidator ControlToValidate="UserName"
➥ ErrorMessage="User Name is required."
                        ID="UserNameRequired" runat="server" ToolTip=
➥"User Name is required."
➥ValidationGroup="CreateUserWizard1">*</asp:RequiredFieldValidator>
                    <cc1:ValidatorCalloutExtender
ID="ValidatorCalloutExtender1"
➥runat="server" TargetControlID="UserNameRequired">
                    </cc1:ValidatorCalloutExtender>
              </td>
            </tr>
            <tr>
              <td align="right">
                <label class="ContentSmall" for="Password">
                  Password:</label></td>
              <td>
                <asp:TextBox ID="Password" runat="server"
➥TextMode="Password"></asp:TextBox>
                <cc1:PasswordStrength ID="PasswordStrength1"
➥runat="server" TargetControlID="Password">
                    </cc1:PasswordStrength>
                <asp:RequiredFieldValidator ControlToValidate="Password"
➥ ErrorMessage="Password is required."
                        ID="PasswordRequired" runat="server"
➥ToolTip="Password is required."
➥ValidationGroup="CreateUserWizard1">*</asp:RequiredFieldValidator>
              </td>
            </tr>
            <tr>
              <td align="right">
                <label class="ContentSmall" for="ConfirmPassword">
                  Confirm Password:</label></td>
              <td>
```

```
                        <asp:TextBox ID="ConfirmPassword" runat="server"
➥TextMode="Password"></asp:TextBox>
                        <asp:RequiredFieldValidator
➥ControlToValidate="ConfirmPassword"
➥ErrorMessage="Confirm Password is required."
                        ID="ConfirmPasswordRequired" runat="server"
➥ToolTip="Confirm Password is required."
                        ValidationGroup="CreateUserWizard1">*
➥</asp:RequiredFieldValidator>
                      </td>
                    </tr>
                    <tr>
                      <td align="right">
                        <label class="ContentSmall" for="Email">
                        E-mail:</label></td>
                      <td>
                        <asp:TextBox ID="Email" runat="server"></asp:TextBox>
                        <asp:RequiredFieldValidator ControlToValidate="Email"
➥ErrorMessage="E-mail is required."
                        ID="EmailRequired" runat="server" ToolTip=
➥"E-mail is required."
➥ValidationGroup="CreateUserWizard1">*</asp:RequiredFieldValidator>
                      </td>
                    </tr>
                    <tr>
                      <td align="right">
                        <label class="ContentSmall" for="Question">
                        Security Question:</label></td>
                      <td>
                        <asp:TextBox ID="Question" runat="server"></asp:TextBox>
                        <asp:RequiredFieldValidator ControlToValidate="Question"
➥ ErrorMessage="Security question is required."
                        ID="QuestionRequired" runat="server"
➥ToolTip="Security question is required."
➥ValidationGroup="CreateUserWizard1">*</asp:RequiredFieldValidator>
                      </td>
                    </tr>
                    <tr>
                      <td align="right">
                        <label class="ContentSmall" for="Answer">
                        Security Answer:</label></td>
                      <td>
                        <asp:TextBox ID="Answer" runat="server"></asp:TextBox>
                        <asp:RequiredFieldValidator ControlToValidate="Answer"
➥ErrorMessage="Security answer is required."
                        ID="AnswerRequired" runat="server" ToolTip="Security
➥answer is required."
➥ValidationGroup="CreateUserWizard1">*</asp:RequiredFieldValidator>
                      </td>
                    </tr>
                    <tr>
                      <td align="center" colspan="2">
                        <asp:CompareValidator ControlToCompare="Password"
➥ControlToValidate="ConfirmPassword"
                        Display="Dynamic" ErrorMessage="The Password and
➥Confirmation Password must match."
                        ID="PasswordCompare" runat="server"
➥ValidationGroup="CreateUserWizard1"></asp:CompareValidator>
```

```
                    </td>
                  </tr>
                  <tr>
                    <td align="center" colspan="2" style="color: red">
                      <asp:Literal EnableViewState="False" ID="ErrorMessage"
➥ runat="server"></asp:Literal>
                    </td>
                  </tr>
                  <tr>
                    <td colspan="2">
                    </td>
                  </tr>
                </table>
              </ContentTemplate>
            </asp:CreateUserWizardStep>
            <asp:CompleteWizardStep ID="CompleteWizardStep1" runat="server">
              <ContentTemplate>
                <table border="0">
                  <tr>
                    <td align="center" colspan="2">
                      Complete</td>
                  </tr>
                  <tr>
                    <td>
                      Your account has been successfully created.</td>
                  </tr>
                  <tr>
                    <td align="right" colspan="2">
                      <asp:Button CausesValidation="False"
➥CommandName="Continue" ID="ContinueButton" runat="server"
                        Text="Continue" ValidationGroup="CreateUserWizard1" />
                    </td>
                  </tr>
                </table>
              </ContentTemplate>
            </asp:CompleteWizardStep>
          </WizardSteps>
```

We need to register the Ajax control toolkit as we are using the controls from this toolkit. This is done by adding the following snippet at the top of the Register.aspx page:

```
<%@ Register Assembly="AjaxControlToolkit" Namespace="AjaxControlToolkit"
➥TagPrefix="cc1" %>
```

In the UserName field, we have added a TextBoxWaterMarkExtender. The TargetControlID property should be set to the UserName textbox. When the textbox is empty, it displays the message as set in this extender, and the message is wiped out when the focus is on the textbox. You can also set the CSS style for the watermark. The field Password has an extender PasswordStrengthExtender, which signifies the strength of the password when the user types in the password. The styling and formatting are configurable. The third extender used is the ValidatorCalloutExtender. This is used for the UserName field. This extender is to be set for a `RequiredFieldValidator`. Because `UserName` already has one, we have set this extender to it. The significance of this extender is that the message pops out in a graphical fashion, and images can be set. Certainly, these cool little features add to your application. The design view of the `Register.aspx` is shown in Figure 22.8.

FIGURE 22.8
Registering a
customer

Set the `Default.aspx` as the start-up page and run the application. Click the `Register Now` link, click the `Create User` button without entering values and see how the extenders play their role, and then add a customer to the site for later use in the application. Now that we have the users ready in the system, we need to take care of the navigational aspects of the application. This is the focus of the next section.

Navigating the Site

Navigation is an important part of any site, which helps the user go to any page of the web site from the home page. Because this application is based on e-commerce, we will definitely have links such as Products, View Cart, and Order, which directly takes the user to the requested page. As discussed earlier, we have three types of users for our application: Administrator, Manager, and Customer. The Administrator and Manager have similar kinds of privileges, except that the Administrator has control over all the Managers, and the Customer shops at the site to purchase products. Therefore, we have designed a `Menu` control that helps the respective user in navigating the site.

The `Menu` control is a new control in ASP.NET 2.0 that requires a `SqlDataSource` or `XmlDataSource` to bind the data to the control. If we specify a `SqlDataSource` to it, the `Menu` control, by default, looks for a `Web.sitemap` file, which has all the menu items listed. This `Web.sitemap` file is an XML file that has `siteMapNode` tags holding the menu item in the attributes `url`, `title`, `description`, and so on. But the problem we have is that we have two different sets of navigational items—one each for Administrator/Manager and Customer—and we have defined two sitemap files, `Admin.sitemap` and `Customer.sitemap`, which are described next:

`Admin.sitemap`:

```
<?xml version="1.0" encoding="utf-8" ?>
<siteMap>
        <siteMapNode url="~/AdminHome.aspx" title="Home" description=
➥"Home page" />
        <siteMapNode url="~/ManageCategories.aspx" title="Product Categories"
➥        description="Manage Product Categories" />
        <siteMapNode url="~/ManageImages.aspx" title="Images"
➥     description="Manage Images" />
        <siteMapNode url="~/ManageProducts.aspx" title="Products"
➥      description="Manage Products" />
        <siteMapNode url="~/PendingOrders.aspx" title="Pending Orders"
➥ description="Pending Orders" />
        <siteMapNode url="~/OrderHistory.aspx" title="Order History"
➥description="Order History" />
</siteMap>
```

`Customer.sitemap`:

```
<?xml version="1.0" encoding="utf-8" ?>
<siteMap>
        <siteMapNode url="~/Default.aspx" title="Home"
➥description="Home page" />
        <siteMapNode url="~/Products.aspx" title="Products"
➥description="Products offered" />
        <siteMapNode url="~/Cart.aspx" title="Shopping Cart"
➥description="Items to purchase" />
        <siteMapNode url="~/Order.aspx" title="Place Order"
➥description="Order the selected items" />
        <siteMapNode url="~/TrackOrder.aspx" title="Track Your Order"
➥description="Track your Order" />
</siteMap>
```

Because we are going with our custom-defined sitemap files in `Admin.sitemap` and `Customer.sitemap`, and not with the standard `Web.sitemap` file, we have to use `XmlDataSource` to bind data to the `Menu` control. We will be using the same `Menu` control to bind the Admin and Customer.sitemap files based on who logs in. By default, we will load the Customer.sitemap file into the Menu control when the web site is opened, and we will retain the Customer.sitemap file when the customer logs in. But when the Administrator/Manager logs in, we will load the Admin.sitemap file into the Menu control.

Now let's load the sitemap files into the Menu control dynamically when the page is loaded. This is done in the MasterPage.master code-behind file. The following is the code listing for loading these sitemap files into the Menu control:

```
public enum SiteMapMenuType
    {
        Customer,
        Admin
    }
protected void Page_Load(object sender, EventArgs e)
    {
        this.lblTime.Text = DateTime.Now.ToString();
        //this.lblErrorMessage.Text = string.Empty;
        if (!Page.IsPostBack)
            this.BindCategories();
        if (Page.User.Identity.IsAuthenticated == false)
        {
            this.LoginStatus1.Visible = false;
            this.Menu1.DataSource = this.GetMenuDataSource
➥(SiteMapMenuType.Customer);
            this.Menu1.DataBind();
        }
        else
        {
            this.LoginStatus1.Visible = true;
            if (Page.User.IsInRole("Customer"))
            {
                this.Menu1.DataSource = this.GetMenuDataSource
➥ (SiteMapMenuType.Customer);
                this.Menu1.DataBind();
                MembershipUser myObject = Membership.GetUser();
                if (this.Menu1.Items[2] != null && this.Menu1.Items[2].
➥NavigateUrl == "~/Cart.aspx")
                    this.Menu1.Items[2].NavigateUrl = "~/Cart.aspx?UserId="
➥+ myObject.ProviderUserKey.ToString();
                if (this.Menu1.Items[3] != null && this.Menu1.Items[3].
➥NavigateUrl == "~/Order.aspx")
                    this.Menu1.Items[3].NavigateUrl = "~/Order.aspx?UserId="
➥+ myObject.ProviderUserKey.ToString();
                if (this.Menu1.Items[4] != null &&
this.Menu1.Items[4].NavigateUrl
➥== "~/TrackOrder.aspx")
                    this.Menu1.Items[4].NavigateUrl =
"~/TrackOrder.aspx?UserId="
➥+ myObject.ProviderUserKey.ToString();
            }
            else
            {
```

```
                      this.Menu1.DataSource = this.GetMenuDataSource
➥ (SiteMapMenuType.Admin);
                      this.Menu1.DataBind();
              }
        }
    }
    XmlDataSource GetMenuDataSource(SiteMapMenuType menu)
    {
        XmlDataSource source = new XmlDataSource();
        source.XPath = "siteMap/siteMapNode";
        switch (menu)
        {
            case SiteMapMenuType.Customer:
                source.DataFile = @"~\Customer.sitemap";
                break;
            case SiteMapMenuType.Admin:
                source.DataFile = @"~\Admin.sitemap";
                break;
            default:
                break;
        }
        source.DataBind();
        return source;
    }
```

In the preceding code listing, we've written a method GetDataSourceName, which
returns an XmlDataSource required to bind it to the Menu control. This method
returns the XmlDataSource containing Admin.sitemap if the authenticated user is
Administrator/Manager; otherwise, it returns the Customer.sitemap into the
XmlDataSource. If no user is authenticated, the method still returns
Customer.sitemap in the XmlDataSource, as this is the navigation to be shown for
every user who visits the site.

After this code is written, we need to set the DataBindings to the Menu control in the
HTML source. Here is the snippet for it:

```
<asp:Menu ID="Menu1" runat="server" Orientation="Horizontal"
➥BackColor="#B5C7DE" DynamicHorizontalOffset="2" Font-Names="Verdana"
➥Font-Size="0.8em" ForeColor="#284E98" StaticSubMenuIndent="10px"
➥Width="60%">
                      <DataBindings>
                          <asp:MenuItemBinding DataMember="siteMapNode"
➥TextField="title" NavigateUrlField="url" />
                      </DataBindings>
                      <StaticMenuItemStyle HorizontalPadding="5px"
➥VerticalPadding="2px" />
                      <DynamicHoverStyle BackColor="#284E98" ForeColor="White" />
                      <DynamicMenuStyle BackColor="#B5C7DE" />
                      <StaticSelectedStyle BackColor="#507CD1" />
                      <DynamicSelectedStyle BackColor="#507CD1" />
                      <DynamicMenuItemStyle HorizontalPadding="5px"
➥VerticalPadding="2px" />
                      <StaticHoverStyle BackColor="#284E98" ForeColor="White" />
              </asp:Menu>
```

This snippet is placed just below the Label lblPageSubHeading in the MasterPage.master HTML source. We set the attributes of MenuItemBinding's DataMember, TextField, and NavigateUrlField to siteMapNode, title, and url, respectively, as set in the sitemap files defined previously. Now we are ready with navigation for the site. Run the application, and you can see the home page loaded with Customer.sitemap in Figure 22.9.

FIGURE 22.9
Home page displaying the navigation bar for the Customer

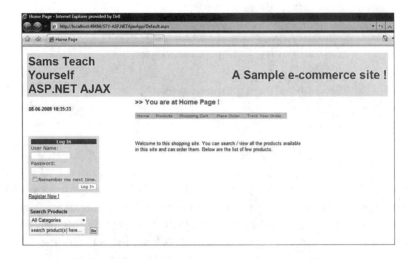

This helps the user navigate to the home page, products page, view cart page, and order page from any part of the web site. Log in with the Administrator username that we created earlier in the hour—that is, sriram with password sriram@24h. You'll find that the sitemap has changed to point to the navigational items administering the site. Figure 22.10 illustrates this.

By the Way

We have not yet added pages to the different links presented in the menu. Therefore, clicking these pages would end up throwing an ASP.NET error. As we progress along building the application, we would add each of those pages.

The application is beautifully set up to take off to the next step of performing some operations on products and adding to the cart. The next hour focuses on managing categories and products from the administration point of view and searching the products and adding it to the cart from the shopping point of view.

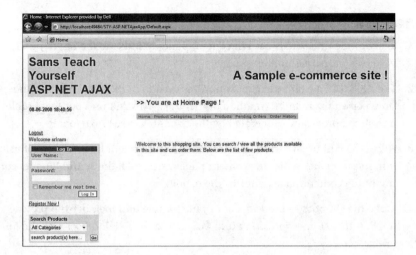

FIGURE 22.10
Home page
displaying the
navigation bar
for the
Administrator/
Manager of the
site

Summary

This hour kick-started the application development of the sample e-commerce application. It covered creating the basic infrastructure required, such as css files, developing master pages for use in all the other pages of the site, creating roles and users for the system by using the custom ASP.NET membership and role providers, registering customers in the site, and providing navigation to all the users in the system. In the next hour, we will concentrate on searching and shopping for the products.

Workshop

Quiz

1. What is a `MasterType` attribute?

2. What is the use of ASP.NET role and membership API?

3. True or False: You cannot use a `ScriptManager` control in a content page after using it in a master page?

4. What should be done to point the ASP.NET role and membership provider to point to an existing database?

5. What is the control `ValidatorCalloutExtender` used for?

6. What is the control `TextBoxWatermarkExtender` used for?

Answers

1. `MasterType` attribute is used in content pages to indicate the use of public variables/properties of master page.

2. The ASP.NET role and membership API is used to manage roles, users and store personalization information of the users. This API uses database tables and stored procedures generated by the `aspnet_regsql.exe` tool.

3. False. You can use a ScriptManager control in a content page in spite of using it in master page. When the content page is accessed, the ScriptManager control in the content page performs the action.

4. Make the changes to the `web.config` file for role and membership providers to point to a connection string that points to a desired database. See the following code:

```
<roleManager enabled="true" defaultProvider="CustomizedRoleProvider">
      <providers>
<add connectionStringName="MyConn" name="CustomizedRoleProvider"
➥type="System.Web.Security.SqlRoleProvider" />
      </providers>
 </roleManager>
   <membership defaultProvider="CustomizedMembershipProvider">
      <providers>
<add name="CustomizedMembershipProvider"
➥type="System.Web.Security.SqlMembershipProvider"
➥connectionStringName="MyConn" />
      </providers>
   </membership>
```

5. `ValidatorCalloutExtender` is used in conjunction with a `RequiredFieldValidator` to validate the input data in a control. The following code uses this extender to validate the textbox `txtProductName`:

```
<asp:TextBox ID="txtProductName" runat="server"></asp:TextBox>
                  <asp:RequiredFieldValidator
➥ControlToValidate="txtProductName" ErrorMessage=
➥"Product Name is required." ID="ProductNameRequired"
➥runat="server" ToolTip="Product Name is
➥required.">*</asp:RequiredFieldValidator>
                        <cc1:ValidatorCalloutExtender ID=
➥"ValidatorCalloutExtender1" runat="server" TargetControlID="
➥ProductNameRequired ">
                  </cc1:ValidatorCalloutExtender>
```

6. `TextBoxWatermarkExtender` is used to notify the user with a message in the textbox. The user needs to mention the textbox name in the attribute `TargetControlID`. When the textbox gets focus, the message is automatically wiped out. See the following code to implement this extender:

```
<asp:TextBox ID="UserName" runat="server"></asp:TextBox>
                    <cc1:TextBoxWatermarkExtender ID=
➡"TextBoxWatermarkExtender1" runat="server" Enabled="True"
                        TargetControlID="UserName" WatermarkText=
➡"Enter User Name" WatermarkCssClass="Transparent">
                    </cc1:TextBoxWatermarkExtender>
```

Searching and Shopping for the Products

What You'll Learn in This Hour:

▶ Setting up categories and products in the site
▶ Searching for products
▶ Adding to the cart and managing the cart

The previous hour set up the application in terms of users, roles, login, the home page, and navigation. The next step is the display of products in the home page, the search functionality for products, the products detail page, and adding products to the cart. For this to happen, we need the products to be set up in the site. Therefore, this hour initially focuses on setting up the categories and products in the site. Later, the user operational flow discussed previously will be put into action.

> This hour contains code snippets for the pages `MasterPage.master`, `Default.aspx`, `ProductDetails.aspx`, and `Cart.aspx`. Only the snippets important in the context of application functionality and snippets related to ASP.NET Ajax are provided. The missing code can be found in the application provided on this book's web site (www.informit.com/ title/9780672329678). Copy the missing code from the web site, paste it in the application you are building here, and run the application.

Setting Up the Categories, Images, and Products

If we look at the data model we have designed for the application, the `Product` table is a child table to the `Categories` and `Images` tables. The `Product` table holds the foreign keys

CategoryId and ImageId, respectively. Figure 23.1 depicts the data model of these three tables.

FIGURE 23.1
Data model of
categories,
images, and
product

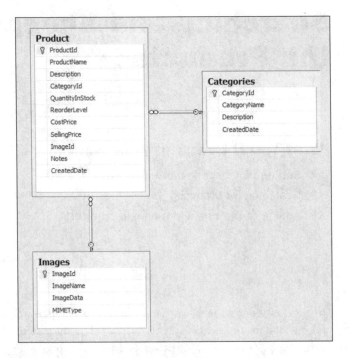

Therefore, before we create a page to add products, we need to create pages for adding categories and images, since the products page will hold the fields' category and image. The three new ASPX pages we will be creating are ManageCategories.aspx, ManageImages.aspx, and ManageProducts.aspx. These three pages are more or less similar, in the sense that all of them are add/edit/delete pages—typical master data setup pages in any application. We will be using the GridView control for viewing the records, and the DetailsView control for adding/updating the records. Let's start off by creating categories in the application.

Open the solution STY-ASP.NETAjaxApp created in the previous hour. Add a new web form and name it ManageCategories.aspx. As usual, the first task is to associate this page with the MasterPage.master file. Then go to the source view and create two panels, pnlMain and pnlDetails. The pnlMain panel holds the GridView control responsible for displaying the categories that are to be used in the application. You can also delete a specific category using this control. The pnlDetails panel holds a DetailsView control, which is used to perform the addition of a new category or editing an existing category. The following is the code snippet of the pnlMain panel in the source view:

```
<asp:Panel ID="pnlMain" runat="server">
    <asp:Button ID="btnAddNew" runat="server" Text="Add New Category"
OnClick="btnAddNew_Click" /><br />
    <asp:GridView ID="gvCategories" runat="server" CssClass="Table"
DataSourceID="GridViewDataSource"
    DataKeyNames="CategoryId" AllowSorting="true" AutoGenerateColumns="false"
    SelectedIndex="0" OnSelectedIndexChanged="gvCategories_SelectedIndexChanged"
RowStyle-CssClass="ContentSmall"
    OnPageIndexChanged="gvCategories_PageIndexChanged"
OnRowDeleted="gvCategories_RowDeleted"
    OnSorted="gvCategories_Sorted" OnRowDataBound="gvCategories_OnRowDataBound">
        <Columns>
            <asp:CommandField ButtonType="Button" ShowSelectButton="true"
ShowDeleteButton="true" />
            <asp:BoundField DataField="CategoryId" HeaderText="Category ID"
ReadOnly="True"
SortExpression="CategoryId" />
            <asp:BoundField DataField="CategoryName" HeaderText="Category Name"
SortExpression="CategoryName" />
            <asp:BoundField DataField="Description" HeaderText="Category Description"
SortExpression="Description" />
        </Columns>
    </asp:GridView><br />
  <asp:ObjectDataSource ID="GridViewDataSource" runat="server"
DeleteMethod="Delete"
        SelectMethod="GetAllCategories"
TypeName="ShoppingCartTableAdapters.CategoriesTableAdapter">
        <DeleteParameters>
            <asp:Parameter Name="CategoryId" Type="Int32" />
        </DeleteParameters>
    </asp:ObjectDataSource>
</asp:Panel>
```

In the preceding code snippet, the GridView control gvCategories uses BoundFields to display the columns, and also uses a CommandField that displays two buttons: Select and Delete. Clicking the Select button displays the category record in editable mode in the DetailsView control. Clicking the Delete button deletes the corresponding category from the data store.

Before we look into the DetailsView and its code for addition and deletion, we have to understand the binding mechanism of categories to the GridView control. This is done with the help of an ObjectDataSource control. This control holds a business object, which binds data to the GridView control. This business object is mentioned in the TypeName attribute of the ObjectDataSource control. In this case, the business object is ShoppingCartTableAdapters.CategoriesTableAdapter. Throughout this application, we will be using different adapters to perform operations in the site. These adapters are created using a typed DataSet object.

Building the Business Objects for the Application

To create a typed DataSet, right-click the project file, click Add New Item, and create a new DataSet object named ShoppingCartDAL.xsd.

This object is created to hold different TableAdapters to be used for the application. In essence, this object acts as a data access layer for the application performing select/insert/update/delete operations. That's the reason you find the naming convention with a suffix "DAL" to ShoppingCart. After adding ShoppingCart.xsd file, this is found in the App_Code folder.

Go to the DataSet designer view of ShoppingCart.xsd and view its properties. Give the Name property as ShoppingCart. Now, this is the name of the dataset, and ShoppingCartTableAdapters is the namespace created automatically for this dataset class. Use this namespace in all the code behind files which are using TableAdapters.

Let's create CategoriesTableAdapter to understand how these adapters are built and used with the ObjectDataSource control.

To create a CategoriesTableAdapter, follow these steps:

1. Right-click the DataSet designer and click Add, TableAdapter.

2. Specify the connection string required to connect to the database. If already configured, the connection string can be chosen in the list provided; else the user can create a new connection. In our case, it is already configured as MyConn (which holds the connection to the shoppingcart database in SQL Server 2005).

3. Choose a command type. The command type specifies the option through which a TableAdapter has to access data. The following are the options:

   Use SQL statements.

   Create new stored procedures.

   Use existing stored procedures.

   In this application, we concentrate on using SQL statements.

4. The next step in the wizard is the query builder. You can either enter the SQL query or use the query builder wizard. Figure 23.2 displays the SQL query in the wizard used to fetch all categories using the CategoriesTableAdapter.

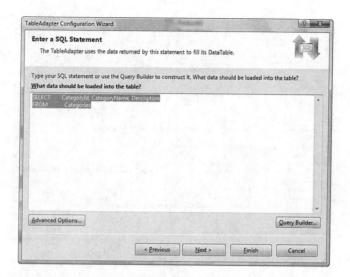

FIGURE 23.2
Configuring
CategoriesTab
leAdapter

5. The next step is to choose the methods to be generated. The TableAdapter methods load and save data between your application and the database. You will have options to return a DataTable and also to create methods to send updates directly to the database (GenerateDBDirectMethods). Let's check the option Return DataTable and name the method GetAllCategories. Check the option to generate insert, update, and delete queries.

You are done with creating a TableAdapter. Go to the properties window of this TableAdapter and name it CategoriesTableAdapter. This TableAdapter automatically generates a CategoriesDataTable with columns mentioned in the SQL statement.

We can also have user-defined insert/update/delete queries by right-clicking the TableAdapter and clicking Add, Query. Now that we are done with creating the CategoriesTableAdapter, you can see the properties of it in the Properties window (see Figure 23.3).

Figure 23.3 displays the properties of the CategoriesTableAdapter, which generated the queries for insert/update/delete commands, apart from the select query. We'll not go into too much detail about TableAdapters in this hour. Rather, we'll just have an overview of how they are built and the operations they perform with respect to our sample application. Similar to the CategoriesTableAdapter, we will have to create ImagesTableAdapter to manage images, ProductTableAdapter to manage products and stock, and CartTableAdapter and CartDetailsAdapter to manage products in the cart. Figure 23.4 displays the TableAdapters in the ShoppingCartDAL.xsd file.

FIGURE 23.3
Properties of
CategoriesTab
leAdapter

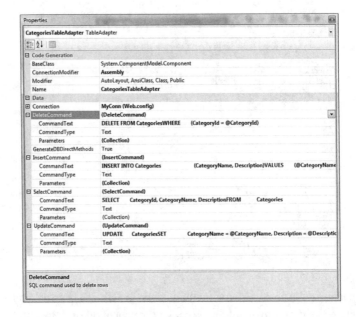

FIGURE 23.4
The
TableAdapters
used in the
sample applica-
tion

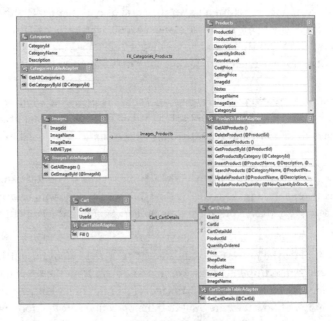

Let's briefly discuss the operations of the TableAdapters we mentioned previously.
These are the methods that are executed while performing operations on the site.
The source is provided on the book's product page (go to www.informit.com/title/
9780672329678 to access the code).

`CategoriesTableAdapter:`

▶ `GetAllCategories()`—Fetches all the categories from the site.

▶ `GetCategoryById(@CategoryId)`—Fetches the category based on the input ID.

Insert, update, and delete methods are generated automatically.

`ImagesTableAdapter:`

▶ `GetAllImages()`—Fetches all the images used in the site.

▶ `GetImageById(@ImageId)`—Fetches images based on the input ID.

Insert, update, and delete methods are generated automatically.

`ProductsTableAdapter:`

▶ `GetAllProducts()`—Fetches all the products available in the site.

▶ `DeleteProduct(@ProductId)`—Deletes a product from the store.

▶ `GetLatestProducts()`—Fetches the five newly added products to the site. These products are displayed in the home page.

▶ `GetProductById(@ProductId)`—Fetches a product based on the input Id.

▶ `GetProductsByCategory(@CategoryId)`—Fetches the products based on the selected category.

▶ `InsertProduct(@ProductName, @Description, @CategoryId, @QuantityInStock, @ReorderLevel, @CostPrice, @SellingPrice, @ImageId, @Notes)`—This method executes an insert statement into the products database.

▶ `SearchProducts(@CategoryName, @ProductName)`—This method searches for the products in the store that matches the entered `CategoryName` or `ProductName`.

▶ `UpdateProduct(@ProductName, @Description, @CategoryId, @QuantityInStock, @ReorderLevel, @CostPrice, @SellingPrice, @ImageId, @Notes, @ProductId)`—This method executes an insert statement into the products database.

▶ `UpdateProductQuantity(@NewQuantityInStock, @ProductId)`—This method updates the stock of the products, when a product is sold out from the site.

CartDetailsTableAdapter:

▶ GetCartDetails(@UserId)—Fetches a user's products from the cart.

▶ AddProductToCart(@CartId, @ProductId, @QuantityOrdered, @Price, @ShopDate)—Adds a product and its details to the cart.

▶ DeleteProductInCart(@CartDetailsId)—Deletes a product from the cart.

▶ UpdateProductInCart(@QuantityOrdered, @Price, @ShopDate, @CartDetailsId)—Updates a product details in the cart.

Now that we understand the business objects built for the application using TableAdapters, we'll get back to the ManageCategories.aspx page, where the CategoriesTableAdapter is used with the ObjectDataSource control to bind data to the GridView control, to display categories information to the user. The TypeName attribute in the ObjectDataSource control holds the business object CategoriesTableAdapter. This ObjectDataSource is used to bind the data to the GridView control gvCategories. The DataSourceID property of gvCategories holds the ID of the ObjectDataSource control—that is, GridViewDataSource. The best part of this process is that the data binding is done without writing a single line of code.

Adding/Editing Categories

Let's discuss the second panel in ManageCategories.aspx, pnlDetails; this displays the DetailsView control, which holds the elements to add or edit categories. The source view for the DetailsView control in pnlDetails is as follows:

```
<asp:Panel ID="pnlDetails" runat="server">
<asp:DetailsView AutoGenerateRows="False" DataSourceID="DetailsViewDataSource"
➥DataKeyNames="CategoryId"
    CssClass="Table" HeaderText="Category Details"
➥RowStyle-CssClass="ContentSmall" ID="dvCategory" runat="server"
➥AutoGenerateEditButton="True"
    AutoGenerateInsertButton="True" OnItemInserted="dvCategory_ItemInserted"
➥OnItemUpdated="dvCategory_ItemUpdated"
    OnDataBound="dvCategory_DataBound" OnModeChanging="dvCategory_ModeChanging"
➥ Width="367px">
    <Fields>
        <asp:TemplateField HeaderText="Category Name"
➥SortExpression="CategoryName">
            <EditItemTemplate>
                <asp:TextBox ID="EditCategoryName"
➥runat="server" Text='<%# Bind("CategoryName") %>'></asp:TextBox>
                <asp:RequiredFieldValidator ControlToValidate="EditCategoryName"
➥ErrorMessage="Category Name is required."
                        ID="CategoryNameRequired" runat="server"
➥ToolTip="Category Name is required.">*</asp:RequiredFieldValidator>
```

```
                        <cc1:ValidatorCalloutExtender ID=
➥"ValidatorCalloutExtender2" runat="server"
➥TargetControlID="CategoryNameRequired">
                        </cc1:ValidatorCalloutExtender>
            </EditItemTemplate>
            <InsertItemTemplate>
                    <asp:TextBox ID="InsertCategoryName" runat="server"
➥Text='<%# Bind("CategoryName") %>'></asp:TextBox>
                    <asp:RequiredFieldValidator
ControlToValidate="InsertCategoryName"
➥ ErrorMessage="Category Name is required."
                        ID="CategoryNameRequired" runat="server"
➥ToolTip="Category Name is required.">*</asp:RequiredFieldValidator>
                    <cc1:ValidatorCalloutExtender ID="ValidatorCalloutExtender1"
➥runat="server" TargetControlID="CategoryNameRequired">
                        </cc1:ValidatorCalloutExtender>
            </InsertItemTemplate>
            <ItemTemplate>
                    <asp:Label ID="Label1" runat="server"
➥Text='<%# Bind("CategoryName") %>'></asp:Label>
            </ItemTemplate>
        </asp:TemplateField>
        <asp:TemplateField HeaderText="Category Description"
➥SortExpression="Description">
            <EditItemTemplate>
                    <asp:TextBox ID="EditDescription" runat="server"
➥Text='<%# Bind("Description") %>'></asp:TextBox>
                    <asp:RequiredFieldValidator ControlToValidate="EditDescription"
➥ErrorMessage="Description is required."
                        ID="DescriptionRequired" runat="server" ToolTip="Category
➥Description is required.">*</asp:RequiredFieldValidator>
                    <cc1:ValidatorCalloutExtender
ID="ValidatorCalloutExtender4"
➥runat="server" TargetControlID="DescriptionRequired">
                        </cc1:ValidatorCalloutExtender>
            </EditItemTemplate>
            <InsertItemTemplate>
                    <asp:TextBox ID="InsertDescription" runat="server"
➥Text='<%# Bind("Description") %>'></asp:TextBox>
                    <asp:RequiredFieldValidator
ControlToValidate="InsertDescription"
➥ErrorMessage="Description is required."
                        ID="DescriptionRequired" runat="server"
➥ToolTip="Category Description is required.">*</asp:RequiredFieldValidator>
                    <cc1:ValidatorCalloutExtender ID=
➥"ValidatorCalloutExtender3" runat="server"
➥TargetControlID="DescriptionRequired">
                        </cc1:ValidatorCalloutExtender>
            </InsertItemTemplate>
            <ItemTemplate>
                    <asp:Label ID="Label2" runat="server"
➥Text='<%# Bind("Description") %>'></asp:Label>
            </ItemTemplate>
        </asp:TemplateField>
    </Fields>
  </asp:DetailsView><br />
  <asp:ObjectDataSource ID="DetailsViewDataSource" runat="server"
➥DeleteMethod="Delete"
```

```
        InsertMethod="Insert" OldValuesParameterFormatString="{0}"
➥SelectMethod="GetCategoryById"
        TypeName="ShoppingCartTableAdapters.CategoriesTableAdapter"
➥UpdateMethod="Update">
        <SelectParameters>
            <asp:ControlParameter ControlID="gvCategories"
➥Name="CategoryId" PropertyName="SelectedValue"
                Type="Int32" />
        </SelectParameters>
        <DeleteParameters>
            <asp:Parameter Name="CategoryId" Type="Int32" />
        </DeleteParameters>
        <UpdateParameters>
            <asp:Parameter Name="CategoryName" Type="String" />
            <asp:Parameter Name="Description" Type="String" />
            <asp:Parameter Name="CategoryId" Type="Int32" />
        </UpdateParameters>
        <InsertParameters>
            <asp:Parameter Name="CategoryName" Type="String" />
            <asp:Parameter Name="Description" Type="String" />
        </InsertParameters>
    </asp:ObjectDataSource>
</asp:Panel>
```

By the Way

We would be using controls from the Ajax control toolkit in most of the pages in the application. As a reminder, please register the Ajax control toolkit in pages that uses the toolkit's controls. Here is the code to register:

```
<% @ Register Assembly="AjaxControlToolkit" Namespace="AjaxControlToolkit"
➥TagPrefix="cc1" %>
```

In the preceding code snippet, the DetailsView control dvCategory used TemplateFields to display the fields. The TemplateField holds ItemTemplate, InsertItemTemplate, and EditItemTemplate. The values in ItemTemplate will be ReadOnly. This is generally used to display values, and no operations can be performed here. If the mode is Insert, then InsertItemTemplate will be displayed, and if the mode is Edit, the EditItemTemplate will be displayed. At any point of time, only one mode can be displayed to the user.

Let's take a closer look at the InsertItemTemplate in the two TemplateFields of the DetailsView. The first one holds the Textbox CategoryName. Because this field is mandatory, we add validations to it in the form of RequiredFieldValidator, and also an Ajax extender ValidatorCalloutExtender, which displays a graphic message to the user when no entry is made for the field on submission of the page. We have already discussed the features of this extender in the previous hour when creating the registration page. Likewise, we also use this validation for the CategoryDescription field since this field also is mandatory. We apply the same validation model when editing the category as well. This can be found in the `EditItemTemplate` for each of the `TemplateFields` in the `dvCategory`.

The next important thing to look at in the `pnlDetails` is the `ObjectDataSource` control used for the `DetailsView` control `dvCategory`.

This `ObjectDataSource` control holds the business object `CategoriesTableAdapter` in the `TypeName` attribute. The four interesting attributes to be looked at are `SelectMethod`, `InsertMethod`, `UpdateMethod`, and `DeleteMethod`. These attributes hold the methods to be executed in the `CategoriesTableAdapter`. For example, the `SelectMethod` attribute holds the method name `GetCategoryById`. This method requires a parameter `CategoryId` to be executed. This is mentioned in the `SelectParameter` tag in the `ObjectDataSource` control. In this case, the `CategoryId` is fetched from the selected value of the row in the `GridView` control `gvCategories`. Similarly, for insert, update, and delete operations, parameters can be defined in `InsertParameters`, `UpdateParameters`, and `DeleteParameters` tags, respectively. These parameters will be used in the respective methods defined in the `CategoriesTableAdapter`. The insert, update, and delete methods inside this `TableAdapter` have straightforward SQL queries to perform the respective task in the categories of the application. The source of the SQL queries for insert, update, delete, and select can be viewed on this book's web site.

Following are the events associated with the `GridView` and `DetailsView` controls for the categories in the `ManageCategories.aspx` code-behind file:

```
protected void btnAddNew_Click(object sender, EventArgs e)
{
    this.pnlMain.Visible = false;
    this.pnlDetails.Visible = true;
    this.dvCategory.ChangeMode(DetailsViewMode.Insert);
}
protected void gvCategories_SelectedIndexChanged(object sender, EventArgs e)
{
    this.pnlMain.Visible = false;
    this.pnlDetails.Visible = true;
    dvCategory.ChangeMode(DetailsViewMode.Edit);
}
protected void gvCategories_PageIndexChanged(object sender, EventArgs e)
{
    dvCategory.ChangeMode(DetailsViewMode.ReadOnly);
}
protected void gvCategories_RowDeleted(object sender,
➥GridViewDeletedEventArgs e)
{
    if (e.Exception != null)
    {
        this.Master.ErrorMessage.Text = "Delete operation failed.";
        e.ExceptionHandled = true;
    }
}
```

```
    protected void dvCategory_ItemInserted(Object sender,
➥System.Web.UI.WebControls.DetailsViewInsertedEventArgs e)
    {
        if (e.Exception != null)
        {
            this.Master.ErrorMessage.Text = "An error occured while
➥entering this record.  Please verify the data you have entered.";
            e.ExceptionHandled = true;
        }
        this.gvCategories.DataBind();
        this.pnlMain.Visible = true;
        this.pnlDetails.Visible = false;
    }
    protected void dvCategory_ItemUpdated(Object sender,
➥System.Web.UI.WebControls.DetailsViewUpdatedEventArgs e)
    {
        this.gvCategories.DataBind();
        this.pnlMain.Visible = true;
        this.pnlDetails.Visible = false;
    }
    protected void dvCategory_ModeChanging(Object sender,
➥System.Web.UI.WebControls.DetailsViewModeEventArgs e)
    {
        if (e.CancelingEdit)
        {
            this.pnlMain.Visible = true;
            this.pnlDetails.Visible = false;
        }
    }
```

The different events in the preceding code listing perform various UI related operations such as displaying and hiding of panels, changing the mode from add to edit and vice-versa, and refreshing the data after performing an add, update, or delete operation.

Let's run the application; log in as sriram/sriram@24h (the Administrator account), and click the Product Categories menu item. This will load the ManageCategories.aspx page. Initially, this will display all the categories in the GridView control, as shown in Figure 23.5. Just to display the GridView control with data initally, we have added a few records directly in the database. The database is provided as shoppingcart.mdf file on this book's web site. You can attach this database in your SQL Server 2005 to use this data.

To add a new category:

1. Click the button Add New Category. This hides the pnlMain panel and displays the pnlDetails panel, which holds the DetailsView control (see Figure 23.6).

2. Enter values and click insert. The Insert method of the CategoriesTableAdapter is called, and the new values are added to the database and reflected in the GridView control.

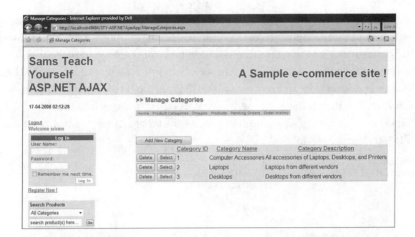

FIGURE 23.5
Displaying
product cate-
gories.

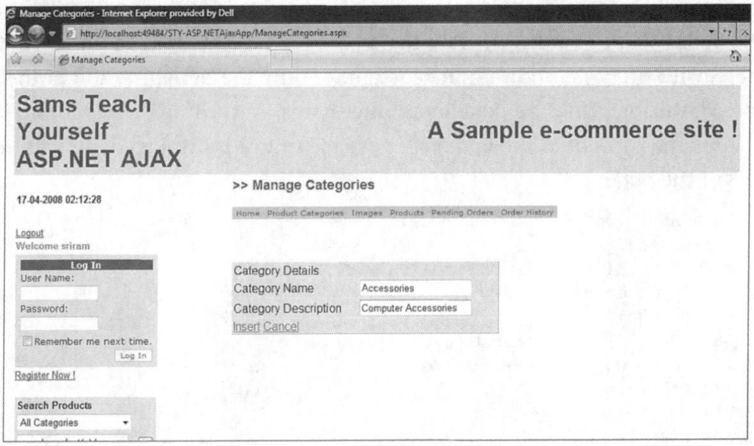

FIGURE 23.6
Adding a
category.

To edit a category:

1. Click the Select button in the GridView control for the record you intend to edit. This will again show the DetailsView now in Edit mode.

2. Change the values and click the Update button. This will call the Update method in the CategoriesTableAdapter.

To delete a category, click the Delete button in the GridView control for the record you intend to delete. This will call the Delete method in the CategoriesTableAdapter and update the database with this deletion. After the record is deleted, the GridView is refreshed, and the deleted value will not be seen.

Because this is an e-commerce application, there will be hundreds and thousands of users logging in and using the system simultaneously. To improve the performance of the application, and to reduce the response times of the page to make it more interactive, we can use partial-page postback here in the form of UpdatePanel. And while the updating is in progress, we can display the UpdateProgress control, which indicates the progress. To use this ASP.NET Ajax feature, add the UpdateProgress control in the Content tag of the ManageCategories.aspx page. The HTML source is as follows:

```
<asp:UpdateProgress ID="progress1" runat="server"
➥AssociatedUpdatePanelID="pnlContent" DisplayAfter="0">
                        <ProgressTemplate>
                        <div class="Table">
                            Loading...
                        </div>
                        </ProgressTemplate>
                        </asp:UpdateProgress>
```

Add the UpdatePanel control to hold the pnlMain and pnlDetails panel controls. Therefore, with any operation on the categories, only the panel portion of the page is rendered, thus making the page more interactive. And while this updating is being done, the content of the UpdateProgress control is displayed, indicating the progress of the page:

```
<asp:UpdatePanel ID="pnlContent" runat="server">
<ContentTemplate>
        <asp:Panel ID="pnlMain" runat="server">
        . . . . . GridView control . . . .
        </asp:Panel>
        <asp:Panel ID="pnlDetails" runat="server">
        . . . . . DetailsView control . . . .
        </asp:Panel>
</ContentTemplate>
</asp:UpdatePanel>
```

After the categories are set up, the next step is to set up images and then products. We'll not go into detail of how this is done for images and products in this hour—it is done in exactly the same way as it is done for the categories. You can find the source for this on this book's web site. We have listed the TableAdapters for images and products earlier in this hour. Figures 23.7–23.10 show snapshots of the images and products after the records have been added from the application.

FIGURE 23.7
Displaying the images that are used in the application

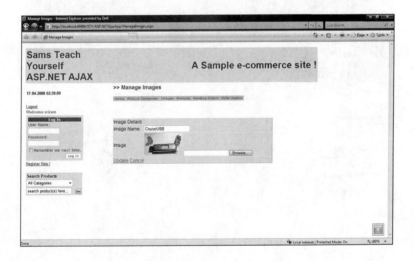

FIGURE 23.8
Updating the image that is used in the application

FIGURE 23.9
Displaying the products that are used in the application

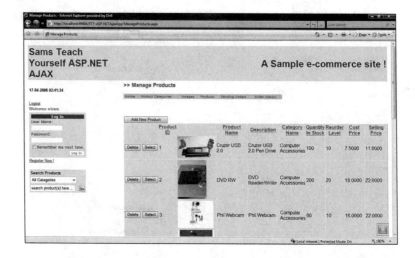

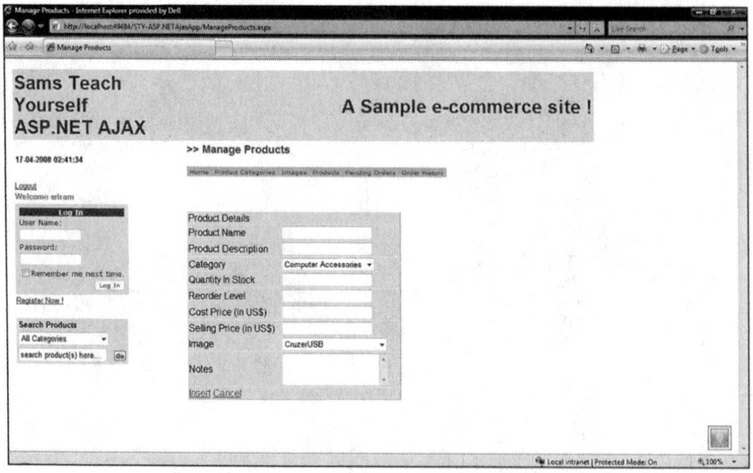

FIGURE 23.10
Adding a new product to the site

With this, the categories, images, and product set up is done. The Administrator/Manager of the site has the permission to perform this task. This is generally done when the site is first hosted. Later, additions and modifications can be done. Now that the products are set up, we will shift our focus to the major focus of this hour—searching for products and adding them to the cart.

Searching for Products

Searching for products is the key part of the application, as this is the most frequently used operation on any e-commerce site. For the figures used in this hour, every figure has a search panel to the left of the page. As discussed in the previous hour, the search panel consists of a category drop-down list and a product textbox, and this panel is placed in the `masterpage.master` page. This is done to facilitate searching in every page of the application, as the `masterpage.master` page is used in every content page in the site. The categories drop-down list is bound with the categories defined in the site. The code to bind categories is shown next. This code is present in the code-behind file of `masterpage.master`:

```
private void BindCategories()
    {
        CategoriesTableAdapter CategoriesAdapter = new CategoriesTableAdapter();
        ShoppingCart.CategoriesDataTable Categories;
        Categories = CategoriesAdapter.GetAllCategories();
        ddlCategories.DataSource = Categories;
        ddlCategories.DataBind();
        this.ddlCategories.Items.Insert(0, new ListItem
➥("All Categories", string.Empty));
    }
```

To search for product(s) in the site, just click the Go button in the search box. The results of the search are displayed in the content page `Default.aspx`. Because the `masterpage.master.cs` and `default.aspx.cs` are two different classes, you cannot have a direct event handler to catch the search results. Therefore, we will implement an event delegate to achieve this.

A delegate is a class that can hold a reference to a method. Unlike other classes, a delegate class has a signature, and it can hold references only to methods that match its signature. A delegate is thus equivalent to a type-safe function pointer or a callback.

Here is the definition of the search delegate we are talking about:

```
public delegate void SearchClickHandler(object sender, System.EventArgs e);
public event SearchClickHandler SearchClick;
```

This is declared in the code-behind of the `masterpage.master` file.

We will also define two properties—CategoryName and ProductName—in the MasterPage.master code-behind file, that will hold the values keyed in the search panel. These values will be used to bind the search results in the default.aspx page:

```
private string _categoryName;
    private string _productName;
    public string CategoryName
    {
        get { return _categoryName; }
        set { _categoryName = value; }
    }
    public string ProductName
    {
        get { return _productName; }
        set { _productName = value; }
    }
```

After the Go button is clicked, the CategoryName and ProductName properties are set with the values in the Category drop-down list and ProductName textbox, respectively. Then the searchClick event handler is fired to an existing delegate. This is subscribed in default.aspx.cs. The following is the code illustrating the Go button click, and firing the event handler:

```
protected void btnSearchProduct_Click(object sender, EventArgs e)
    {
        if (ddlCategories.SelectedValue == string.Empty)
            CategoryName = string.Empty;
        else
            CategoryName = ddlCategories.SelectedItem.Text;
        ProductName = txtSearchProduct.Text.Trim();

        //Fire event to existing delegate
        OnSearchClick(e);
    }
    protected virtual void OnSearchClick(EventArgs e)
    {
        if (SearchClick != null)
        {
            //invokes the delegates
            SearchClick(this, e);
        }
    }
```

Here is the code to initialize the subscription of the event searchClick. This is done in the Page_Load event of the Default.aspx page:

```
Master.SearchClick += new MasterPage.SearchClickHandler(Master_SearchClick);
```

The code for subscribing the event is as follows:

```
void Master_SearchClick(object sender, EventArgs e)
    {
        ProductsTableAdapter ProductsAdapter = new ProductsTableAdapter();
        ShoppingCart.ProductsDataTable Products;
        Products = ProductsAdapter.SearchProducts(Master.CategoryName,
➡Master.ProductName);
        ProductDataList.DataSource = Products;
        ProductDataList.DataBind();
    }
```

In the preceding code, the values from CategoryName and ProductName are used to bind the products list to a DataList control in the default.aspx page. The method SearchProducts of the ProductsTableAdapter retrieves products from the database based on the input values CategoryName and ProductName given to it. The source of the DataList control in Default.aspx used to bind these products is as follows:

```
<asp:DataList ID="ProductDataList" runat="server" RepeatColumns="3"
➡RepeatDirection="Horizontal">
        <ItemTemplate>
            <div class="ProductList">
                <a href='ProductDetails.aspx?ProductId=<%# Eval("ProductId")
%>'>
                    <img src="ImageHandler.ashx?ImageId=<%# Eval("ImageId")
➡%>" alt='<%# Eval("ImageName") %>' width="150" height="100" />
                </a>
                <a href='ProductDetails.aspx?ProductId=<%# Eval("ProductId")
%>'>
                    <div class="ContentMedium"><%# Eval("ProductName") %></div>
                    <div class="ContentMedium">Price (US $) :<%#
➡String.Format("{0:##.00}", Eval("SellingPrice")) %></div>
                </a><br />
            </div>
        </ItemTemplate>
    </asp:DataList>
```

By default, when the site is opened, only six products are listed in the home page. These are the latest ones added to the site. To view the entire list of products, you are provided with a link called More. Clicking this will redirect the user to the products list page.

Set the default page to Default.aspx and run the application. This will show the home page displaying the six latest records added to the site. For the convenience of the reader, I've already added around 10 products through the add products page from the administrator login (see Figure 23.11).

FIGURE 23.11
Products display
in home page

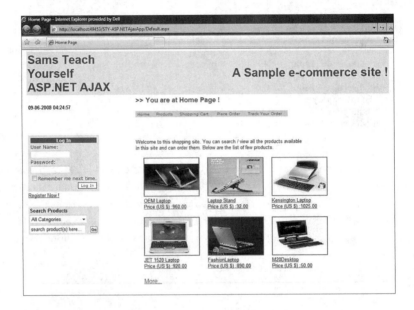

Now let's search for a set of USB-related products in the site. This can be done by the user keying in **usb** in the Product Name text box and clicking Go. The output is shown in Figure 23.12.

FIGURE 23.12
Searching prod-
ucts with key-
word "usb"

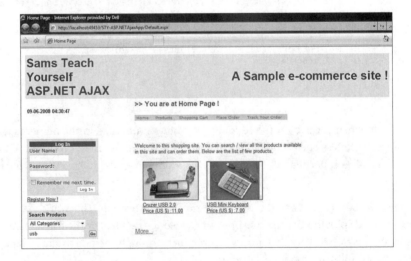

Now let's add a little bit of Ajax to the search functionality. We will do this with the help of UpdatePanel and UpdateProgress controls as done earlier in the hour. All we have to do is modify the MasterPage.master file to add these controls to embed the Login and Search panels. See the following snippet:

```
<asp:UpdateProgress ID="UpdateProgress1" runat="server"
➥AssociatedUpdatePanelID="pnlMaster" DisplayAfter="0">
                        <ProgressTemplate>
                        <div class="Table">
                            Loading...
                        </div>
                        </ProgressTemplate>
                        </asp:UpdateProgress><br />
<asp:UpdatePanel ID="pnlMaster" runat="server">
<ContentTemplate>
        <!--........table containing Login Panel à
        <!--........table containing Search Panel à
</ContentTemplate>
</asp:UpdatePanel>
```

The html table for Login and Search panels can be found in the snippets of Hour 22. Now, when user enters search criteria and clicks the Go button, partial-page rendering happens, and the `UpdateProgress` controls shows the progress of the update. Figure 23.13 displays the progess of the update operation in a text "Loading..." just above the `Login` control.

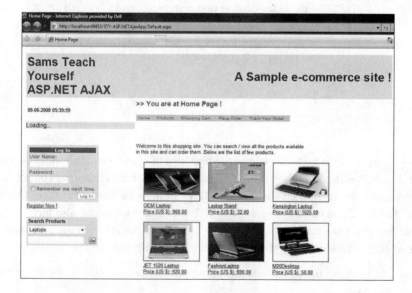

FIGURE 23.13
UpdateProgress and UpdatePanel controls in action while searching for a product

Product Details Page

Now that the home page and the search results are implemented, the next step for the user is to view the details of the product he/she intends to purchase. If you have observed the code snippet of the `DataList` control holding the products list in the

Default.aspx file, there is an anchor tag holding every product that is being displayed. This anchor tag holds a reference to the product details page for a product. Therefore, clicking a product in this list redirects the user to the products details page, ProductDetails.aspx. This page holds a FormView control displaying the details of the product selected. Here is the source of the control:

```
<asp:FormView ID="FormView1" runat="server" DataSourceID="FormViewDataSource"
➥EnableViewState="false">
        <ItemTemplate>
        <table width="600">
            <tr>
                <td style="width:300px">
                    <img src="ImageHandler.ashx?ImageId=<%# Eval("ImageId")
➥%>" alt='<%# Eval("ImageName") %>' />
                </td>
                <td style="width:300px">
                    <div class="ContentMedium">Product ID :
➥<%#Eval("ProductId") %></div><br />
                    <div class="ContentMedium">Product Name :
➥<%#Eval("ProductName") %></div><br />
                    <div class="ContentMedium">Description :
➥<%#Eval("Description") %></div><br />
                    <div class="ContentMedium">Category :
➥<%#Eval("CategoryName") %></div><br />
                    <div class="ContentMedium">Price (US $) :<%#
➥String.Format("{0:##.00}", Eval("SellingPrice")) %></div><br />
                    <div class="ContentMedium">Notes : <%#Eval("Notes")
➥%></div><br />
                </td>
            </tr>
        </table>
        </ItemTemplate>
    </asp:FormView>
```

This control holds a table displaying the image of the product, along with the product details. The data to this control is bound by the ObjectDataSource control, which has a SelectMethod "GetProductById" of the type ProductsTableAdapter. The queries can be viewed on the book's web site. This data source also has QueryString parameter, which holds the productId passed from the home page. Based on this QueryString, the products details are displayed.

Figure 23.14 shows the product details of the product Cruzer USB 2.0 selected from the home page.

FIGURE 23.14
Displaying the details of the product Cruzer USB 2.0 in the ProductDetails .aspx page

Adding Products to Cart

The next step for the user is to add the selected product to the cart.

> If you are new to the concept of a cart, a *cart* is a collection of different products selected in the site while shopping.

By the Way

This can be done by clicking the Add to Cart button provided in the product details page. This operation requires a user to be logged in to the site—that is, he/she must be a registered user at the site. Here is the workflow for adding products to a cart:

1. Must be a registered user with the site.

2. Checks whether the user already has a cart that is not yet ordered. If Yes, go to step 3. If No, creates a new cart.

3. If the cart already exists for this user, checks whether this product is already added to the cart. If Yes, updates the quantity of this product in the cart. If No, adds the product to the cart.

The code for the preceding workflow is as follows:

```
protected void AddToCart_Click(object sender, EventArgs e)
    {
        if (Page.User.Identity.IsAuthenticated)
        {
            if (Page.User.IsInRole("Customer"))
            {
```

```
            CartTableAdapter CartAdapter = new CartTableAdapter();
            MembershipUser myObject = Membership.GetUser();
            Guid UserID = (Guid)myObject.ProviderUserKey;
            ShoppingCart.CartDataTable CartTable =
➥CartAdapter.IsCartExists(UserID);
            object CartId = null;
            if (CartTable.Rows.Count == 0)
                CartId = CartAdapter.Add(UserID);
            else
                CartId = int.Parse(CartTable.Rows[0]["CartId"].ToString());
            int ProductId = int.Parse(Request.QueryString["ProductId"].
➥ToString());
            ProductsTableAdapter ProductsAdapter = new
ProductsTableAdapter();
            ShoppingCart.ProductsDataTable Products;
            Products = ProductsAdapter.GetProductById(ProductId);
            decimal Price =
➥decimal.Parse(Products.Rows[0]["SellingPrice"].ToString());
            CartDetailsTableAdapter CartDetailsAdapter = new
➥CartDetailsTableAdapter();
            ShoppingCart.CartDetailsDataTable CartDetailsTable =
➥CartDetailsAdapter.IsProductExistsInCart(UserID, ProductId);
            if (CartDetailsTable.Rows.Count == 0)
                CartDetailsAdapter.AddProductToCart(int.Parse
➥ (CartId.ToString()), ProductId, 1, Price, DateTime.Now);
            else
            {
                int newQuantity =
➥int.Parse(CartDetailsTable.Rows[0]["QuantityOrdered"].ToString()) + 1;
                decimal newPrice = newQuantity * Price;
                int CartDetailsId =
➥int.Parse(CartDetailsTable.Rows[0]["CartDetailsId"].ToString());
                CartDetailsAdapter.UpdateProductInCart(newQuantity,
➥newPrice, DateTime.Now, CartDetailsId);
            }
            Response.Redirect("Cart.aspx?UserId=" + UserID.ToString());
        }
        else
        {
            this.Master.ErrorMessage.Text = "You are not authorized to shop.
➥Login as a Customer to shop for products.";
        }
    }
    else
    {
        this.Master.ErrorMessage.Text = "** Login to shop for products **";
    }
}
```

Manipulating the Cart

Log in as rajesh/rajesh@24h and add the product Cruzer USB 2.0 to our cart
by clicking the Add to Cart button. This executes the workflow discussed in the

preceding section and will display the cart in the Cart.aspx page. The Cart.aspx page holds a GridView control to display the cart. The source of the control is as follows:

```
<asp:GridView ID="gvCart" runat="server" CssClass="Table"
➥ DataSourceID="GridViewDataSource"
    DataKeyNames="CartDetailsId" AutoGenerateColumns="false" SelectedIndex="0"
➥ OnRowDataBound="gvCart_RowDataBound"
    OnRowDeleted="gvCart_RowDeleted" ShowFooter="true" HeaderStyle-
➥CssClass="ContentMedium"
    RowStyle-CssClass="ContentSmall" FooterStyle-CssClass="ContentSmall"
➥CellPadding="3">
    <Columns>
      <asp:CommandField ButtonType="Button" ShowDeleteButton="true" />
      <asp:TemplateField>
        <ItemTemplate>
            <asp:TextBox ID="CartDetailsId" runat="server" Text='<%#
Eval("CartDetailsId") %>' Width="30" Visible="false"></asp:TextBox>
        </ItemTemplate>
      </asp:TemplateField>
      <asp:BoundField DataField="ProductId" HeaderText="Product ID"
➥ReadOnly="True" SortExpression="ProductId" />
      <asp:BoundField DataField="ProductName" HeaderText="Product Name"
➥SortExpression="ProductName" />
      <asp:TemplateField HeaderText="Quantity">
        <ItemTemplate>
            <asp:TextBox ID="Quantity" runat="server" Text='<%#
➥Eval("QuantityOrdered") %>' Width="30"></asp:TextBox>
        </ItemTemplate>
      </asp:TemplateField>
      <asp:TemplateField HeaderText="Unit Price">
        <ItemTemplate>
            <asp:TextBox ID="UnitPrice" runat="server" dir="rtl" Text='<%#
Eval("UnitPrice") %>' Width="70" Enabled="false"></asp:TextBox>
        </ItemTemplate>
        <FooterTemplate>
            <div class="ContentMedium" style="text-align:right">Total Price :
➥</div>
        </FooterTemplate>
      </asp:TemplateField>
      <asp:TemplateField HeaderText="Price">
        <ItemTemplate>
            <asp:TextBox ID="Price" runat="server" dir="rtl" Text='<%#
➥Eval("Price") %>' Width="70" Enabled="false"></asp:TextBox>
        </ItemTemplate>
        <FooterTemplate>
            <asp:TextBox ID="txtTotalPrice" runat="server" Width="70"
➥dir="rtl" Enabled="false" />
        </FooterTemplate>
      </asp:TemplateField>
    </Columns>
    </asp:GridView><br />
```

This `GridView` control is bound to an `ObjectDataSource` control that has `SelectMethod` as `GetCartDetails` from the type `CartDetailsTableAdapter`. This method fetches all the products that are present in the current cart. The cart, after adding the product `Cruzer USB 2.0`, is shown in Figure 23.15.

FIGURE 23.15
Cart after adding a product

Here is the source of the `ObjectDataSource` control bound to the preceding GridView control:

```
<asp:ObjectDataSource ID="GridViewDataSource" runat="server"
➥DeleteMethod="DeleteProductInCart"
        SelectMethod="GetCartDetails"
➥TypeName="ShoppingCartTableAdapters.CartDetailsTableAdapter">
        <SelectParameters>
            <asp:QueryStringParameter Name="UserId" DefaultValue=
➥"01be2d91-f762-4847-bde2-c4457789ddb0" QueryStringField="UserId"
➥ /></SelectParameters>
        <DeleteParameters>
            <asp:Parameter Name="CartDetailsId" Type="Int32" />
        </DeleteParameters>
    </asp:ObjectDataSource>
```

Let's add one more product called `DVD RW` to the cart, just to make a purchase on multiple products at a time. This can be done by clicking the Continue Shopping button and following the same process of adding a product to the cart, as discussed earlier in the hour. Your updated cart output is shown in Figure 23.16.

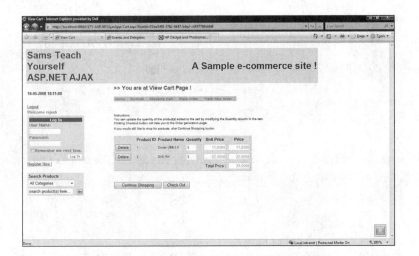

FIGURE 23.16
The updated cart with one more product in it

The cart in Figure 23.15 displays ProductID, Product Name, Quantity, Unit Price, and Price. Here, the user can manipulate the cart by changing the quantity of a product (if he/she wants to buy more quantity of this product) and deleting a product if he/she does not want to buy it. The last column, Price field, is the unit price of the product multiplied by the quantity. This is implemented by the Ajax feature called *page methods*. This feature was discussed previously in Hour 14, "Working with Web Services Using Ajax."

When the user changes the quantity column, we'll raise the OnKeyUp event of JavaScript and call a JavaScript method called UpdatePrice by passing the parameters Quantity textbox ID, Price textbox ID, Price value, and the internal ID CartDetailsID.

CartDetailsID is a unique ID for a row in the CartDetails database table.

By the Way

Because the textboxes in each row are in a GridView control, the OnKeyUp attribute for the textbox Quantity is assigned in the RowDataDataBound event of the GridView control. The code for this is as follows:

```
protected void gvCart_RowDataBound(object sender, GridViewRowEventArgs e)
    {
        if (e.Row.RowType == DataControlRowType.DataRow)
        {
            totalPrice += decimal.Parse(((TextBox)e.Row.FindControl
➡("Price")).Text);
            if (e.Row.FindControl("Quantity") != null)
                ((TextBox)e.Row.FindControl("Quantity")).Attributes.Add
➡ ("onkeyup", "UpdatePrice(" + ((TextBox)e.Row.FindControl
```

```
➥ ("Quantity")).ClientID + ", " + ((TextBox)e.Row.FindControl
➥ ("Price")).ClientID + ", " + ((TextBox)e.Row.FindControl("Price")).
➥Text + ", " + ((TextBox)e.Row.FindControl("CartDetailsId")).Text + ");");
        }
        if (e.Row.RowType == DataControlRowType.Footer)
        {
            ((TextBox)e.Row.FindControl("txtTotalPrice")).Text =
➥totalPrice.ToString();
        }
    }
```

The variable totalPrice is declared as a private variable in the scope of the class Cart. The declaration is shown here:

```
decimal totalPrice = 0;
```

The source for the JavaScript function UpdatePrice is as follows:

```
function UpdatePrice(txtQty, txtPrice, OriginalPrice, CartDetailsId)
    {
        if (txtQty.value != "")
        {
            txtPrice.value = txtQty.value * OriginalPrice;
            PageMethods.UpdateCart(txtQty.value, txtPrice.value,
➥CartDetailsId, OnSucceeded, OnFailed);
        }
    }
```

The page method for updating the product price is invoked from the UpdatePrice JavaScript function.

By the Way

> For page methods to work, we have to set EnablePageMethods attribute to true in the ScriptManager control. We have done this in the MasterPage.master file, and this file is included in the cart content page. Therefore, the PageMethods feature is enabled for us in the cart page.

Here is the code-behind for the PageMethod updating the cart:

```
[WebMethod]
    public static void UpdateCart(int Quantity, decimal Price, int
CartDetailsId)
    {
        CartDetailsTableAdapter CartDetailsAdapter = new
CartDetailsTableAdapter();
        CartDetailsAdapter.UpdateProductInCart(Quantity, Price,
➥DateTime.Now, CartDetailsId);
    }
```

As we've added a WebMethod attribute, we will have to include the namespaces System.Web.Services.

Therefore, without posting the page back for updating the cart, we have implemented a cool Ajax feature to update the cart using page methods.

Also if you observe the RowDataBound event of GridView, we keep updating the Total Price of all the products when the GridView is rendered.

As discussed earlier in the hour, we have implemented UpdatePanel and UpdateProgress controls in ManageCategories.aspx file, and MasterPage.master for Login and Search panels. Instead of using these controls in every content page, we can use them in the MasterPage.master file around the ContentPlaceHolder control, which holds every content page of this application. Here is how we implement this:

```
<asp:UpdateProgress ID="UpdateProgress2" runat="server"
➥AssociatedUpdatePanelID="pnlContent" DisplayAfter="0">
                    <ProgressTemplate>
                    <div class="Table">
                        Loading...
                    </div>
                    </ProgressTemplate>
                    </asp:UpdateProgress><br />
            <asp:UpdatePanel ID="pnlContent" runat="server">
            <ContentTemplate>
                <asp:Label ID="lblErrorMessage" runat="server"
➥CssClass="ErrorText"></asp:Label><br />
                    <asp:contentplaceholder id="ContentPlaceHolder1"
runat="server">
                </asp:contentplaceholder>
            </ContentTemplate>
            </asp:UpdatePanel>
```

This way every content page of this application has implemented the UpdatePanel and UpdateProgress controls, thereby making the application more interactive and responsive.

This ends the current hour. The next hour focuses on generating and managing orders.

Summary

This hour focused on setting up the categories, images, and product data in the application. We have utilized the features of ASP.NET 2.0 to program the pages. Every data setup page had a `GridView` and `DetailsView` control for display and add/edit of items, respectively. All the operations are done using `TableAdapters` for each entity (category/image/product). These `TableAdapters` used SQL queries to perform operations on the database. Every add/edit page used Ajax extenders to validate the input from the user. Also the performance, interactivity, and response times of the pages improved with the use of the `UpdatePanel` control. After the products were set up, we have coded the default.aspx page to support the searching of products and displaying the products in detail. Later, several products were added to the cart. The cart page showed the product name, quantity and price, and total price of the order. The user can manipulate the quantity and update the cart here. The next step is to generate the order, which will be discussed in the next hour.

Workshop

Quiz

1. What is the use of `UpdateProgress` control?

2. What is a `TableAdapter`?

3. True or False: You can use only one `UpdateProgress` control for each `UpdatePanel` control.

4. When using master pages and content pages, what is the better way of using `ScriptManager`, `UpdateProgress`, and `UpdatePanel` controls?

5. What is a `PageMethod`?

Answers

1. The `UpdateProgress` control provides status information about partial page updates in `UpdatePanel` controls.

2. A `TableAdapter` is a strongly typed equivalent of a standard `DataAdapter`. More specifically, a `TableAdapter` connects to the database, executes queries, and returns a `DataTable`.

3. False. You can use one `UpdateProgress` control and associate with all the `UpdatePanel` controls in the page.

4. Make use of the `ScriptManager` control in the master page as this can be used across all the content pages. If you would like to use different properties of this `ScriptManager` control for a specific content page, then use the `ScriptManagerProxy` control for this content page. Similarly, `UpdateProgress` and `UpdatePanel` controls can be wrapped around the `ContentPlaceHolder` in the master page. This way, a single `UpdateProgress` and `UpdatePanel` control will be sufficient for all the content pages.

5. A `PageMethod` is a static method in a page class. This is an alternative to web service method. Sometimes, you may not have the need or even want to create a web service to do some basic functionality; you may just want to use a method in your page class. This is when `PageMethods` will be useful.

HOUR 24

Generating and Managing Orders

What You'll Learn in This Hour:

- ▶ Order generation
- ▶ Tracking orders
- ▶ Managing pending orders and order history

We've finally come to the last stage of the application development, which focuses on the order-generation process to the tracking of the orders. The process starts after the customer checks out of the cart to place an order on the site. The customer is prompted to fill in his/her personal details, such as shipping address and credit card information. After the details are entered, the customer places an order on the site. This is the workflow at the front end. Coming to the management of orders, the Administrator or Manager looks into all the orders generated by the customer and starts the shipment process to deliver the order to the customer. This hour completely focuses on the development of pages for the preceding workflow.

> **By the Way**
>
> This hour contains code snippets for the pages Order.aspx, TrackOrders.aspx, PendingOrders.aspx, and OrderHistory.aspx. Only the snippets important in the context of application functionality and snippets related to ASP.NET Ajax are provided. The missing code can be found in the application provided in this book's web site (www.informit.com/title/9780672329678). Copy the missing code from the web site, paste it in the application you are building here, and run the application.

Placing an Order

In the previous hour, we added a few items to the cart, and now we are ready to check out to order them.

By the Way

> "Check out" is a term popular in e-commerce sites. This is an action performed to finalize the items that are shopped in the cart and signifies that the customer is ready to place an order.

Let's create a page, `Order.aspx`, which holds the customer's order information, shipping address, and credit card information. If the customer is shopping for the first time, the shipping address needs to be entered, and this will be saved for subsequent orders. We will not build code that deals with credit card processing in our application, as that is beyond the scope of the hour. We will just have the user interface displaying the credit card-related fields to make the order page look complete.

We've divided the order page into three sections: Review the Order, Enter Shipping Address, and Payment Details.

Review the Order

This section presents the items added to the cart along with tax, discount, and shipping charges. The Cart Items for review will be presented in a `GridView` control called gvCart. The following code listing is the aspx source of the `GridView` control in `Order.aspx` page:

```
<h4>Review the Order</h4>
<asp:GridView ID="gvCart" runat="server" CssClass="Table"
➥DataSourceID="GridViewDataSource"
    DataKeyNames="CartDetailsId" AutoGenerateColumns="false" SelectedIndex="0"
➥OnRowDataBound="gvCart_RowDataBound" HeaderStyle-CssClass="ContentMedium"
    RowStyle-CssClass="ContentSmall" FooterStyle-CssClass="ContentSmall"
➥ShowFooter="true" CellPadding="5">
    <Columns>
      <asp:TemplateField>
        <ItemTemplate>
            <asp:TextBox ID="CartDetailsId" runat="server" Text='<%#
➥Eval("CartDetailsId") %>' Width="30" Visible="false"></asp:TextBox>
        </ItemTemplate>
      </asp:TemplateField>
      <asp:BoundField DataField="ProductId" HeaderText="Product ID"
➥ReadOnly="True" SortExpression="ProductId" />
      <asp:BoundField DataField="ProductName" HeaderText="Product Name"
➥SortExpression="ProductName" />
      <asp:TemplateField HeaderText="Quantity">
        <ItemTemplate>
            <asp:Label ID="Quantity" runat="server" Text='<%# Eval
➥("QuantityOrdered") %>' Width="30"></asp:Label>
```

```
            </ItemTemplate>
        </asp:TemplateField>
        <asp:TemplateField HeaderText="Unit Price"
➡ItemStyle-HorizontalAlign="Right">
            <ItemTemplate>
                <asp:Label ID="UnitPrice" runat="server" Text='<%#
➡Eval("UnitPrice") %>' Width="70"></asp:Label>
            </ItemTemplate>
            <FooterTemplate>
                <asp:Label ID="lblSubTotal" runat="server"
➡Text="Sub Total : "></asp:Label><br />
                <asp:Label ID="lblTax" runat="server" Text="Tax :
➡"></asp:Label><br />
                <asp:Label ID="lblDiscount" runat="server" Text="Discount :
"></asp:Label><br />
                <asp:Label ID="lblShippingCharges" runat="server"
➡Text="Shipping & Handling Charges : "></asp:Label><br /><br />
                <asp:Label ID="lblTotalAmount" runat="server"
➡Text="Total Amount (in US$) : "></asp:Label>
            </FooterTemplate>
        </asp:TemplateField>
        <asp:TemplateField HeaderText="Price" ItemStyle-HorizontalAlign="Right">
            <ItemTemplate>
                <asp:Label ID="Price" runat="server" Text='<%# Eval
➡ ("Price") %>' Width="70"></asp:Label>
            </ItemTemplate>
            <FooterTemplate>
                <asp:Label ID="SubTotal" runat="server" Width="70" dir="rtl"/><br />
                <asp:Label ID="Tax" runat="server" Width="70" dir="rtl"
➡Text="30.00"/><br />
                <asp:Label ID="Discount" runat="server" Width="70" dir="rtl"
➡Text="5.00"/><br />
                <asp:Label ID="ShippingCharges" runat="server" Width="70"
➡dir="rtl" Text="15.00"/><br /><br />
                <asp:Label ID="TotalAmount" runat="server" Width="70" dir="rtl"/>
            </FooterTemplate>
        </asp:TemplateField>
    </Columns>
    </asp:GridView><br />
  <asp:ObjectDataSource ID="GridViewDataSource" runat="server"
        SelectMethod="GetCartDetails"
➡TypeName="ShoppingCartTableAdapters.CartDetailsTableAdapter">
        <SelectParameters>
            <asp:QueryStringParameter Name="UserId" DefaultValue=
➡"01be2d91-f762-4847-bde2-c4457789ddb0" QueryStringField="UserId"
➡/></SelectParameters>
    </asp:ObjectDataSource>
```

The preceding code uses the business object CartDetailsTableAdapter's
GetCartDetails method to bind the cart information of the corresponding customer. The QueryString in the SelectParameters tag is identified by the UserId
placing the order. Currently, the values for tax, discount, and shipping charges have
been hard coded in this page in the FooterTemplate of the Price column. Later, you
can extend this application, and create your own configuration for these values in

the Admin part. This `GridView` displays all the products and the quantity, price, taxes, and total amount for the order. After the customer reviews this, he/she has to enter the shipping address in the next section.

Enter Shipping Address

If the customer is shopping on this site for the first time, then he/she has to enter the shipping address—or else it will be loaded as you see in this section. This section holds the content in a table tag. All fields are mandatory here and are validated using the Ajax extender `ValidatorCalloutExtender`. Here is the code listing for this section of the `Order.aspx`:

```
<h4>Enter Shipping Address</h4>
<table width="500" class="Table">
    <tr>
        <td>
            <asp:TextBox ID="AddressId" runat="server" Visible="false">
➡</asp:TextBox>
            <div class="ContentSmall">Address : </div>
            <asp:TextBox ID="Address" runat="server" TextMode="MultiLine"
➡Rows="3" Columns="25"></asp:TextBox>
            <asp:RequiredFieldValidator ControlToValidate="Address"
➡ErrorMessage="Address is required."
                    ID="AddressRequired" runat="server"
➡ToolTip="Address is required.">*</asp:RequiredFieldValidator>
                    <cc1:ValidatorCalloutExtender ID=
➡"ValidatorCalloutExtender1" runat="server"
➡TargetControlID="AddressRequired">
                    </cc1:ValidatorCalloutExtender>
        </td>
        <td>
            <div class="ContentSmall">City : </div>
            <asp:TextBox ID="City" runat="server"></asp:TextBox>
            <asp:RequiredFieldValidator ControlToValidate="City"
➡ErrorMessage="City is required."
                    ID="CityRequired" runat="server"
➡ToolTip="City is required.">*</asp:RequiredFieldValidator>
                    <cc1:ValidatorCalloutExtender ID=
➡"ValidatorCalloutExtender2" runat="server"
➡TargetControlID="CityRequired">
                    </cc1:ValidatorCalloutExtender>
        </td>
    </tr>
    <tr>
        <td>
            <div class="ContentSmall">State : </div>
            <asp:TextBox ID="State" runat="server"></asp:TextBox>
            <asp:RequiredFieldValidator ControlToValidate="State"
➡ErrorMessage="State is required."
                    ID="StateRequired" runat="server"
➡ToolTip="State is required.">*</asp:RequiredFieldValidator>
                    <cc1:ValidatorCalloutExtender ID=
➡"ValidatorCalloutExtender3" runat="server"
➡TargetControlID="StateRequired">
```

```
                  </cc1:ValidatorCalloutExtender>
        </td>
        <td>
            <div class="ContentSmall">Country : </div>
            <asp:TextBox ID="Country" runat="server"></asp:TextBox>
            <asp:RequiredFieldValidator ControlToValidate="Country"
➥ErrorMessage="Country is required."
                     ID="CountryRequired" runat="server"
➥ToolTip="Country is required.">*</asp:RequiredFieldValidator>
                  <cc1:ValidatorCalloutExtender
ID="ValidatorCalloutExtender4"
➥runat="server" TargetControlID="CountryRequired">
                  </cc1:ValidatorCalloutExtender>
        </td>
    </tr>
    <tr>
        <td>
            <div class="ContentSmall">Zipcode : </div>
            <asp:TextBox ID="Zipcode" runat="server"></asp:TextBox>
            <asp:RequiredFieldValidator ControlToValidate="Zipcode"
➥ErrorMessage="Zipcode is required."
                     ID="ZipcodeRequired" runat="server"
➥ToolTip="Zipcode is required.">*</asp:RequiredFieldValidator>
                  <cc1:ValidatorCalloutExtender
ID="ValidatorCalloutExtender5"
➥runat="server" TargetControlID="ZipcodeRequired">
                  </cc1:ValidatorCalloutExtender>
        </td>
        <td>
            <div class="ContentSmall">Contact No : </div>
            <asp:TextBox ID="ContactNo" runat="server"></asp:TextBox>
            <asp:RequiredFieldValidator ControlToValidate="ContactNo"
➥ErrorMessage="Contact Number is required."
                     ID="ContactNumberRequired" runat="server"
➥ToolTip="Contact Number is required.">*</asp:RequiredFieldValidator>
                  <cc1:ValidatorCalloutExtender
ID="ValidatorCalloutExtender6"
➥runat="server" TargetControlID="ContactNumberRequired">
                  </cc1:ValidatorCalloutExtender>
        </td>
    </tr>
</table>
```

Payment Details

This section accepts the payment information in the form of a credit card. As mentioned earlier, these are just dummy fields in the application, and we are not processing this through any payment gateway. When you are ready to make your e-commerce application online, you can integrate this code with any payment gateway to process credit card transactions. For example, if you want to use PayPal for processing all credit cards, there is source code available in the starter kits and community projects, in Microsoft's asp.net site, http://asp.net/community/. The project name is PayPal eCommerce Starter Kit. The HTML source we used for this section on our order page is as follows:

```
<h4>Payment Details</h4>
<table width="500" class="Table">
    <tr>
        <td>
            <div class="ContentSmall">Credit Card No : </div>
            <asp:TextBox ID="CreditCardNo" runat="server"></asp:TextBox>
            <asp:RequiredFieldValidator ControlToValidate="CreditCardNo"
➥ErrorMessage="Credit Card Number is required."
                        ID="CreditCardNoRequired" runat="server"
➥ToolTip="Credit Card Number is required.">*</asp:
➥RequiredFieldValidator>
                    <cc1:ValidatorCalloutExtender ID=
➥"ValidatorCalloutExtender7" runat="server"
➥TargetControlID="CreditCardNoRequired">
                    </cc1:ValidatorCalloutExtender>
        </td>
    </tr>
    <tr>
        <td>
            <div class="ContentSmall">CVV Number : </div>
            <asp:TextBox ID="CVVNo" runat="server" TextMode="Password">
➥</asp:TextBox>
            <asp:RequiredFieldValidator ControlToValidate="CVVNo"
➥ErrorMessage="CVV Number is required."
                    ID="CVVNoRequired" runat="server" ToolTip="CVV Number is
➥required.">*</asp:RequiredFieldValidator>
                    <cc1:ValidatorCalloutExtender
ID="ValidatorCalloutExtender8"
➥runat="server" TargetControlID="CVVNoRequired">
                    </cc1:ValidatorCalloutExtender>
        </td>
    </tr>
    <tr>
        <td>
            <div class="ContentSmall">Expiry Date : </div>
            <asp:DropDownList ID="ExpiryDate" runat="server"></asp:DropDownList>
            <asp:RequiredFieldValidator ControlToValidate="ExpiryDate"
➥ ErrorMessage="Expiry Date is required."
                    ID="ExpiryDateRequired" runat="server" ToolTip="Expiry
Date
➥is required.">*</asp:RequiredFieldValidator>
                    <cc1:ValidatorCalloutExtender
ID="ValidatorCalloutExtender9"
➥runat="server" TargetControlID="ExpiryDateRequired">
                    </cc1:ValidatorCalloutExtender>
        </td>
    </tr>
</table>
```

Figure 24.1 showcases the Order Review form at runtime before placing the order.

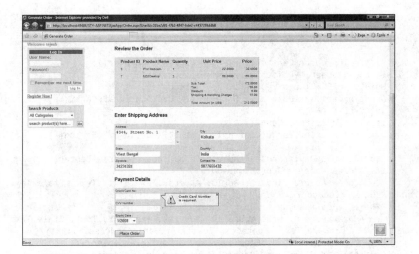

FIGURE 24.1
Reviewing the order

As usual, we've used the Ajax extender `ValidateCalloutExtender` to perform input validations in this page.

After filling in the payment details, click the button Place Order. This will confirm the order and display the message, as shown in Figure 24.2.

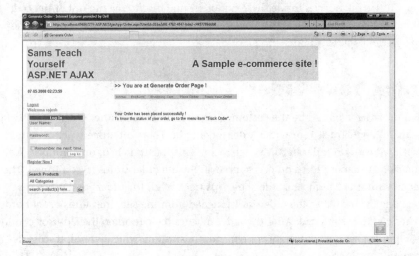

FIGURE 24.2
Order confirmation

The code-behind for executing the Place Order is as follows:

```
protected void btnPlaceOrder_Click(object sender, EventArgs e)
    {
        CartTableAdapter CartAdapter = new CartTableAdapter();
        MembershipUser myObject = Membership.GetUser();
        Guid UserID = (Guid)myObject.ProviderUserKey;
        ShoppingCart.CartDataTable CartTable = CartAdapter.IsCartExists(UserID);
        int CartId = 0;
        if (CartTable.Rows.Count > 0)
            CartId = int.Parse(CartTable.Rows[0]["CartId"].ToString());

        AddressTableAdapter AddressAdapter = new AddressTableAdapter();
        if (AddressMode == Operation.Add)
            AddressAdapter.Insert(UserID, Address.Text, City.Text, State.Text,
➥Country.Text, Zipcode.Text, ContactNo.Text);
        else if (AddressMode == Operation.Update)
            AddressAdapter.Update(UserID, Address.Text, City.Text, State.Text,
➥Country.Text, Zipcode.Text, ContactNo.Text, int.Parse(AddressId.Text));
        OrderTableAdapter OrderAdapter = new OrderTableAdapter();
        OrderAdapter.PlaceOrder(CartId, tax, discount, shippingCharges,
➥totalAmount, "Confirmed");
        this.pnlOrder.Visible = false;
        this.pnlConfirm.Visible = true;
    }
```

`AddressTableAdapter` and `OrderTableAdapter` are the new adapters created to add/update the shipping address of a customer and to place/manage orders, respectively. To see the queries inside these adapters, and also to see the rest of the code-behind in `Order.aspx`, view this book's web site. It is not possible to have all the code presented in this hour.

Track Your Order

After an order is placed by the customer, he/she can track his/her order by clicking the menu item, Track Your Order, after logging in. There are three types of status associated with an order in this system: Confirmed, Dispatched, and Shipped. As soon as a customer places an order successfully, the order status is Confirmed. The Administrator or Manager of the site keeps track of all the orders and processes them one by one. After the order is dispatched from the site, the status of that order is changed to Dispatched. After the order reaches the customer, the status is changed to Shipped. These activities are done in Administration, which we will discuss in upcoming sections.

Let's create the page `TrackOrder.aspx` to track the orders of a customer. This page also has three sections. The first block holds a drop-down list containing `OrderIds` generated by the customer so far. The second block holds the `OrderId` and `Order Generated` date and its status. The third block holds the Order details of the selected

order. The *aspx* source for the first two blocks is shown in the following code. The
source for the third block—that is, the Order details, is not pasted here as it is the
same as in the Review Order section of the `Order.aspx` page. Refer to the book's
web site for the entire source:

```
<table cellpadding="3" class="Table" width="300">
<tr>
    <td><div class="ContentMedium">Select Order Id : </div></td>
    <td align="left"><asp:DropDownList ID="OrderId" runat="server"
➥DataSourceID="OrderDataSource" DataValueField="OrderId"
➥DataTextField="OrderId" AutoPostBack="true"></asp:DropDownList></td>
</tr>
</table>
<asp:ObjectDataSource ID="OrderDataSource" runat="server"
➥SelectMethod="GetOrderIds"
➥TypeName="ShoppingCartTableAdapters.OrderTableAdapter">
        <SelectParameters>
            <asp:QueryStringParameter Name="UserId"
➥DefaultValue="01be2d91-f762-4847-bde2-c4457789ddb0"
➥QueryStringField="UserId" /></SelectParameters>
</asp:ObjectDataSource>
<h4>Your Order Status :</h4>
<asp:FormView ID="FormView1" runat="server" DataSourceID="FormViewDataSource"
➥EnableViewState="false" CssClass="Table">
        <ItemTemplate>
        <table width="300">
            <tr>
                <td style="width:300px">
                    <div class="ContentMedium">Order ID : <%#Eval("OrderId")
➥%></div><br />
                    <div class="ContentMedium">Order Date : <%#Eval("OrderDate")
➥ %></div><br />
                    <div class="ContentMedium">Order Status :
➥<%#Eval("OrderStatus") %></div><br />
                </td>
            </tr>
        </table>
        </ItemTemplate>
    </asp:FormView>
<asp:ObjectDataSource ID="FormViewDataSource" runat="server"
        SelectMethod="GetOrderDetails"
➥TypeName="ShoppingCartTableAdapters.OrderTableAdapter">
        <SelectParameters>
            <asp:ControlParameter ControlID="OrderId" Name="OrderId"
➥PropertyName="SelectedValue"
                Type="Int32" />
        </SelectParameters>
    </asp:ObjectDataSource>
    <br />
    <div class="ContentSmall">
    ** Notes : The are 3 status' associated with an order in this system. <br />
    1. Status "Confirmed" indicates Order Placed by the Customer.<br />
    2. Status "Dispatched" indicates the Order dispatched from the location of
➥the site. i.e., Shipment in progress.<br />
    3. Status "Shipped" indicates Shipment delivered to the customer.
    </div>
```

Figure 24.3 displays the Track Your Order page of the customer rajesh after placing the order.

FIGURE 24.3
Tracking your
order

This is the end of the operations that can be performed by the customer.

Manage Pending Orders

This is an administration activity performed by the Administrator or Manager of the site. All the orders placed by the customers can be viewed here. The Administrator or Manager's job is to look at these orders and start the dispatch process of the order. Initially, all the orders here will be in Confirmed status—that is, an order has been placed by customer. After an order is dispatched, the status should be modified as Dispatched; once it reaches the customer, the status of the order should be modified as Shipped. So in essence, the pending orders are all the orders that are not in Shipped status.

Now, let's create a page named PendingOrders.aspx. This page should display each order, with the customer name, address, and order status in each row of the GridView. This is bound to a panel pnlMain. To view the details of the order and to change the status of the order, we will provide a button called Change Status; by clicking it, we will display the details panel pnlDetails, which holds a DetailsView control displaying OrderId, OrderDate, and Status drop-down lists to allow modification. Apart from the DetailsView, the panel pnlDetails also holds a GridView displaying the items of the selected order. Here is the source of the panel pnlMain:

```
<asp:Panel ID="pnlMain" runat="server">
    <div class="ContentSmall">
        The following list of orders are pending, meaning the orders have been
➥placed by the customer,<br />
        but are yet to be shipped to the customers.<br />
        The Administrator or the Manager of the site have to co-ordinate
➥the dispatch and delivery of the order,<br />
        and update the status of the order accordingly in this page. <br />
        The Customer can track the order in the site, only if you update
➥the status here.
    </div><br /><br />
    <asp:GridView ID="gvPendingOrders" runat="server" CssClass="Table"
➥DataSourceID="GridViewDataSource"
    DataKeyNames="OrderId" AllowSorting="true" AutoGenerateColumns="false"
    SelectedIndex="0" OnSelectedIndexChanged="gvPendingOrders_
➥SelectedIndexChanged"
    OnPageIndexChanged="gvPendingOrders_PageIndexChanged" RowStyle-
➥CssClass="ContentSmall"
    OnSorted="gvPendingOrders_Sorted" OnRowDataBound="gvPendingOrders_
➥OnRowDataBound">
        <Columns>
            <asp:CommandField ButtonType="Button" ShowSelectButton="true"
➥SelectText="Update Status" />
            <asp:BoundField DataField="OrderId" HeaderText="Order ID"
➥ReadOnly="True" SortExpression="OrderId" />
            <asp:BoundField DataField="OrderDate" HeaderText="Order Date"
➥SortExpression="OrderDate" />
            <asp:BoundField DataField="OrderStatus" HeaderText="Order Status"
➥SortExpression="OrderStatus" />
            <asp:BoundField DataField="TotalAmount" HeaderText="Total Amount"
➥ SortExpression="TotalAmount" />
            <asp:BoundField DataField="UserName" HeaderText="Customer Name"
➥SortExpression="UserName" />
            <asp:TemplateField HeaderText="Customer Address" SortExpression="City">
                <ItemTemplate>
                    <asp:Label ID="CustomerAddress" runat="server"></asp:Label>
                </ItemTemplate>
            </asp:TemplateField>
        </Columns>
    </asp:GridView><br />
  <asp:ObjectDataSource ID="GridViewDataSource" runat="server"
➥SelectMethod="GetPendingOrders"
    TypeName="ShoppingCartTableAdapters.PendingOrdersTableAdapter">
    </asp:ObjectDataSource>
</asp:Panel>
```

The preceding source uses a new business object, PendingOrdersTableAdapter, which binds the pending orders to the GridView using the GetPendingOrders method. Please refer to the book's web site for more details on this adapter.

Clicking the Change Status button will display the details of order, and the Administrator or Manager also can change the status of the order accordingly. Here is the source of the panel pnlDetails. This excludes the source of the order items, as this was already presented in the Order.aspx page earlier in the hour:

```
<asp:DetailsView AutoGenerateRows="False" DataSourceID="DetailsViewDataSource"
➥DataKeyNames="OrderId"
    CssClass="Table" ID="dvOrderStatus" RowStyle-CssClass="ContentSmall"
➥runat="server" AutoGenerateEditButton="True"
    OnItemUpdated="dvOrderStatus_ItemUpdated" OnModeChanging="dvOrderStatus
➥ModeChanging" Width="367px" EnableViewState="false">
    <Fields>
        <asp:TemplateField HeaderText="Order ID" SortExpression="OrderId">
            <EditItemTemplate>
                <asp:Label ID="EditOrderId" runat="server" Text='<%#
➥Bind("OrderId") %>'></asp:Label>
            </EditItemTemplate>
            <ItemTemplate>
                <asp:Label ID="OrderId" runat="server" Text='<%#
➥Bind("OrderId") %>'></asp:Label>
            </ItemTemplate>
        </asp:TemplateField>
        <asp:TemplateField HeaderText="Order Status"
➥SortExpression="OrderStatus">
            <EditItemTemplate>
                <asp:DropDownList ID="EditOrderStatus" runat="server"
➥SelectedValue='<%# Bind("OrderStatus") %>'>
                    <asp:ListItem Value="Confirmed" Text="Confirmed">
➥</asp:ListItem>
                    <asp:ListItem Value="Dispatched" Text="Dispatched">
➥</asp:ListItem>
                    <asp:ListItem Value="Shipped" Text="Shipped"></asp:ListItem>
                </asp:DropDownList>
            </EditItemTemplate>
            <ItemTemplate>
                <asp:Label ID="OrderStatus" runat="server" Text='<%#
➥Bind("OrderStatus") %>'></asp:Label>
            </ItemTemplate>
        </asp:TemplateField>
    </Fields>
  </asp:DetailsView><br />
  <asp:ObjectDataSource ID="DetailsViewDataSource" runat="server"
      OldValuesParameterFormatString="{0}" SelectMethod="GetOrderDetails"
➥OnUpdating="DetailsViewDataSource_Updating"
      TypeName="ShoppingCartTableAdapters.OrderTableAdapter"
➥UpdateMethod="UpdateOrderStatus" >
        <SelectParameters>
            <asp:ControlParameter ControlID="gvPendingOrders"
➥Name="OrderId" PropertyName="SelectedValue"
                Type="Int32" />
        </SelectParameters>
        <UpdateParameters>
            <asp:Parameter Name="OrderId" Type="Int32" />
        </UpdateParameters>
    </asp:ObjectDataSource>
```

Log in with Administrator account sriram/sriram@24h and click the menu Pending Orders. Figure 24.4 shows three pending orders for the customer rajesh.

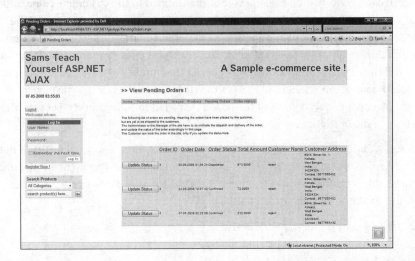

FIGURE 24.4
Viewing pending orders

Click the Update Status button to view the details. Also you can change the status of the order. Figure 24.5 illustrates this.

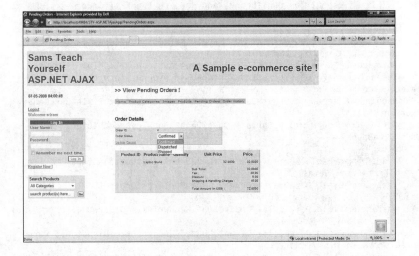

FIGURE 24.5
Viewing the order details and changing the order status

After the status is changed to Shipped, this record is moved out of pending orders. Now this becomes a fulfilled order to the customer and thus can be found in the Order History menu item, which is described in the next section.

Order History

As discussed previously, all the orders that are shipped to the customers come under the Order History category. This report gives the Administrator and Manager the complete history of the order. It maintains the ordered date, dispatched date, and shipped date of an order to a customer. This is helpful data in many cases. One such case is that the site Administrator can find out the number of days taken to dispatch and ship an order to different places (as the customer address is also displayed here). This data is also a proof of the orders delivered to the customer. Let's go ahead and create the OrderHistory.aspx.

This has a similar layout to the PendingOrders.aspx. Here the panel pnlMain holds a GridView control holding the information of Ordered Date, Dispatched Date, and Shipped Date of an Order to a customer. The details panel pnlDetails holds the OrderId, its status, and the order items.

Here is the source of the panel pnlMain:

```
<asp:Panel ID="pnlMain" runat="server">
    <div class="ContentSmall">
        The Order History defines, the phases, the Order has been through,
➡after it has been placed by the Customer.<br />
        This history displays only the Shipped Orders.<br />
        It displays the Ordered Date, Dispatched Date, and Shipped Date of
➡an Order.<br />
        This is useful for monitoring, and keeping track of Order
➡transactions in the site.
    </div><br /><br />
    <asp:GridView ID="gvOrderHistory" runat="server" CssClass="Table"
➡ DataSourceID="GridViewDataSource"
    DataKeyNames="OrderId" AllowSorting="true" AutoGenerateColumns="false"
    SelectedIndex="0" OnSelectedIndexChanged="gvOrderHistory_
➡SelectedIndexChanged"
    OnPageIndexChanged="gvOrderHistory_PageIndexChanged" RowStyle-CssClass=
➡"ContentSmall"
    OnSorted="gvOrderHistory_Sorted" OnRowDataBound="gvOrderHistory_
➡OnRowDataBound">
    <Columns>
        <asp:CommandField ButtonType="Button" ShowSelectButton="true"
➡SelectText="View Details" />
        <asp:BoundField DataField="OrderId" HeaderText="Order ID"
➡ReadOnly="True" SortExpression="OrderId" />
        <asp:BoundField DataField="OrderDate" HeaderText="Ordered Date"
➡ SortExpression="OrderDate" />
        <asp:BoundField DataField="DispatchDate" HeaderText="Dispatched Date"
➡SortExpression="DispatchDate" />
        <asp:BoundField DataField="ShippedDate" HeaderText="Shipped Date"
➡SortExpression="ShippedDate" />
        <asp:BoundField DataField="TotalAmount" HeaderText="Total Amount"
➡ SortExpression="TotalAmount" />
        <asp:BoundField DataField="UserName" HeaderText="Customer Name"
➡SortExpression="UserName" />
        <asp:TemplateField HeaderText="Customer Address" SortExpression="City">
```

```
        <ItemTemplate>
            <asp:Label ID="CustomerAddress" runat="server"></asp:Label>
        </ItemTemplate>
      </asp:TemplateField>
    </Columns>
    </asp:GridView><br />
  <asp:ObjectDataSource ID="GridViewDataSource" runat="server"
➡SelectMethod="GetOrderHistory"
   TypeName="ShoppingCartTableAdapters.OrderHistoryTableAdapter">
    </asp:ObjectDataSource>
</asp:Panel>
```

This GridView uses a new business object OrderHistoryTableAdapter to bind order history data to the control. Refer to the accompanying web site for query and code-behind details.

The panel pnlDetails holds a DetailsView control that contains OrderId and Order Status, both of which are ReadOnly, and a GridView control holding the order items. Here is the source of the panel pnlDetails:

```
<h4>Order Details</h4>
    <asp:DetailsView AutoGenerateRows="False"
DataSourceID="DetailsViewDataSource"
➡ DataKeyNames="OrderId"
    CssClass="Table" ID="dvOrderStatus" RowStyle-CssClass="ContentSmall"
➡runat="server" AutoGenerateEditButton="false"
    OnModeChanging="dvOrderStatus_ModeChanging" Width="367px"
➡EnableViewState="false">
    <Fields>
        <asp:TemplateField HeaderText="Order ID" SortExpression="OrderId">
            <ItemTemplate>
                <asp:Label ID="OrderId" runat="server" Text='<%# Bind("OrderId")
➡ %>'></asp:Label>
            </ItemTemplate>
        </asp:TemplateField>
        <asp:TemplateField HeaderText="Order Status"
SortExpression="OrderStatus">
            <ItemTemplate>
                <asp:Label ID="OrderStatus" runat="server" Text='<%#
➡Bind("OrderStatus") %>'></asp:Label>
            </ItemTemplate>
        </asp:TemplateField>
    </Fields>
    </asp:DetailsView><br />
  <asp:ObjectDataSource ID="DetailsViewDataSource" runat="server"
      OldValuesParameterFormatString="{0}" SelectMethod="GetOrderDetails"
      TypeName="ShoppingCartTableAdapters.OrderTableAdapter">
      <SelectParameters>
          <asp:ControlParameter ControlID="gvOrderHistory"
➡Name="OrderId" PropertyName="SelectedValue"
              Type="Int32" />
      </SelectParameters>
      <UpdateParameters>
          <asp:Parameter Name="OrderId" Type="Int32" />
      </UpdateParameters>
    </asp:ObjectDataSource>
```

As usual, the preceding code snippet excludes the order items GridView, as this is already presented in the Order.aspx page earlier in the hour. Add the missing code in your application from the application provided on the book's web site and run the application. Log in as sriram/sriram@24h [Administrator account] and click the Order History menu. Figure 24.6 shows the history of all orders.

FIGURE 24.6
View order history

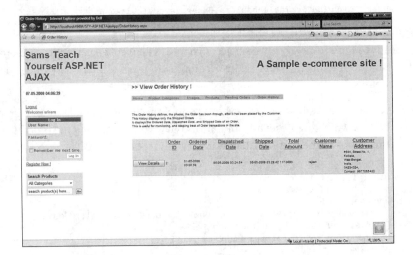

Click the View Details button to display the details of the order. This is shown in the Figure 24.7.

FIGURE 24.7
Details of the order in order history

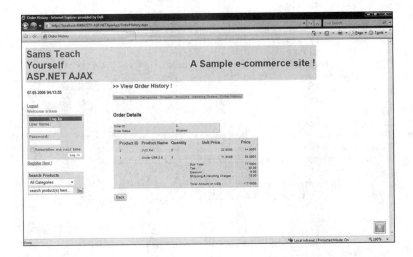

After you run the application, all the order-related pages developed in this hour are already Ajaxified, as the `ScriptManager`, `UpdateProgress`, and `UpdatePanel` controls are placed in the master page `MasterPage.master` file.

This ends development of all the pages in the application. Hours 22, 23, and 24 contain code snippets/listings of portions of all the pages in the application. These hours explained the core functionality of the applications and focused on explaining and providing these snippets/listings relevant to ASP.NET Ajax to develop the application. However, you need to refer to the book's web site to completely build the application, as there are pieces of code missing in the snippets/listings provided here.

Summary

This hour focused on the development of pages for placing orders by customers and tracking those orders. In addition, we discussed developing pages for managing pending orders and maintaining the order history. With this, the sample application has been completed using ASP.NET Ajax. The entire source code for this application is provided on the book's web site.

We now have come to the end of the book, which we hope has helped you to thoroughly understand the concepts of ASP.NET Ajax. As we progressed through the hours, you have been exposed to several real-time examples of different concepts covered in the book. We hope these examples, along with the sample application, will assist you in building your own applications in ASP.NET Ajax with ease. Thank you for reading!!

Workshop

Quiz

1. What is the use of the attribute `dir` for a `Label` control?

2. What is an `ObjectDataSource` control?

3. True or False: `DetailsView` control can be used only for insert, update, or deletion of records.

4. What are the different statuses maintained for an order in the sample application we've built?

5. What does Order history page display?

Answers

1. The `dir` attribute is used to display the value in the Label in two of the available directions: `rtl` meaning right to left or `ltr` meaning left to right direction. If we do not use this attribute, it is by default `ltr`.

2. `ObjectDataSource` is an ASP.NET data source control to enable declarative data binding against underlying data stores. In the application we built in this book, we have used the `ObjectDataSource` that holds a business object that eventually binds to a `GridView` or a `DetailsView` control.

3. False. `DetailsView` control can also be used for ReadOnly purpose.

4. Confirmed, Dispatched, and Shipped.

5. Order history displays all the orders that have been confirmed, dispatched, and shipped along with the dates of the transactions.

Index

S

Sams **Teach Yourself**

When you only have time
for the answers™

Whatever your need and whatever your time frame, there's a Sams **Teach Yourself** book for you. With a Sams **Teach Yourself** book as your guide, you can quickly get up to speed on just about any new product or technology—in the absolute shortest period of time possible. Guaranteed.

Learning how to do new things with your computer shouldn't be tedious or time-consuming. Sams **Teach Yourself** makes learning anything quick, easy, and even a little bit fun.

Visual Basic 2008 in 24 Hours

James Foxall
ISBN-13: 978-0-672-32984-5

C++ in One Hour a Day

Jesse Liberty
Bradley Jones
Siddhartha Rao
ISBN-13: 978-0-672-32941-8

SQL in 24 Hours, Fourth Edition

Ryan Stephens
Ron Plew
Arie Jones
ISBN-13: 978-0-672-33018-6

ASP.NET 3.5 in 24 Hours

Scott Mitchell
ISBN-13: 978-0-672-32997-5

WPF in 24 Hours

Rob Eisenberg
Christopher Bennage
ISBN-13: 978-0-672-32985-2

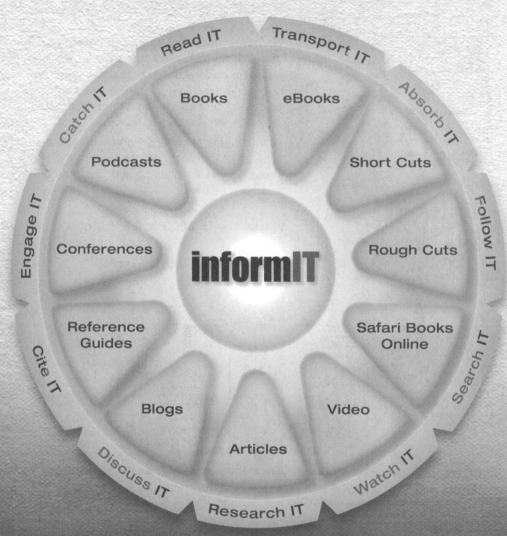